Welfare and Human Nature

Also by Martin Hewitt

WELFARE, IDEOLOGY AND NEED

Welfare and Human Nature

The Human Subject in Twentieth-Century Social Politics

Martin Hewitt
Senior Lecturer in Social Policy
University of Hertfordshire

First published in Great Britain 2000 by
MACMILLAN PRESS LTD
Houndmills, Basingstoke, Hampshire RG21 6XS and London
Companies and representatives throughout the world

A catalogue record for this book is available from the British Library.

ISBN 0–333–80305–1

 First published in the United States of America 2000 by
ST. MARTIN'S PRESS, LLC,
Scholarly and Reference Division,
175 Fifth Avenue, New York, N.Y. 10010

ISBN 0–312–23409–0

Library of Congress Cataloging-in-Publication Data
Hewitt, Martin.
Welfare and human nature : the human subject in twentieth-century social politics / Martin Hewitt.
p. cm.
Includes bibliographical references and index.
ISBN 0–312–23409–0 (cloth)
1. Social policy—Philosophy. 2. Public welfare—Philosophy. 3. Human behavior—Philosophy. 4. Political psychology. I. Title.

HN28 .H45 2000
361.6'1'01—dc21
                                                            00–023342

© Martin Hewitt 2000

All rights reserved. No reproduction, copy or transmission of this publication may be made without written permission.

No paragraph of this publication may be reproduced, copied or transmitted save with written permission or in accordance with the provisions of the Copyright, Designs and Patents Act 1988, or under the terms of any licence permitting limited copying issued by the Copyright Licensing Agency, 90 Tottenham Court Road, London W1P 0LP.

Any person who does any unauthorised act in relation to this publication may be liable to criminal prosecution and civil claims for damages.

The author has asserted his right to be identified as the author of this work in accordance with the Copyright, Designs and Patents Act 1988.

This book is printed on paper suitable for recycling and made from fully managed and sustained forest sources.

10 9 8 7 6 5 4 3 2 1
09 08 07 06 05 04 03 02 01 00

Printed and bound in Great Britain by
Antony Rowe Ltd, Chippenham, Wiltshire

To Ann, Matthew and Thomas

Contents

Acknowledgements — viii

1 Introduction — 1

Part I Mainstream Traditions in Social Policy — 19

2 Social Democracy and Human Nature — 29
3 Equality and Difference in the Postwar Years — 47
4 Human Nature and the Right — 74

Part II Critical Perspectives on Human Nature — 103

5 Marx and Human Nature — 105
6 Marxism, Human Nature and Need — 118
7 Feminism, the Politics of Recognition and Social Policy — 139
8 Conclusion — 163

Notes — 185
Bibliography — 187
Index — 196

Acknowledgements

This book began life as a doctoral thesis. I am indebted to Ted Benton, my supervisor, for his consistent support, sensitive interventions and guidance, especially at those critical points when the project was becoming overwhelming and the direction ahead unclear. I would also like to thank Ian Craib, University of Essex, and Peter Dickens, University of Sussex, for their comments and discussion. My colleagues at the University of Hertfordshire are owed much gratitude: Derrick Dale for his unstinting support for my attending the doctorate programme at Essex; colleagues who commented on several seminar presentations based on what eventually became this book; and Agnes Michel for updating material in Chapter 1. Lastly, I would like to thank Ann, Matthew and Thomas who had to endure my mental absenteeism from our home for long periods of time. I owe them a big apology for this and as small recompense dedicate the book to them.

1
Introduction

As we move into the twenty-first century, governments throughout the developed world are concluding a crucial phase in the history of welfare reform – reforms that in earlier times represented the culmination of the democratic process of governing social needs. Reflecting this global trend, the British Labour and Conservative Parties appear to have abandoned their traditional welfare and ideological commitments, including their commitment to specific views of human nature, and to be embarking on the construction of new programmes. Both have undergone significant shifts in ideological principle. First, in the 1970s the Conservative Party adopted neo-liberal principles that continued to drive its policies in government until May 1997. Then Labour adopted a new constitution that abandoned the traditional commitment to 'common ownership'. Now both parties have concluded a radical review of the welfare state, of its philosophical justification and policies. At the same time neither party has yet settled in its new ideological guise. The Tories have suffered a prolonged loss of public support and growing disenchantment with their policies that began in 1992 and culminated in their overwhelming defeat in the 1997 election. Although New Labour appears more united, and its principles move apparent, its relationship to the Social Democratic tradition is still in question.

A significant aspect of the crisis besetting politics is the widespread doubt, outside as well as inside mainstream politics, about the traditional Social Democratic and neo-liberal conceptions of human nature that have defined political thought and public policy this century. Traditionally Social Democrats believed that individuals share basic needs which government protects and that they enjoy a range of abilities which government nurtures with universal education, health and social security policies. By contrast, the Right believes that individuals have needs which are fulfilled in the market place except for a minority deficient in abilities of self-reliance and moral strength. This minority is the target of selective welfare provisions. Continuing doubts about these two projects have led to questions about the kind of ideology and welfare policies required at the turn of the new century, and has raised concerns about what conceptions of human nature, purpose and need should inform future policy.

By the early 1990s, New Labour and the post-Thatcherite Right, as well as academics debating the state of politics 'beyond Left and Right', were suggesting that a new society can unleash untapped human potential. Tony Blair, for example, foresaw a socialism combining 'social advance and individual achievement' which 'gives each citizen their chance to develop their potential to the full' (1994). In a similar vein Raymond Plant talked of a 'new covenant between individual and society' (1993). Somewhat to the right, John Gray's notion of a market order and publicly enriched civil society that promotes 'positive' self 'autonomy' (1992) likewise assumed a potential for enlarging human nature. Further, Gray and other erstwhile advocates of Thatcherism were becoming increasingly critical of its achievements and its limited view of human potential. For example, David Green criticized Thatcherism for its 'too narrow view of human character' which encouraged a largely self-interested form of individualism to the detriment of the mutual obligations necessary for a healthy civil society (1993, 1).

In academic discourse, several writers proposed new forms of social and political action that would enhance individual and social human-nature after three decades of social change. For example, Anthony Gidden's 'self reflexivity' (1994), Len Doyal and Ian Gough's 'critical autonomy' (1991), Paul Hirst's self-empowering 'associationalism' (1994), and Hiliary Wainwright's notion of the 'distinct role of purposive human agency, and creativity' (1994), all shared a concern about the future development of human potential. These concepts of human nature and fulfilment, with their talk of liberating 'human agency', 'autonomy', 'potential' and 'creativity', though far from clearly defined, echoed earlier radical traditions of Marxism, as well as more recent traditions of feminist thought, which have remained less visible and underdeveloped in mainstream politics and policy.

At the same time as traditional notions of human nature have been questioned and new ones advanced, several political thinkers have revived the generic concept of human nature as a central concern of political thought and policy (e.g. Hollis 1977; Plant 1991; Gray 1992; Le Grand 1997). This revival has occurred after a period when political theory was dominated by a more scientific outlook (Hollis 1977, 2). If, presently, thinkers are rediscovering that the purpose of political and moral thought is the 'realisation of the possibilities of human nature' (Vincent and Plant 1984, 71), then the study of the different conceptions of human nature becomes central.

Human nature and social policy

Accounts of human nature inform the formation of social policy, from its initial conception of needs and aims, through its definition of tasks and responsibilities, to its assessment of outcomes and its overall appraisal. Broadly, the aims of social policy presented in textbooks are to enable individuals to meet their needs for health, social integration, education, housing and employment, and thereby to realize their capabilities as fully as possible. On this view, government makes policies in the belief that a healthy, integrated and fulfilled population contributes to the greater wellbeing of society – though of course what individuals perceive as their needs and what government deems individuals need often diverge. At the heart of government social programmes are two normative conceptions of the human subject, often conceived implicitly in the aims of social policy. First is the subject whose life is one of individual and social fulfilment: the good worker, the concerned parent and the dutiful citizen, found for example in policies developing 'active citizenship', 'enterprise culture', 'welfare-to-work' and parental responsibility. The second is the antithesis of the first, the subject unable to perform socially expected roles because of unmet needs and deficient competencies. The aim of social policy is normally defined as providing resources to meet the needs and competencies that these individuals lack, so that they can become fulfilled in the sense applying to the former normative subjects.

Normative conceptions of the human subject in policy have often been posed in negative terms – of individuals lacking health, education, the skills of parentcraft, etc. – in relation to an implied *other* idealizing the competent subject that government expects of its citizens. However, the radical shifts in Tory social policy between 1979 and 1997 gave rise to an *explicit* moral agenda depicting the ends of policy in terms of positive conceptions of the human qualities that are meant to replace more negative conceptions of lack. For example, in the late-1980s a raft of policies in education, employment, training, health and social security sought to develop enterprise in the human subject. This represented both a concerted attempt to replace what government considered Britain's serious skills deficit in an increasingly competitive world, and an attack on the 'dependency culture' caused by welfare policies that were believed to sap self-reliance, the work-ethic and family life (Keat and Abercrombie 1991; Heelas and Morris 1992). The attack on the dependency culture was associated with the government's concern to address the related problem of the underclass. This concern was characterized by some on both the Left and Right in motivational terms as the problem of individuals suffering from 'personal pathologies' (Field 1989, 8) and social 'disease' (Murray 1990, 23).

These concerns in social policy about needs and abilities point to the legitimate interest of the academic discipline of social policy in the different constructions of human nature and the human subject found in policy. They also point to the normative role these constructions play in shaping government policy. One approach therefore to the study of social policy is via the notions of human nature that inform welfare and other programmes. Of course, social policy has followed other approaches, such as identifying social needs and problems, or services and provisions needed, or defining the role welfare plays in achieving or impeding wider political and economic goals. Each approach enables the student to address important aspects of social policy. However, the question of human nature arises whatever approach one takes in social policy. This is not to say, however, that analysing discourses of human nature is an essential part of social policy from whatever perspective studied. Nor is this to say that there is an inexorable logic in the formation of social policy that proceeds from reasoning about the foundations of human nature to the translation of this reasoning into policy and its implementation. Social policy develops in response to a wide range of contingencies occasioned by changing patterns of social structure, population, income distribution and poverty, employment opportunities, changes in public expectation and wider economic developments. The study of these empirical trends is a necessary part of understanding social policy. Consequently, human nature reasoning is rarely stated in the form of logically coherent propositions about human abilities and needs. Rather this reasoning is expressed in the form of statements about human motivation that often use conflicting propositions to address real-life contingencies. We discuss the structure of this reasoning later in the chapter.

Despite the difficulties of studying human nature in social policy, there is a particular feature of the present political climate that recommends its study as important. We have already referred to this climate as one of uncertainty about the fate of welfare. In addition, the climate can be characterized by a narrowing of political perspectives and policy options. For some, the aims of welfare are no longer as challenging and clear-cut as they once were. There is a post-Enlightenment mood, associated with the influence of postmodern thought and with a new pragmatism in mainstream politics, which discounts the classic choices that once shaped modern politics, between universal and selective welfare, between the state and market, and between collective responsibility and individual freedom. In this climate, questions about the nature of the 'good society' and human existence, which seemed relevant to earlier times, are now being replaced by more practical questions about surviving economic and political change. The issues today are more pragmatic, provisional and piecemeal in pursuing the practical options that policy can offer. As an example of the collapse into pragmatism, Gray argues that

> There is no one set of policies, no one structure of institutions, in which an enabling welfare state is embodied. There is instead a diversity of local settlements, never final and always provisional, in which conflicting claims are given a temporary reconciliation, and the values of autonomy and community are accorded a more or less complete embodiment and expression.
>
> (1992, 63)

In his *adieu* to the old welfare state, Mishra likewise concludes that now that the majority of people have given way to the values of consumerism, free enterprise and economic growth,

> it is unlikely that universality as a principle of social provision can survive for long. And once we bid farewell to full employment as well as to universality, the 'welfare state' as a distinct phase in the evolution of social policy in the West will have come to an end.
>
> (1993, 36)

Yet this pragmatic turn in social policy does not square easily with the recent moralizing discourse in mainstream politics and with the concern of politicians and academics addressed earlier to set out political agendas and policy objectives that realize new qualities of human potential.

The aims of the book

In the context of these issues, the book examines developments in the notion of human nature in social policy, during the twentieth century, culminating in speculation about the future direction social policy might take towards meeting human need and securing human fulfilment.

Specifically, the aims are three-fold:

(i) to trace the different conceptions of human nature in Social Democratic and Radical Right thought and policy, drawing connections between political theory and policy, and identifying the limits some of these conceptions have imposed on government policy and the potential they offer for future goals of fulfilment overlooked by official policy. The Social Democratic notion of human nature is discussed in Chapters 2 and 3 and the Radical Right's notion in Chapter 4.

(ii) to examine other theories of human nature which have had less influence on politics than Social Democracy and the Radical Right, but which have provided alternative critiques of mainstream political thought and policy – namely Marxism in Chapters 5 and 6 and feminism in Chapter 7.

(iii) to develop a notion of human nature as involving mutual co-operation, examine the relevance of mutualism for social policy, and examine the relationship between this and other notions of human nature. Chapters 5, 6, 7 and 8 develop the mutualist view of welfare, drawing on notions of praxis and reciprocity in modern Marxism and feminism, as well as in Social Democratic thought. The underlying belief is that the idea of human mutuality provides insights into problems faced by the welfare state, and will contribute towards designing new conceptions of human need and policy in a newly emerging welfare state, as Chapter 8 argues.

Social and economic transformation

The questioning of traditional notions of human nature and the need for new conceptions that enlarge the scope of human fulfilment have arisen in response to several processes of change in recent decades. These processes have contributed to undermining the main political projects of social reform advanced by Liberals, Social Democrats and Conservatives the twentieth century. For each process of change, the question arises about what new vision of human nature can be advanced.

1 The increasing globalization of capitalism

This has been associated with the supra-national powers of multi-national corporations and with the emergence of new foreign competitors in the Far East and elsewhere. Globalization has undermined the viability of the nation state as a sustainable economic force. As a consequence of these developments, capitalism is becoming a universal system of production, marketing and consumption, though expressing itself in diverse forms throughout the world (Gray 1998). Capitalism is approaching the proportions of a new world system (Wallerstein 1974).[1] The ubiquity and diversity of globalization raise important issues of an economic, political and cultural nature (see Waters 1995).

These trends have had a profound and widespread impact on labour markets and welfare states in the West, of which the transformation of Britain's is typical. Britain has seen the long-term decline in its manufacturing sector and the expansion of its 'social reproduction' sector of health, social care, education and personal services especially those provided by small enterprises in hairdressing, catering and cleaning (Jordan 1998, 37). It has gradually moved from being a leading industrial nation of the postwar years to being a minor competitor who by the 1980s had become relatively low in skill, productivity and labour costs (Nolan and Walsh 1995, 66). One consequence of these trends has been the transformation of traditional labour relations in Britain, typified by the emergence of a dual labour market with a declining core of full-time, long-term employees and a growing periphery of employees on part-time or short-term contracts. Although there are competing accounts of the causes of this process, it has been aided and abetted throughout the 1980s and 1990s by legislation curtailing trade union powers, deregulating industrial relations and financial markets, and privatizing nationalized industries, by employers imposing new forms of employment flexibility and managerialism, and by declining trade union membership (1995, 64). Throughout Western nations, traditional class struggles have abated, social alliances fractured and labour markets restructured, resulting in increased insecurity for the employed, growing poverty (Oppenheim and Harker 1996), and widening inequalities in income and wealth (Barclay 1995).

These new insecurities have stretched the social protection of the classic welfare state to its limits, revealing gaps in its comprehensive cover. Beveridge's compact with the British public, replicated in various guises throughout Western welfare states, involved a pledge to protect the income of individuals whose earnings were disrupted for various reasons with national insurance provisions based on the contributory principle. High levels of regular employment in the early postwar decades sustained the national insurance system, which in turn helped to slow down the rates of dependency that began to rise in the 1960s and to secure a floor for the poorest in the 1990s (Glennerster 1995, 221). However, decoupling long-term benefits and wages in 1980 reduced the beneficial effect benefits had on lessening income inequalities (Barclay 1995, 25). Fundamental changes in the labour market in the last three decades have now ended this effect producing a declining number protected for long periods of time by 'universal' social insurance and a growing number dependent on selective means-tested benefits. Chamberlayne has described the emerging pattern of crisis in welfare systems caused by 'the increasing detachment of many individuals from "regularized" employment, lengthening periods of claim from those with established entitlements, and increasing demands for social citizenship rights from those who had never been attached to the "regular" labour market' (1991/92, 8). In addition, the growth in employer-provided benefits such as occupational pensions has contributed to new forms of non-state protection, which have improved the prosperity of pensioners and reduced their reliance on means-tested benefits (Webb 1994). However, at the same time the gap between the richest and poorest pensioners has grown and inequalities in old age widened (DSS 1998b, 14). More recently, mounting evidence of growing concentrations of poverty on council estates and the polarization of poor and affluent neighbourhoods (Green 1996; Noble and Smith 1996) has supplemented more general evidence of widening inequalities (see Barclay 1995, 29 *et passim*). Further, policies introducing internal markets in the NHS and local authorities, formula-funding and opting-out in schools, and greater reliance on means-testing in social security, among other reforms, have done little to reverse widening inequalities since the mid-1970s (*ibid.*). These changes have undermined earlier policies that met common basic needs by providing universal provision in health, national insurance and education.

2 Changes in gender relations

These represent a further development that has questioned the traditional accounts of human nature found in British policy. Such changes have occurred principally in the spheres of work and domestic relations, and have been associated with feminist critiques of ideologies purporting to justify the traditional structure of gender relations on grounds of men's and women's *natural* differences (Williams 1989).

The transformation of the labour market described above has also been characterized by an increasing number and proportion of women becoming economically active. Between 1951 and 1998 women as a percentage of the total labour force rose from 31 to 44 per cent (Hakim 1978, 1265; Thair and Risdon 1999, 103) – a trend that is likely to continue rising to 46 per cent in 2011 (Armitage and Scott 1998, 281). This trend has its reverse image in the decline in the proportion of men in employment over the last half century. Increasing employment among women has been possible largely because of the changing structure of the labour market towards greater flexibility in employment, associated with the growth in part-time, temporary, contracted-out, home working and other non-standard patterns of employment. In 1998, 81 per cent of people of working age who worked part-time were women (Thair and Risdon 1999, 108). These new patterns of work are also associated with continuing low rates of pay among female workers and with prolonged inequalities of income between men and women, despite equal pay legislation introduced in the UK in 1970.

The predominant presence of women in low-paid occupations such as catering, cleaning, hairdressing, nursing and social care reflects an ideological view about what tasks are appropriate for women based on their traditional role in the domestic division of labour (Lonsdale 1992, 97). In this sense, a naturalistic view of women's nature and capabilities – i.e. gifted in personal nurturing and caring tasks – reinforces their low wages, insecurity and subjugation, and the demeaning nature of their work, and perpetuates gender inequalities in income, power and socially perceived value.

These naturalistic assumptions about women's capabilities have influenced social policy. The 'familialist' assumptions of much twentieth century social policy about 'normal' family life formed part of the consensual thinking of Conservative and Labour welfare policy (Williams 1989, 6). This thinking meant that policies should support the gendered division of labour where men are the principal wage earners concentrating on the outer world of work, and women the domestic workers focusing on the inner life of family, child care, homekeeping and the emotional nourishment of male partners. These assumptions about gender relations in the domestic sphere imply that women are financially dependent on the male head of the household (*ibid.*). Given these assumptions, the aims of social policy throughout the twentieth century can be understood as supporting the gender roles and relations of the normal family and re-installing them when family life is threatened. Fiona Williams charts the role of Rightist thinkers (1989, 118–20), and Liberal and Social Democratic thinkers such as the Webbs, Beveridge and Titmuss (123–4, 127–9), in perpetuating these assumptions in modern social policy. Assumptions about women's domestic capabilities have for some time shaped views about the resources available in the informal, voluntary and private sectors of the new mixed economy as it increasingly takes over welfare responsibilities from the state (Finch and Groves 1980).

However, the changing role of women in work, family and welfare places new demands on their repertoire of competencies and raises new expectations which challenge traditional ideological assumptions about women's 'nature'. Women are expected to participate in new areas of paid work as well as performing their traditional roles in the family. The British Social Attitudes survey shows 'little evidence that the increase of women in paid employment has been matched by a commensurate change in the way domestic tasks are divided within the household', with 79 per cent of households reporting that doing the laundry remains a predominantly female task (Scott *et al*. 1998, 31–3). The latter division of labour continues to hold for dual earning couples (*ibid*.). Yet, despite the enduring expectations of women that accompany their growing involvement in paid work, social policy has recently begun to place further demands on women. Under the Labour government's New Deal, welfare now plays a more active role than previously in encouraging lone mothers to enter the labour market (DSS 1998a, 26). Women fulfil the important role of 'returners' to work which helps to defuse the 'demographic time bomb' produced by the retirement of skilled workers and the insufficient supply of young entrants to the labour market (Callender 1996). They are expected to act as the front line in providing informal, voluntary and private forms of welfare. Women are also expected to provide an increasing range of abilities associated with flexible labour to a degree that threatens to undermine the very naturalistic qualities that patriarchal society has traditionally assigned to them. These changes also undermine the traditional view of men's roles in society. The new challenges to male and female nature are addressed in Chapter 7.

3 The decline of postwar welfare states

In Liberal, Christian Democratic and Social Democratic nations in Europe the decline of postwar welfare states has undermined a commitment to meet basic needs (Esping-Andersen 1996). The 'classic welfare state' of Beveridge sought to protect all citizens from want and to strengthen their universal rights. In this it was based on a particular account of human nature comprising shared basic needs (described in Chapter 2). The question therefore arises about what new accounts of human nature inform the 'reconstructed' welfare state today with its notion of meeting residual rather than universal needs and its much reduced (or redefined) conception of citizenship.

Unearthing different notions of human nature in political thought has become a pressing concern in the light of the transformation of Social Democratic and Radical Right welfare politics. Social Democracy, for example, has been associated with the history of welfare in the twentieth century and was central to the postwar consensus, which evaporated in the wake of the world recession of the early 1970s, and the ascendancy of the New Right in the 1980s. Several commentators have described the establishment of a 'new welfare state' based on a 'new settlement' that replaced the 'classic welfare state' of the first postwar Labour government (e.g. Wilding 1992; Taylor-Gooby and Lawson 1993). However, in the early 1990s other commentators argued persuasively that the postwar welfare state had in some crucial respects outlasted the Right's attack on it (e.g. Le Grand 1990, 350; Glennerster 1991, 172). By the late 1990s, Glennerster continues to insist that despite tightly constrained budgets for two decades state welfare 'has continued to deliver many of its traditional objectives' (1998, 318). If this remains true, it suggests that, if the institution that most embodied Social Democratic values – the welfare state – remains intact in some form, then so do some of the tenets of Social Democracy. However, against this speculation, it is undoubtedly the case that the Labour government is ploughing new furrows in policy that significantly depart from the traditional path of universal welfare.

The transformation of traditional Rightist and Social Democratic politics puts into question the accounts of human nature and welfare these politics rest on, and suggests that the revival of either's fortune requires inventing new accounts. The contrasting accounts of the human subject as consumer or citizen, which respectively underlie the welfare programmes of the Radical Right and Social Democratic Left, serve as examples of attempts to reinvent their different notions of human nature. For the Right the consumer represents the self-interested subject whose interests are best exercised in the market where the needs of individuals and families can be met. For the Left, the citizen is traditionally the universal subject of the political community whose basic needs are protected by the state on condition that the duties of good citizenship are upheld. Revisionism on the Left is seen in the way it acknowledges that new market freedoms should be available to citizens who, once their basic needs are met, are free to expand their autonomy beyond the realm of the state. Likewise, New Labour is advancing a conditional notion of citizenship, which makes social rights to benefits and social housing contingent on responsible behaviour at work, and in the community (Dwyer 1998). These revised notions have been constructed in tune with the changing political, social and economic demands facing social policy in the 1990s.

4 The emergence of post-traditional or late-modern societies

According to several writers recently, one of the consequences of the emergence of post-traditional or late-modern societies, where tradition is open to critical interrogation, is the presence of new 'manufactured uncertainties' accompanying global climactic, environmental and economic threats resulting from human interventions in science, technology and industrialization (Giddens 1994, 4; Beck 1992). Human-made risks are of a different order and origin from traditional externally imposed risks. They challenge the Enlightenment belief that humankind has the power to exercise increasing control over its destiny (for which the welfare state was one such means) and overcome a fateful submission to nature. Moreover manufactured risks require individuals who have developed human attributes which Giddens calls 'self-reflexivity' to enable him or her to filter vast amounts of information and be more sensitively attuned to the impact they can have on the social and natural worlds. Thereby, Giddens argues, personal autonomy is reconciled with social interdependency, which together contribute to new forms of solidarity that are less dependent on traditional roles and modes of compliance. Consequently, new forms of 'generative politics' emerge that tackle poverty and social exclusion by engendering active trust between government and private organizations in providing welfare (13–15). If the traditional view of humankind was based on the notion of a rational and purposeful human nature, what concept of human nature is suggested by the 'reflexive' and 'autonomous' individuals of post-traditional societies who are subject to greater degrees of unpredictable risk?

Each of these four shifts in social and political culture betokens the end of a particular phase of modern history and arguably augurs the development of new powers of human nature to replace those that once equipped human life for the modern age. Each poses a challenge to humankind to develop powers to satisfy the new needs that society at the beginning of the twenty-first century faces. We will return to this important theme about human nature in the concluding chapter. It is reasonable, however, to question the genesis of the new qualities of human nature that postmodern and post-traditional societies brings forth. The book will argue that the core notions of mutual recognition and praxis in human labour, derived from Hegel and Marx, describe essential qualities of human nature which provide precisely this bridge between the endurability of human agency and the experiences of contingency, neediness and risk that characterize contemporary life. Specifically, the book will argue that universal features of human nature are located, in large part, *immanently* in mutual interaction and praxis. We will return to these questions in Chapters 7 and 8.

Reading human nature

The study requires a method of reading that makes explicit the assumptions about human nature in policy discourse and contributes towards a theoretical reconstruction of accounts of human nature. The reconstruction of implicit notions of human nature is important, for example, in making explicit the theories of need that are constitutive of social policy (see Berry 1986, 82).

Theories, accounts or propositions about human nature do several things. First, they furnish models of human nature based on core – or axial – assumptions characterizing the way individuals behave in different settings such as social, political and economic ones. Models make explicit the logic of social action based on the assumption of how individuals behave in each setting. The individualist model of human motivation, for example, is characterized by an assumption that people behave in ways oriented to the interest of self and immediate others and that this informs the different spheres of moral, social, political and economic action. Models, secondly, act like *gestalt* by establishing patterns among points of reference, or propositions in discourse, that refer to the object world, so helping to stabilize the relationship between discourse and the world. These patterns are present in the structure of proposition and argumentation that constitute a given discourse. The individualist model, for example, portrays different individuals seeking out their best interests by competing with each other or combining in voluntary associations to maximize their interests in concert with others. Such a model of action represents an atomistic pattern or structure of individuals working together in firms and competing against other firms to maximize their separate interests. It is a model found in the writings of classical political economists like Adam Smith. Further, this model portrays processes of production and consumption driven by the individual's experience of need that motivates him or her to embark on projects that seek to satisfy this need. Once satisfied the individual must work further to maintain the level of satisfaction or move onto new projects that satisfy other, perhaps higher, interests. In this way, a model also presents a sequential pattern of action. This sequencing of events represents a third feature of human nature accounts, namely narratives that portray the unfolding of individual or collective action directed at using objects to satisfy needs, and sometimes being thwarted in the process. Like models these narratives give shape to the process of events in the external world of which the human subject is a part.

Fourthly, a theory of human nature specifies a particular metaphysical view of humankind, or theory about the purpose of human existence, which affects not only our understanding of the nature of human existence (our ontology), but also what can be known about human existence (our epistemology). For example, the metaphysical view that sees humankind as fundamentally motivated towards individual self-interest carries implications about the kind of knowledge of the human and natural worlds available to us. It implies that only knowledge emanating from the individual's personal standpoint is valid – a viewpoint addressed later in relation to Hayek's theory of knowledge.

Fifthly, a theory of human nature functions in ideological ways as filters in a discourse that privileges certain human qualities over others and that screens out discussion of other supposedly unwarranted or unsubstantiated qualities. This process of filtering involves filling out as well as eclipsing gaps in knowledge. The ideology of the Right routinely eclipses or fails to address action motivated by altruistic concerns and represents it as action driven by some form of self-interest.

These five features point to the coherence of accounts of human nature that depends on a structure of argument that links together three component types of statement:

(i) factual generalizations about the needs, desires and interests which characterize the motivation of individual and collective subjects: e.g., for the Right, individual self-interest; and for Social Democrats, public-spiritedness, altruism and a belief in the 'common good' of all.
(ii) theories of human motivation that explain the way these needs, desires and interests motivate human action; e.g. self-interest leads to possessive forms of behaviour. These statements ascribe causal properties to particular agencies or subjects that are motivated to act in certain ways, and to particular objects, human and non-human, that are acted upon (Dryzak 1996, 109).
(iii) normative statements about the forms of conduct required of humans in order that they, given their dominant motivation, fulfil their lives with others. For the Right, for example, prudence and competitiveness in the market place, respect for the rule of law, and obedience to the moral order. Normative characterizations of human conduct lay down ideal standards about the way humans should conduct themselves in specific situations such as in markets and parliaments (Berry 1986, 41).

This account of the argumentation of human nature sees the way normative statements are derived from empirical or factual premises in a particular light. Instead of seeing facts and values as belonging to separate domains of analysis, it sees them as aspects of the same totality of human analytical faculties that are geared to achieving specific purposes or projects. Berry refers to this particular stance in political and moral philosophy as 'ethical naturalism' (1986, 50). Being human entails committing our natural faculties to courses of action directed at fulfilling our needs, wants and desires. By virtue of this commitment or interest, a normative or ideal state of goodness or rightness is posited (53). Our moral values are thus contingent on the needs humans must satisfy to secure life and fulfilment. In Berry's words, a theory of human nature implies 'an unavoidable structure to what humans do and what they value' (54); it 'possesses a descriptive and prescriptive duality', two elements 'like the warp and weft of a fabric, that constitute a conceptual whole' (37, 36). This would imply, for example, that if a particular account of human nature – such as Social Democracy's – argues that there are certain basic needs that are common to all, then social arrangements ought to be underwritten by the state. In this the state would be expressing the collective interests of all, to secure need-fulfilment and the right of all citizens to basic provisions.

Argumentation or reasoning that ties empirical, theoretical and normative components together into a coherent account of human nature represents a

14 *Welfare and Human Nature*

metaphysical theory of human nature, providing ontological and epistemological propositions about humankind.

To demonstrate how the three components are combined to produce a metaphysical theory of human nature, we can examine their role in two different theories found in Rightist thought, namely theories based on either institutional or epistemic arguments for human conduct – examined more fully in Chapter 4. (We will subsequently show in more general terms that these two arguments are indicative of two different kinds of argumentation in human nature theory, namely primary and secondary accounts.) In the first theory, seen in Milton Friedman's work, the examples appended to the factual and theoretical components of human nature discourse above – i.e. (i) and (ii) – suggest that human nature is governed by the dominant motivation of self-interest, which drives individuals to engage in acts of personal possession and satisfaction (Friedman, M. and R. 1980). However, when Rightist thinkers consider the normative implications of this view for social life – i.e. (iii) above – they argue that the dangers of social breakdown posed by unfettered acquisitiveness require that individuals must be constrained by an institutional order that limits selfish appetites. This can be by, for example, impressing on individuals the risks as well as gains of the market, the restrictions on individual liberty that accompany law-breaking, and the stigma assigned to moral wrong-doing. A metaphysical account of human nature emerges that portrays individual motivation as tending towards anarchy, but which at the same time is subject to a self-imposed ordinance that renders self-interested behaviour into a regular, predictable but dynamic social arrangement by the imposition of the institutions of the market, the rule of law and moral regulation.

However, in the second theory, found in Hayek's work (e.g. 1943, 44), human nature is endowed with a diversity of needs and talents and is not in principle predominantly self-interested. Nonetheless, Hayek contends, an individual's knowledge of need is confined to oneself and others known personally. This is not because of self-interest. It is an unavoidable fact of knowledge. Only individuals or groups of individuals in proximity can hold knowledge about their different needs and ends. Hence, satisfying the needs of all is best achieved through co-operation between individuals in the market place which enables them to buy and sell on the basis of knowledge communicated by prices, and which motivates sellers to compete for custom and buyers to shop around. Without access to knowledge of everyone's needs, market prices provide the best information that each individual can go on. This arrangement produces the most efficient allocation of scarce resources without central direction, without knowledge of everyone's needs and circumstances, and with each individual making decisions on extremely limited knowledge (about a range of commodity prices to be paid to meet their particular needs). This knowledge is nonetheless rapidly disseminated by the price system to other actors throughout the entire economy. It is because of this limitation on knowledge that human existence is best organized according to the institutional designs of the market, the rule of law and moral custom. Here, a metaphysical account describes the diverse motivations characterizing human nature, rather than its singular self-interest. Further, unlike the first theory, it characterizes individuals principally in *epistemic* terms acting on limited knowledge of human needs. It is this particular approach that leads Hayek to an individualist theory of human nature and action – which it shares with the former neoliberal account of human nature. This metaphysical theory provides the basis for an account of human knowledge and a specific set of normative prescriptions based on a market order supporting competition and voluntary association. The three types of statement listed above hold for Hayek as for Friedman. However, the particular reasoning Hayek adopts with respect to human knowledge links these propositions together to produce a different metaphysical account of human nature, one that stresses the epistemic rather than institutional grounds (or social ontology) for social action. We can summarize this difference by calling Hayek an epistemic individualist and Friedman an ontological individualist.

In the first theory, the single dominant motivation of self-interest is rendered into a dynamic order of competition and voluntary co-operation by means of the institution of the market. In the second, diverse human motivations to satisfy unlimited needs are constrained by the epistemic fact of human ignorance (rather than by the motivation of self-interest) which can only be overcome by the dynamic price system of the market.

These two examples of reasoning about human nature point to a pivotal distinction governing our understanding of human nature. The first example offers a coherent model of human nature based on a direct line of argument from the initial premise about the self-interested motivation of individuals to the need for social order. The second offers a more complex, and potentially unsteady, account that flows from the epistemological premise of human ignorance about the diverse nature of human ends and needs. It is Hayek's acknowledgement of diverse and unpatterned human needs and unbounded human nature that poses the problem. For the market, characterized by individual competition and voluntary co-operation, may be insufficient to achieve a satisfactory social order among people who possess motivations and talents that are not only those of self-interest and competitiveness. Whatever facility the market has for satisfying self-interest, this may not extend to differently motivated individuals whose proclivities – such as altruism, care, spirituality – will not fare well in a market society, even though these form part of Hayek's 'unbounded human nature'. The contention of Hayek (1943, 44) and Friedman (Friedman M. and R. 1980, 47) that these qualities can be commodified and provided in the market place is not convincing, resting on a metaphysics of human nature which fundamentally limits the scope of human need, experience and fulfilment.

The first type we call a primary account or theory of human nature. Here there is a consistent line of reasoning which links empirical, theory of motivation and normative propositions to provide a coherent metaphysical argument. The second is called a secondary or meta-theory of human nature describing features that in a primary theory would contradict each other, but which in this theory are addressed *as if* they can operate coherently. The fact that these features are unsettled raises issues about how the theory would need reconstructing to advance a more coherent one. This type of theory seeks to construct a consistent line of reasoning to describe the diverse attributes of human nature. Yet, this can result in certain propositions that stretch reasoning beyond its logical limits, for example, in seeking to understand altruism in a theory of human nature based on the dominance of self-interest. Being in itself diverse, human nature is described in terms of characteristics that do not provide a coherent picture of human motivation.

Humankind encounters developments in history that demand new responses over time, and which challenge primary conceptions of human nature which assume that certain dominant attributes have persisted over time. The significant changes in late-twentieth century capitalist society, described earlier, generate processes – e.g. social class reconfigurations, new gender and ethnic identities, and new social movements around these identities – that have challenged the established notions of human nature produced by political ideologies. In human nature discourse, these material changes are represented in propositions that unsettle established or primary notions about human nature and make demands for secondary theoretical reconstruction. In this respect, we will argue in Part II that concepts that until recently have been on the margins of social theory, about 'reflexivity', 'mutuality' and 'praxis', should play a more central part in theoretical reconstruction. When a theory stands in need of reconstruction, it becomes increasingly clear that its conception of human nature's unchanging status is no longer tenable. The idea that human nature consists in unchanging attributes has become especially problematic in the context of the fundamental social transformation described earlier and witnessed during the last thirty years.

In the face of historical contingencies that challenge the idea of endurable and eternal human attributes, a secondary or meta-theory can develop in one of two ways. First it can be reduced in scope to a set of first-order propositions about human nature in which 'rogue' or conflicting propositions are abandoned to re-establish a logically cogent discourse. Having asserted his unbounded model of human capabilities, Hayek frequently comes down on the side of stressing the essential competitive nature of humankind at the cost of overlooking the implications of the non-competitive side. Secondly, rogue propositions that depart from a coherent set of primary propositions may open the account to alternative readings by suggesting surplus meanings that have the power to radically re-order it. For example, what impact would Hayek's conception of the diversity of human attributes have on a theory of social order based on the workings of the market, the rule of law and conservative morality? For here other-regarding interests would have to hold equal sway alongside self-regarding ones.

Hiliary Wainwright has attempted such an alternative reading, namely of Hayek's proposition about the tacit knowledge that individuals have of their needs and technologies. The result of this re-reading is to render his individualist account of human nature into a fundamentally different one. She argues that if this important knowledge can be owned by associating individuals and groups rather than exclusively by individuals, then this would form the basis for radically different forms of social and political practice, and for different types of social order, and so contribute to more creative forms of human fulfilment than those described by Hayek (Wainwright 1994, 58; see Gamble 1996, 211–12). However, by rendering his meta-account in dogmatically individualist terms, Hayek produces a fundamentally delimited conception of tacit knowledge that premises an institutional order primarily on the market and that delivers a severely bounded conception of human purposiveness.

In conclusion, secondary or meta-theories posit new and over-arching propositions that lead to greater coherence, to potentially new ways of understanding human nature, and to new ideals that humankind is capable of achieving; that is, to new explanatory and normative propositions. These propositions encompass a wider range of normative and descriptive content and posit a wider field of reference than are found in primary theories.

The argument

In Part I we outline four models of human nature that have underpinned social policy in the twentieth century, namely the organic, atomistic, basic needs and mutualist accounts. For Social Democracy and the Right, a theory of human nature, drawing on these models, is described first in terms of a primary account, and, secondly, as an unsteady account that grapples with the effects of social change on social thought and the need to develop new notions of human nature that are more commensurate with recent developments. The result is a secondary theory that strives to reach new levels of intellectual integrity in the context of conflicting principles and shifting contingencies. Chapter 2 discusses the formation of theories of human nature in early twentieth century, Social Democratic social policy, focusing especially on the thought of Sidney and Beatrice Webb and Richard Tawney. Here the organic notion a human nature is clearly present. This account has given rise to the two major ideas about human needs and abilities that have shaped social policy in the twentieth century, namely that all of humankind shares common basic needs, and that individuals must engage in mutual acts of recognition, labour and service, by using their talents for the benefit of each other's needs. In Chapter 3 these themes are explored in the context of the development of Social Democratic thought during the second half of the twentieth century, focusing especially on the problem posed by the emergence of new social differences in the context of welfare policies wedded to the notion of common basic need. The chapter examines the ideas especially of Beveridge, Crosland, Titmuss and Rawls. Chapter 4 outlines the theory of human nature shaping Rightist thought and policy this last half century and especially in the last two decades, and addresses the issues posed by an atomistic theory of human nature.

Part II moves away from influential ideologies of social policy and human nature to examine two accounts that have had only a limited impact on official social policy twentieth century, namely Marxism and feminism – both at best limited to the study of social policy in the Academy, and only feminism beginning to influence policy in recent decades. (Because of limited space, the book does not discuss other theories of human nature such as those present in evolutionist, green and psychoanalytic theory – see Cowen (1994) for a broader perspective.) The account of human nature that emerges from these two strands concerns the notion of human mutuality. For human fulfilment requires acts of labour directed at co-operation between individuals with different as well as common needs. However much social differences of class, gender or race – more than commonality – can be said to characterize humankind, mutual action is required to recognize the nature of need and to produce for need. It can be argued that mutual action thereby produces new needs, new forms of need-satisfaction, and new forms of recognition about the nature of humankind. This insight was fundamental to Marx, especially the early Marx, and is recently being revisited by feminists addressing the 'politics of difference' from the perspective of what Hegel termed the 'struggle for recognition'. The new interpretations that these writers are giving to the notion of human recognition, together with ideas about the nature of basic needs developed by recent Marxists, raise important issues about human nature that have implications for the development of new social policies. The concluding chapter endeavours to draw lessons from these developments for a theory of mutual welfare that incorporates the idea of basic and higher needs.

Part I

Mainstream Traditions in Social Policy

Four models of human nature

The following three chapters examine notions of human nature that have shaped mainstream social policy in the twentieth century. To help map the intellectual terrain covered in Part I and developed later in the book, we outline four models of human nature that have informed twentieth-century social policy, namely, the atomistic, organic, basic needs and mutualist models. The atomistic model characterizes the individualism associated with nineteenth-century Liberalism and with the revival of the Radical Right and neo-liberals who have exercised a decisive influence on Conservative social policy since the 1970s. The organic model had a formative influence at a time when late nineteenth-century Liberalism and twentieth-century Social Democracy were developing a more collectivist approach to government in response to the problems of industrial society. However, the vague conception of the mutual responsibility between individual and society called for more explicit conceptions of collectivism attuned to the administrative tasks of government and to the emergence of mediating institutions of collective welfare such as Friendly Societies, mutual assurance societies and trade unions. The minimum basic needs and human mutuality models respectively were developed in response to these two requirements. The minimum needs model influenced thinking throughout the twentieth century about the government's role in managing social problems, especially in developing universal policies guaranteeing national minimum protection for all. The mutuality model appealed to voluntary forms of collective welfare begun in the late nineteenth century by Friendly Societies, mutual aid, and co-operatives, which survived well into the twentieth century.

As we chart the development of thinking about human nature, and the debates that ensued, we will see that the four models help to distinguish between the different grounds for arguing for specific policies. Although we begin by examining primary accounts of human nature, it is in the nature of practical reasoning in policy and politics that each account does not rest on a single primary model alone, but uses other often conflicting models. As we will see, this was as true for the Right as for Social Democratic policy. In social policy it is rarely the case that singular accounts of human nature, based on first principles alone, fashion the shape and outcome of political reasoning.

1 The atomistic model

This holds that human nature consists of individuals motivated by self-interest in meeting their needs. The market is the most common form of social institution that enables individuals to pursue their different self-interests freely with other individuals, forming voluntary associations where self-interest dictates. Markets operate with minimum external interference, and, according to Hayek, in an ordered and predictable way, and are aided by information disseminated via the price system to maximize the utilities which different individuals gain from purchasing commodities or expending their labour on producing commodities.

An extension of the atomistic conception of human nature argues that some individuals are unable to participate in the labour market because of age, disability or sickness, and require that their minimum needs be met. Nineteenth-century poor law and twentieth-century means-tested provisions have appealed to this *residual* view of human need. This view complements the atomistic view by excluding the non-active 'residuum' from the economically active in the belief that this has a minimum effect on the free circulation of labour in the market. Recently, however, Frank Field (1996) and the Dahrendorf Commission have criticized the human nature reasoning underlying means-testing on the grounds that 'means-tests reward inaction, deceit and dishonesty' (Dahrendorf 1995, 75).

2 The organic model

This represents the basic conception of human nature in the Liberal and Social Democratic tradition, and in some strands of Rightist thought – specifically Conservative – about the sentiments of identity binding the family, community and nation. Adopted by nineteenth-century New Liberals (Freeden 1978, 94) and later by the Webbs, Tawney and Titmuss, the organic model, broadly conceived, sees society as a social unity of different individuals and groups. The fulfilment of individual human nature and the realization of the wider social good are mutually dependent on each other. The common good of the whole depends on the welfare of each individual; and the individual's welfare on the maintenance of the common good. Although this model was present in earlier Liberal and Conservative *laissez-faire* thought, it became more interventionist with the emergence of the British Idealists and New Liberals who began to respond to the social upheavals of nineteenth-century industrialization and urbanization. It also exercised an influence on the newly emerging voluntary organizations represented by the Charity Organization Society whose mission was described by some of its leading members as helping individuals to contribute to the common good (see Vincent and Plant 1984). The recent communitarian movement in American and British politics has deliberately sought to counter the dominance of the atomistic model of Rightist social and economic policies in the 1980s and 1990s by reviving an organic model of human nature (e.g. Etzioni 1995).

3 The basic needs model

This describes the universal basic needs of human nature, and is found, for example, in the ideas of the New Liberals, the Webbs and Beveridge on the national minimum. All individuals have a universal right to sufficient resources and opportunities to fulfil their basic needs; and all in fact rely to some degree on these resources for their survival and flourishing. It therefore implies a moral as well as an empirical demarcation of individuals. Individuals are divided into two groups: those who, once their basic needs are met, have the physical and mental capacities to live independently and to help their less fortunate neighbours; and those who have a claim on collective welfare because they are insufficiently endowed with these capacities, or because these capacities remain unrealized owing to misfortune or deprivation. The model of common basic needs recognizes a level of need-satisfaction that is universal and inclusive of all, unlike the residual model which acknowledges a narrower range and lower level of common needs. Common needs implies a level of satisfaction that is universal to all. Whereas, the residual model holds that the needs of most individuals are best met in the market and that, because it prescribes that only subsistence needs should be met, provision is targeted selectively at the poorest and not indiscriminately at all.

4 The mutualism model

This model of human nature holds that human fulfilment and wellbeing are founded on relationships of reciprocity and co-operation among individuals engaged in works of producing goods for each other. Through co-operative ventures of labour, individuals come to recognize their common human nature in each other. Reciprocity creates the conditions for realizing universality and solidarity among humankind within a framework that includes a large element of voluntary obligation. This model was present in the British Idealists whose ideas, influenced by Hegel's thought, appealed to the New Liberals and the Charity Organization Society. The model is less evident in the Webbs' writings but surfaces later in the writings of Tawney, Beveridge and Titmuss, and in the recent debates on mutualism (e.g. Holman 1993; Blair 1995; Field 1996) and stakeholding (Hutton 1996a, ch. 12; Hutton 1996b, ch. 12; cf. Levitas 1998). Traditionally, the model has referred to the qualities of 'fellowship' and 'comradeship' to designate the third element of 'fraternity' in the socialist trinity of 'equality, liberty and fraternity'. However, in the writings of recent thinkers and politicians associated with New Labour, such as Frank Field, mutualism is not synonymous with altruism alone, but is seen as a new philosophy that conjoins self-interested with other-interested motivations.

A word about terminology. The variety of nineteenth-century political philosophies contributing to the scope of twentieth-century Social Democratic thought and policy – including New Liberalism, Fabianism and ethical socialism – raises issues about defining this trajectory. Cutler *et al.*, have coined the term 'liberal collectivism' to denote the political project that began in the 1930s with the welfare-augmenting initiatives of Keynes and Beveridge in the economic and the social spheres, and ended with the welfare-diminishing initiatives of the 1980s (1986, 150). Both Keynes and Beveridge were part of a project shared with New Liberals and Social Democrats to 'reinvent liberalism' by rejecting the traditional liberal *laissez-faire* hostility to state intervention and by promoting limited state involvement in society and economy. Liberal collectivists therefore

> accepted the traditional philosophical justification of capitalism as a political and economic system whose virtue is that it leaves a man free to do what he wills with his own. At the same time, the Liberal Collectivists accepted that the consequences of this freedom on the market were entirely unacceptable and these consequences would have to be curbed by state intervention in some respects if capitalist freedoms were to survive more generally. (9)

The origins of liberal collectivism go back further than the 1930s to the British Idealists, New Liberals and Fabian Socialists of the late nineteenth century. Social Democracy is presently treated as a major expression of the liberal collectivist project (see Hirst 1994, 2). However, as an expression it reflects the inherently problematic nature of liberal collectivism in seeking the 'happy combination' of minimalist intervention and capitalist freedom (Cutler *et al.* 1986, 153). It is this combination that has framed liberal collectivist discourse since the late nineteenth century, reappearing throughout the twentieth-century discourse of Social Democracy, and shaping the aspirations of New Labour into the new century. We will argue further that it is also this combination of collectivism and individual freedom that represents an unstable element in Social Democracy's meta-theory of human nature.

In contrast with liberal collectivism, neo-liberalism is a political theory seeking to minimize the scope of government intervention, which was revived by the governments of Thatcher, Reagan and other Western leaders in the 1980s. It can be argued that this break with the postwar consensus, the high point of liberal collectivism, also represents a decisive punctuation in the much longer period of liberalism as a global ideology which Wallerstein demarcates between 1789 and 1989 (1995, 1). Neo-liberalism is examined in Chapter 4 on the Radical Right. A further contrast should be noted in passing between, on the one hand, liberal collectivism and Social Democracy, with their belief in co-operating with capitalism, and, on the other, Socialism and Marxism which see capitalism as creating conditions inimical to human fulfilment (discussed in Chapters 5 and 6).

However, the dismantling of national insurance provision and the reconstruction of universal health care and education in the 1980s and 1990s have contributed to the demise of the common needs view of human nature, and the resurrection of market forces and the atomistic view. In these reforms, individuals are treated as consumers exercising choice over public and private provisions by paying for services themselves, by using cost-based vouchers, grants and means-tested subsidies, and by relying on the purchasing decisions of proxy representatives such as general practitioners and local authority social workers operating in quasi-markets. The response of Social Democrats under the banner of New Labour has thus far been to propose policies that draw on the above notions of human nature configured in a different way from the past. There is so far no evidence of a desire by New Labour to revive the national minimum based on the unreconstructed Social Democratic notion of common basic needs as a defining principle of the welfare state.

As we chart the development of thinking about human nature in the twentieth century, and the debates that ensued, the four models will help to distinguish the different positions that emerge. The next chapter explores in more detail the development of the basic needs and mutualist models from the organic conception in Social Democratic thought. Each model represents a distinct account of human nature whose relationship with other models has changed during the century, and is presently giving rise to questions about the future shape of social policy thinking in modern Social Democracy. In subsequent chapters we will examine how these models have been developed in other philosophical traditions and what resources they offer Social Democracy and social policy today.

T.H. Green and the liberal collectivist tradition of human nature

As a prelude to the discussion in Part I and specifically Chapters 2 and 3, we begin by locating an important source for liberal collectivist thought. Although nineteenth-century British Idealism lies outside the scope of the present survey, T.H. Green was important for different intellectual strands in late nineteenth-century Liberalism that were subsequently reconstituted in twentieth-century Social Democracy.[1]

Green's contribution to the Social Democratic account of human nature can be seen in his notion that each individual possesses capacities or powers for recognizing good in each other, and for developing the common good of all by means of reciprocal recognition and co-operation. Each individual has a basic right to this good, a right that derives from qualities residing in human nature and forming the basis of the 'ethical personality'. In *Lectures on the Principles of Political Obligation* (1986), Green identifies universal powers of reason and morality that all individuals possess in some degree – including the sick and mentally retarded (119). These powers form the basis for universal claims for rights which belong to 'every man in virtue of his human nature (the qualities of which render him capable of any fellowship with every other man)' (118), and which form 'a moral capacity without which a man would not be a man' (28). The existence of these moral 'powers', 'capacities' and 'capabilities' in human nature provides a premise for predicating propositions about an individual's moral ends or ideals: such that 'To say that [an individual] is capable of rights, is to say that he *ought* to have them, in that sense of "*ought*" in which it expresses the relation of man to an end conceived as absolutely good' (1986, 26).

T.H. Green and other Idealists believed in a basic moral equality between all individuals, which was based on a Christian view of God's grace imparting qualities of sacredness to all humankind. This belief underpinned their view that each individual possessed the right to the moral and material benefits flowing from the common good which society sought to realize in its spiritual life. This was the basis of the individuals' rights as citizens, an essentially moral and theological conception of equality (see Vincent and Plant 1984, ch. 2).

We can identify the origins of three Social Democratic concepts in Green's thought, namely the social minimum, the common good and social mutuality. Unlike Social Democrats, however, Green does not present an explicit argument that human powers represent needs and abilities that should be supported by a state social minimum. However, in *Prolegomena to Ethics*, he recognizes that individuals have a legitimate interest in arrangements for 'social wellbeing' and that institutional provision is necessary if humankind is to secure its moral development and advance the common good: for 'until life has been so organized as to offer some relief from the pressure of animal want, an interest in what Aristotle calls "living well", or "wellbeing", as distinct from merely "living", cannot emerge' (1986, 275). Further, the idea that the individual's moral capacity is shaped by society imparted a collectivist orientation to Liberal and later Social Democratic thought. For this reason, Green states in the *Lectures* that 'society should secure to the individual every power, that is necessary for realizing this capacity' (1986, 28).

Green believed that all individuals possess moral qualities that contribute to the common good of all. He described the evolution of the common good as progressing in both individual and community in a way that relied on the development of the institutions of state and civil society:

> the establishment of obligation by law or authoritative custom, and the gradual recognition of moral duties have not been separate processes. They have gone on together in the history of man. The growth of the institutions by which more complete equality of rights is gradually secured to a wider range of persons, and of those interests in various forms of social wellbeing by which the will is moralized, have been related to each other as the outer and inner sides of the same spiritual development.
> (1986, 192)

For Green institutions of welfare take on an explicit moral purpose, giving outer form to inner moral impulses.

The individual's recognition of the common good depends on a mutual process of intuiting in the other what the individual knows of him- or herself, by which human co-operation and reciprocity become possible: 'The capacity...on the part of the individual of conceiving a good as the same for himself and others, and of being determined to action by that conception, is the foundation of rights' (1986, 28). Because of these shared capacities, humankind can 'in *mutual helpfulness* conquer and adapt nature, and overcome the influences which would make them victims of chance and accident, of brute force and animal passion' (191, stress added). In the *Prolegomena*, Green argues that the common good is realized in each person's project, whereby 'some practical recognition of personality by another – of an "I" by a "Thou" and a "Thou" by an "I" – is necessary to any practical consciousness of it...as can express itself in act' (1986, 259). Green captures the tone of the common good not only in terms of higher ideals of moral development, but also of the individual's practical ability to empathize with the everyday needs of other individuals: 'Having found his pleasures and pains dependent on the pleasures and pains of others, he must be able in the contemplation of a possible satisfaction of himself to include the satisfaction of others' (264). In this the individual comes to identify with universal needs. To summarize so far, human recognition and reciprocity is the basis for the realization of the individual's personal abilities, for the universal entitlement to exercise rights to the common good, and finally for the betterment of society itself (259).

However, Green did not translate his recognition of the common good as an expression of human capacity into an explicit notion of common needs and an endorsement of social equality. Real equality among humans lay in the moral and not material or economic domain (see Vincent and Plant, 1984, 25–6). This moral form of equalitarianism did not prescribe precise forms of material equality. The Idealists were against the state seeking to limit inequalities which were seen to play a positive role in the formation of 'character', by, for example, enabling those who possessed private property to fulfil their potential, and by encouraging those who did not to aspire by their own efforts to own the material means necessary for their fulfilment. For Green, the ownership of private property provided 'a permanent apparatus for carrying out a plan of life, for expressing ideas of what is beautiful, or giving effect to benevolent wishes' (1986, 170), in short 'the means of realizing a will' (*ibid.*). It followed that individuals possessed fundamental rights to own property and to engage in free trade, based on the fulfilment of human nature that private property allowed (172). The Idealists' organic conception of society could incorporate widely differing individuals, each contributing to the whole and deriving different benefits from the common good. Yet Green was not unaware of the disadvantages faced by the proletariat who in not owning property faced serious obstacles in exercising their will and in fulfilling their duty to contribute to the common good (177). This awareness formed the basis for his belief in the provision of a 'secure minimum'.

Later, Social Democrats recognized the moral claims for individual freedom and diversity in human nature, but argued that material means must provide at least a modicum of wellbeing if moral ends are to be secured. One consequence of the primacy given in Green's thought to moral over material development is an ambiguity about the precise conceptual content of the minimum. Vincent and Plant refer to his 'serious equivocation' over whether the minimum referred to 'merely living' or to 'living well' (1984, 60). For Social Democrats this ambiguity represented a weakness in the Idealists' reasoning that called for more rigorous ways of conceptualizing the basic minimum and implementing it in concrete policies.

Green's account of human nature prefigures much of the thought of the Webbs and other Social Democrats: about moral characteristics common to humankind; the national minimum; society's obligations to advance welfare and the common good; the primacy of the individual's moral purpose; the indivisibility of the individual's moral duties and rights; the organic union of individual and society; and the individual's dependency on social institutions embodying the common good. It was in this spirit that the Webbs argued, for example, that the maintenance of a definite standards of civilized life was dependent on the 'joint responsibility of an indissoluble partnership between the individual and community, in which neither must fail in duty' (1911, 297). In the 1940s Beveridge came to reflect these ideas in his proposals for achieving social security 'by co-operation between the State and the individual' (1942, 6), and in the 1950s Marshall developed his thesis of citizenship as the legal, political and social embodiment of the common good (1963). Most recently, as we will see later, Tony Blair has echoed some of Green's thoughts about the moral relationship between the individual and the common good in developing his thesis about the Third Way (1998).

In this light, twentieth-century Social Democratic thought can be seen to draw on T.H. Green's organic conception of human nature. From this there developed two traditions of thought about human nature, basic needs and mutual needs, both bearing the imprint of the organic view of humankind. One line, developed by the Webbs, describes human nature in organic terms, expressed in the individual's duty to contribute to the common good and the individual's right to collective state welfare. The Webbs' close attention to specific needs and provision transformed the organic discourse into the more concrete discourse of social policy and national minimum provision. Nonetheless, underlying social policy was an organic conception of society whereby individual citizens, in fulfilling their role as national insurance contributors and taxpayers contribute to the common good, and benefit from the common good when claiming national welfare provision.

The tradition of mutual welfare provided an alternative way of developing the organic conception of human nature which was more sensitive to the human qualities of social difference and diversity than the basic needs model. It proposed that, because different individuals possess both common needs and individually different needs, they should co-operate in the labour of satisfying the totality of needs. By co-operating in productive labour to meet their different and shared needs, individuals come to recognize that they belong to an organic whole where each individual contributes to the betterment of all. The reconciliation of commonality and difference among humans is sought through social interaction. Each individual encounters basic and different needs in others, and together they reach agreement on the content of need. The common needs and mutualist accounts of human nature represent alternative approaches in Social Democracy that have influenced the course of twentieth-century social policy.

2
Social Democracy and Human Nature

Introduction

Traditionally, the Social Democratic welfare state has been defined by its commitment to the institutions of democratic government that supplement the market with provisions providing citizens with an increasing range of universal rights to basic standards of living in economic, social and family life (see Briggs 1961, 228; Lowe 1993, 13–14). These provisions aim to circumvent some of the uncertainties of unfettered market capitalism in order to secure a sustainable capitalist economy for the different needs of individuals and basic welfare provision for their shared needs (see Cutler *et al.* 1986). Although this project is often spelt out in concrete social and economic terms, its justification rests on a specific set of metaphysical propositions about human nature, namely arguments about the basic human needs individuals share which must be met to enable them to pursue their own ends as free and responsible citizens in the family, community and economy.

However, this view suggests an uneasy alliance between a notion of human nature characterized by common basic needs, whose responsibility rests ultimately on the state, and a notion characterized by individuals with a diversity of individually different needs who are free to satisfy them in the market. Taken separately, the two propositions represent different primary models of human nature, namely universal and atomistic human nature. Taken together they express a tension requiring resolution – a feature the previous chapter suggested was characteristic of meta-theoretical discourse. This tension recurs at various points in the history of Social Democratic thought and is present in different ways in policy. Different social policy ideologies have attempted to reconcile the two notions. Early Social Democrats like the Webbs employed the notion of the national minimum to formulate standards of provision for basic needs which encouraged individuals above the minimum to use market resources. A more recent philosopher like Rawls formulates principles of justice that seek to reconcile individual liberties with universal rights to basic primary goods. A further approach was adopted in the 1920s and 1930s by Richard Tawney, who emphasized the need for 'fellowship' and co-operation in meeting both shared and individual needs within the public sector. In this Tawney was appealing to a different notion of human nature realized through mutual co-operation, as well as by meeting basic needs, in public services that left little scope for private and voluntary provision.

The chapter argues that Social Democratic thought has advanced two distinct approaches to defining human nature and universalism in welfare provision: namely the provision of welfare for the basic needs of all; and welfare based on mutual reciprocity and co-operation among all members of society whatever their differences. Basic needs and mutualism represent two traditions within Social Democratic thought which were part of the wider movement of liberal collectivism and which were both present in embryo in the writings of T.H. Green and the nineteenth-century British Idealists. The organic view of human nature, based on a vague and at times mystical conception of the common good, and expressing the relationship between the individual and society, was developed in the two more applied concepts of common basic needs and social co-operation. New Liberal and Fabian proposals for national minimum provisions in welfare developed the former. The co-operative provisions of working class self-help found in Friendly Societies and mutual aid collectives in the late nineteenth century developed the latter concept. Currently, debates about notions of human nature underlying social policy have been advanced at a time when Social Democracy is being 'reinvented' in the form of New Labour, and is being reassessed in the context of a British society confronting the social, economic and political transformations traversing the West at the end of the twentieth century (Miliband 1994).

This chapter examines the different notions of human nature found in the first half of the twentieth century within the broad tradition of British Social Democracy, and attempts to locate them in the context of policy developments. This tradition draws on several different philosophical movements in the late nineteenth and twentieth centuries, namely British Idealism, New Liberalism, Fabian Socialism and Ethical and Christian Socialism. The chapter begins by describing the common assumptions about human nature and policy shared by these different contributions which have preserved a line of continuity throughout the twentieth century. At the same time, the basic needs model has almost eclipsed the mutualist model, even though elements of both can be found in influential Social Democratic thinkers in the early part of the century. The chapter ends by comparing the two traditions represented by the Webbs and Tawney, and assesses how compatible mutual and basic need conceptions were in early Social Democratic thought.

The human nature discourse of Social Democracy

The historical context of liberal collectivist thought, and its progeny Social Democracy, has been well documented.[1] The rise of government intervention played a crucial role in the formation of modernity and the modern constitutional state (Freeden 1978, 15). This section focuses on one aspect of this formation which has contributed to political philosophy and policy, namely the adoption by the state of a new conception of human nature, which furnished the metaphysical grounds for the state's authority to intervene in private life and take on new responsibilities towards the individual. Within this Social Democratic conception of human nature we can discern the two moments of basic needs and mutual co-operation. This broad conception of human nature exhibits the following set of empirical, theory of motivation and normative assumptions.

1 Human nature consists of a stratum of shared abilities and needs that form the basis for developing a diverse range of other human attributes

This stratum is identified by scientific investigation and the resources to meet it are met by state social minima. The idea of common abilities and needs stands as a bounded or limited view of human nature, and can be expressed as a coherent set of primary propositions about the empirical properties of human nature. It informs notions of common basic needs and national minimum protection promulgated in the 1906–14 Liberal government and in the Beveridge reforms of the 1940s, and expressed in the writings of the Webbs, Beveridge and postwar Fabians. Similarly, the history of poverty research from Charles Booth to Peter Townsend represents a line of belief that basic needs have a naturalistic basis – for food, warmth, shelter, etc. – which is shaped by culture, and can be identified empirically.

In the British tradition of social administration, the notion of essential needs implies that welfare benefits can be fixed at a minimum subsistence level. This idea was given empirical form in the work of the late nineteenth-century poverty investigations of Charles Booth and Seebohm Rowntree. Rowntree, for example, provided an empirical definition of *physical* deprivation based on the needs for food, housing, clothing, light and fuel (n.d. 119) that influenced subsequent poverty studies. This definition depicted a core of the poorer classes as 'those whose total earnings are insufficient to obtain the minimum necessaries for the maintenance of merely physical efficiency' (n.d. 117), with others in poverty being identified according to conventional and more subjective measures of the investigators.[2]

In addition, poverty was also conceived in terms of psychological necessities. The Webbs, for example, defined destitution as 'the condition of being without one or more of the necessities of life, in such a way that health and strength, and even vitality, is so impaired as to eventually imperil life itself'. This in turn meant that 'it is also a condition of mental degradation', 'the degradation of the soul…in which strength and purity of character are irretrievably lost' (Webb, S. and B. 1911, 1, 2). The Webbs, reflecting Booth and Rowntree's approach, saw need as a set of empirical characteristics identifying social groups by age, illness, ability and so forth. These groups were designated 'with regard to each *natural* class of person' such as 'infants, children of school age, sick, mentally defective, aged and able-bodied unemployed' (311, stress added). This approach enabled social administration to argue for specialist authorities to deal with the natural causes constituting each class (*ibid.*), as exemplified in the 'Minority Report' of the 1909 *Royal Commission on the Poor Laws* (HMSO 1909). The notion of basic needs was later incorporated in the rates of benefit Beveridge devised in his 1942 Report as part of his scientific 'diagnosis of want' (1942, 7) which formed the basis of postwar social policy.

2 Because humankind shares common needs that are social in nature, it endeavours to provide social provisions that ensure that no one's needs go unmet

With this theoretical claim about human motivation in mind – about the type of action that follows from the given facts of human nature – the Webbs argued that 'In a political Democracy, growing ever more conscious of itself, the growth of collective provision for common needs…may be regarded as inevitable' (Webb, S and B. 1911, 329–30; also 331).

Beveridge echoed this commitment to collective welfare in his 1942 Report, specifically in his distinction between what he called 'essential human needs' and less 'uniform and less universal' needs (1942, 273). Essential needs are those which all individuals possess for which Beveridge proposed universal provisions provided by flat-rate national insurance benefits tied to the national minimum and the means-tested safety net of national assistance. Less uniform needs were to be met through voluntary or private provisions according to the individual's command of market resources. All individuals whether rich or poor would have access to the former, whereas only some individuals would have access to the latter.

However, Sydney Webb recognized that the minimum was no more than an administrative convenience for ensuring that benefits were distributed universally to every individual. For example, 'the average citizen…is a mere abstraction, who does not exist' (Webb, S. 1911, 3). In reality government must provide universal services that encompass the needs 'not only for minorities, but even for quite small minorities, and actually for individuals' (*ibid.*). At various points he alludes to the difference between uniform and universal provision – for example in public health (21) – as a distinction between standard provision for all with uniform need and provisions that favour the full inclusion of all in society however different their needs.

The notion that universal benefits are governed by the principle of inclusivity and contribute to social cohesion is a central theme in Social Democracy. However, the distinction between benefits for uniform needs and universal benefits for all with their different needs is symptomatic of a basic tension in Social Democratic thought, which was referred to earlier and to which we return shortly.

For the Webbs, the national minimum constituted a definite standard embracing a broad range of physical, moral and social needs. They frequently talk of an 'ever-growing social consciousness', the 'evolution of civilisation' and 'the Co-operative Commonwealth' to describe this enlightened state of individual and social welfare (Webb, S and B. 1911, 296, 329). It represented 'a recognized standard of civilized life' (331), which was most fully realized in the universal provisions of the post-1945 reforms that established the National Health Service, national insurance and the education system.

3 However, individuals need to develop their different potentials beyond the satisfaction of their basic needs

Individuals will therefore devote their own means to fulfilling personal needs (a further theory of motivation claim). Meeting individual needs beyond basic needs is possible as long as the means used do not conflict with meeting common needs collectively (a normative claim). This involved two different arguments for resolving the tension in Social Democratic thought between the state's minimum and market provision:

(i) an argument that the common good is best represented by a national minimum for the same basic needs of all, in addition to which there is the market where individuals are free to meet needs above the minimum; and

(ii) an argument advancing the notion of the common good based on state provisions alone, such as education and health care, which benefit the individual's common *and* different needs, so strengthening mutual relations among individuals for the benefit of society as a whole.

The Webbs and Tawney represent these two arguments respectively. However, these writers also accepted something of each other's argument, as we will see.

Following the first argument, the Webbs argued that human needs could be met in two different ways which were not necessarily compatible – a tension that characterized Social Democratic discourse thereafter, giving rise to a secondary or meta-discourse whose core propositions required resolution. First, the national minimum fixed a clear division between collective provision for common basic needs and individual self-help for needs above the minimum. The Webbs saw the provision of the minimum as addressing the basic needs of all and requiring collective action by government. The state national minimum provided a uniform level of basic well-being on or above which every one should live, and up to which the 'destitute' should be raised by state provision. For Sidney Webb, it implied a specific range of welfare services in the form of national minima for health, 'sanity', subsistence, leisure, sanitation, education and child care (1911, 8–9). In time, he believed that the range of provision would diversify and standards of welfare rise, commitments shared by other Social Democrats such as Tawney, Beveridge, Marshall, Crosland and Titmuss.

Secondly, the 'national minimum' also implied a different sphere of need *above* the minimum where individuals, state and non-state organizations provided a mix of governmental, private, voluntary and informal welfare arrangements. Whereas the state was seen to have a duty to provide national minimum provision, the mix of provisions above the minimum was governed largely by voluntary choice. Fabian thought has consistently held that the welfare state can accommodate both collective and market principles of social organization. At the turn of the century, the distinction between universal needs and individually different needs justified what the Webbs referred to as the 'extension ladder' of private, voluntary and statutory services built on the national minimum. This superstructure of more diverse and individually attuned provision enhanced personal needs beyond the level provided by universal provision.

However, the Webbs also advanced a different notion of individual needs that relies on a moral argument tying together universal rights and collective duties, and which blurs the institutional distinction between individual and collective needs and provisions, in a way that harks back to T.H. Green and the British Idealists on 'the common good'. Here the Webbs were articulating the second argument above about collective provisions for individually different needs. They argued that only through *collective* provisions for all can individual fulfilment be attained; 'only when the resources of the nation are deliberately organized and dealt with for the benefit, not of particular individuals or classes, but of the entire community ... [can] the maximum aggregate development of *individual* intellect and *individual* character in the community as a whole ... be attained' (Webb, S. and B. 1911, 336–7, stress added). In this way the 'perpetual enlargement of the social purposes of the whole community' is secured (334). Collective provision, for example in health care and education, was not tied to any fixed and uniform notion of minimum needs, but designed for the diversity of basic needs of all individuals. Education and health provision could not be provided on a uniform basis but would have to address the diversity of basic needs found in the population. These provisions were fundamentally redistributive in providing public services for all based on the principle of progressive taxation rather than contributory entitlements accruing to individuals on the basis of their individual earning power.

On balance, however, the Social Democratic tradition saw a clear separation between common basic needs and individually different needs above the minimum, a separation embodied in national minimum provisions that were comprehensively consolidated in the Beveridge reforms of the 1940s. The national minimum approach draws on a rationalist strand in public policy that goes back to the traditions of British empiricism and utilitarianism associated respectively with Hume and Bentham. These traditions were based on an atomistic conception of society as a collection of persons whose individual welfare was understood as the utility-maximization of each, and whose total welfare involved the aggregate of individual welfares and not the advancement of the common good (McPherson 1973, 4–5).

From these factual and theory of motivation claims flow several normative propositions.

4 Welfare provisions based on this human nature discourse should be universally available

This guarantees a modicum of equal provision for all, and embodies the idea of common citizenship rights articulated in the tradition from T.H. Green and the New Liberals to T.H. Marshall and others more recently (see Vincent and Plant 1984). In twentieth-century social policy, this prescription is first explicitly stated in the Fabian writings of the Webbs, especially in their argument that 'the maintenance of a definite standard of civilized life is certainly a universal obligation' incumbent upon the community as well as the individual (Webb, S. and B. 1911, 297). The Webbs believed that universal welfare provision for all should be provided in the form of compulsory insurance, a national health service, education, child care and so forth, which would contribute towards an 'ever-growing social consciousness' (296) and 'prescribed standard of civilized life' (322). Universal welfare, in the sense of state-provided care for the basic needs of all without exclusion, was realized most systematically – though never fully – in the post-Beveridge reforms of the 1940s. Of all the reforms, the 1944 National Health Service White Paper gave the most explicit expression of the spirit of social inclusion and cohesion implied by universalism, ensuring that

> in future every man and women and child can rely on getting all the advice and treatment and care which they may need in matters of personal health; that what they get shall be the best medical and other facilities available; that their getting these shall not depend on whether they can pay for them, or any other factor irrelevant to their real need.
>
> (Ministry of Health 1944, Introduction)

5 Individuals are free to develop their own interests, but they are also bound by obligations to each other and to the common good. Universal welfare plays a central role in raising the moral tone of social life. This implies individual freedom for self-development and flourishing, and a commitment to collective betterment

British Idealists associated with the Charity Organization Society and the Majority Report of the 1909 Poor Law Commission, such as the Bosanquets, believed that on balance universal welfare provision would undermine the individual's sense of self-responsibility and moral independence.[3] In other words, there is a potential conflict between the principles of individual self-reliance and collective support. The Webbs, however, replied that the advantage of universal provision lay in its encouragement of moral strength in both the individual and the collective, in that the advancement of the common good implied the collective support of prevention and treatment in developing individual potential. For example, they argued that it is only by

> the systematic carrying out, by duly co-ordinated public authorities and voluntary agencies, of the policy of prevention – that is, the enforcement on every citizen of his personal obligations whilst simultaneously ensuring, with equal universality, that every citizen shall be able to fulfil them – that we can stimulate the maximum personal independence and develop to the utmost the individual capacity of the people at large.
> (Webb, S. and B. 1911, 40)

The local health authorities, for example, involved 'the steadily growing subordination of personal impulses to the general will…' (302) – a proposal suggesting a more explicitly paternalistic project than that of the Idealists.

Once the universal base was in place, individuals were free to undertake their own projects, unhindered by further governmental restraint and enabled to exercise their own freedom in the market or wherever. Sidney Webb proposed that with national minimum support, individual talent and potential would flourish, without interfering with either 'the pecuniary profits or with the power or the personal development of the exceptional man' (Webb 1911, 11). Beveridge, though sharing this belief in the national minimum, nonetheless believed in more clearly delineating the area of individual responsibility, in that 'The State in organizing security should not stifle incentive, opportunity, responsibility; in establishing a national minimum, it should leave room and encouragement for voluntary action by each individual to provide more than the minimum for himself and his family' (1942, 6–7).

6 These normative arguments suggest that moral rather than material ends govern individuals

The assumption is that by nurturing the moral core of the individual, the community can aspire to the common good and realize the inherent goodness that resides in each individual – a Rousseauan motif about humankind's inherent capacity for goodness. This implies both a belief in human goodness and an awareness of the dangers that social ills can inflict on this goodness.

For the Webbs, destitution was not merely material deprivation, but a moral state affecting the whole of society for which all members held some responsibility: 'a sort of moral malaria and spiritual degradation among the destitute themselves, and ... a distinct lowering of the moral purpose of the whole community, rich as well as poor' (Webb, S. and B. 1911, 294). This moral 'effect' however was the result of a moral 'cause that may be traced in all the immediate and ... material antecedents of Destitution' (*ibid.*); that destitution has, at root, a 'moral factor' (297). To counter any movement of society towards moral decline, the Webbs proposed policies of prevention, such that 'The whole moral effect of the work of the preventive Authorities is ... tending always to increase the consciousness of obligation, and to promote extensive fulfilment of it' (301). Hence, 'It is ... the "Moral Factor" in the problem, whether manifested in the fuller development of individual faculty, the finer tone of family life, or the widening grasp of public spirit, that is and must remain the dominant consideration in every attempt at Social Reconstruction' (333–4).

7 Human freedom implies human wrongdoing as well as doing good, the threat of pernicious evil as well as the beneficence of the common good

Frequently in discourses on human nature, human qualities of morality are contrasted with immoral qualities to provide the elements of a theology of original sin. The Social Democratic discourse is no exception. In their account of the 'moral factor' underlying the problem of destitution, the Webbs identified three different groups characterized by their responsibility for destitution and their capacity for overcoming it – in a way that draws on the Charity Organization Society's distinction between the independent citizen, the 'deserving' and the 'undeserving'. For each group the question of their responsibility implies a specific capacity for moral degradation and potential for redemption.

First, the mass of responsible citizens consisted of for the most part independent members of society contributing to its economic and moral well being. However, as members, these individuals also had a part to play in the genesis of destitution. The causes of destitution were rooted in part in the community's moral indifference towards deprivation. The Webbs described this situation as 'the frequent disjunction between "moral" failure in the community itself, or in some individuals, and the wrecking of the lives of others'. The consequences of this could be seen in the social problems of illness, child neglect and family failure, where the causes lay not only in parental neglect, but also in the neglect of particular classes such as property owners and businessmen who provided inadequate sanitation or managed 'sweated' workshops (Webb, S. and B. 1911, 297). The Webbs' idealist conception of a union of individual and social responsibility implied that all members of the community had some role to play in defeating deprivation.

A second moral category comprised the corrigible poor who were the beneficiaries of welfare policy. Their destitution could be largely prevented if adequate measures were taken. Job training, employment exchanges, national insurance, public health, health care and education, for example, would establish national minima to prevent destitution or raise those who had fallen to a standard where they could become independent and responsible once more. For the responsible poor (the 'deserving' in the language of the 1832 Poor Law Commissioners), such intervention would 'coincide with a systematic enforcement of personal responsibility' (Webb, S. and B. 1910, 303), and would entail clear expectations of responsible conduct. Without state support, these groups were vulnerable to apathy.

Thirdly, a small minority of individuals were deemed incorrigible (the 'undeserving'). For these, the Webbs did not flinch from recognizing that the 'destitution of whole families is caused or aggravated by personal defects or shortcomings' in one or more of the family (Webb, S. and B. 1910, 304). In the case of the unemployed man, 'if it were discovered by actual observation of the man's present behaviour that there was in him a grave moral defect not otherwise remediable, he would have to submit himself, in a detention colony, to a treatment which would be at once curative and deterrent in the old Poor Law sense' (307). In his Report several decades later, Beveridge echoed the same concern about the problem of incorrigibility when dealing with the limited class of men or women with 'weakness or badness of character' (1942, 142).

The Social Democratic tradition, then, recognized the collective responsibility that lies with all members of society for tackling the problems of destitution, a responsibility that when expressed in the form of collective provision can enhance the common good of all. For the majority of poor, welfare intervention appeals to the inner responsibility of the individual to respond to collective support and exert his or her own powers of autonomy. The third group resistant to moral calls is constitutionally impervious to moral persuasion because of some indefinable lack of character and so must be subject to coercive and sometimes custodial intervention. This group defied the logic of scientific administration that the Webbs proposed. In this they represented a problem beyond the scope of scientific and moral understanding that could only be rendered explainable by the notion of original sin. However, the problem of original sin does not belong to them alone, but is shared by the entire community of poor and non-poor who in their different ways are responsible for the common good. In this respect then a modern Social Democrat like Frank Field shares the same concern about engaging in the 'right political activity', which 'is about supporting at every opportunity the age old verities of civic responsibility at the expense of the darker side of human nature, i.e. to provide an environment where those values crucial to a civilized society can flourish' (1997, 145).

We conclude this section by placing the Social Democratic model of human nature in context. The development of industrialization in nineteenth-century Britain gave rise to new social structures of wealth and poverty that challenged the organic view of society. New class alliances questioned the nature of inequalities among individuals who otherwise shared the same essential human nature. This in turn contributed to new ideas within liberal collectivism about human nature, its changing needs and differences, and the role that state and society should play in satisfying needs and ameliorating social inequality. As a consequence of these changes, new ideas about universal human nature, such as common human needs and human mutuality, replaced the organic view. Each idea depicted human equality and difference in different ways and gave rise to different policies. For example, the Idealists, whilst accepting a modicum of universal need, nonetheless believed that, because of the uniqueness of each person, individuals essentially have different talents and propensities which must be harnessed co-operatively for the common good. Individuals therefore had claims to different amounts and types of resources. For exponents of the basic needs theory of motivation, human nature shares a range of empirically identifiable needs and talents which could be defined at the level of the national minimum, as well as a range of different needs which defined individuals differently and which were satisfied through market exchange. This approach relied on the state as the most important agency for meeting human need. The concept of the national minimum represented a principle for reconciling two different propositions about human nature – namely common basic needs and atomistic self-interests – within Social Democracy's meta-theory of human nature.

For ethical socialists like Tawney, human nature possesses universal moral qualities such as dignity and sociality which were the most important of human needs and which enabled different individuals with their different needs to co-operate and live in 'fellowship' with each other. The necessity of human interaction in all areas of social life generated a sense of companionship between individuals from widely different walks of life – a theme Titmuss later described in his official history of social policy during the Second World War (1950). The universal moral worth of humans and the inclusivity of their fellowship was an expression of universal human needs and provided the ground for universalist policies. Whereas the basic needs approach saw the state as the means of realizing human fulfilment, the mutualist model placed the onus of responsibility first and foremost on civil society. These two approaches within Social Democracy imply different ways of configuring the agencies of needs-satisfaction, the state and civil society. However, Tawney, as we will see, believed that mutualism could be nurtured predominantly within the state sector.

Fellowship and equality of consideration: R.H. Tawney

The foregoing account of human nature highlights the tension in Social Democratic thought between basic needs and mutualist notions of humankind. Each of these notions held a particular view of the relationship between common and individually different needs. The mutualist view formed the basis for the case for co-operation in welfare between different individuals. The chapter now turns to Tawney's development of this case.

Though sharing many Fabian beliefs – and close friendships – with the Webbs in supporting the idea of basic human needs, Richard Tawney developed an important strand of Social Democratic thought derived from T.H. Green but largely ignored by basic needs proponents. For Tawney, one of the core features of humankind was its social nature and its need for fellowship among individuals who, though sharing common needs, were also invested with widely differing needs and talents. Human fulfilment required co-operation in life and work among different individuals. Terrill describes Tawney's notion of fellowship as 'right relationships among free and equal individuals' (1974, 217). For Tawney, as for T.H. Green who described fellowship as social service done for others, the imperative of co-operation and fellowship was founded on a Christian morality designed to combat original sin.

In the interwar years, growing awareness of the range of human diversity was influenced by the increasing use of physiological and psychological measurement by government in its social and educational policies (see Rose 1979). The psychological characterization of the individual's educational attainment, skill and intelligence led Fabian social thinkers to address the range of diversity in human attainment and to recognize the role of social, economic and environmental factors shaping human differences and inequalities. The differentiation of environmental influences and human outcomes meant that it was no longer possible to ascribe blanket moral qualities, duties and expectations to different individuals, as the Idealists had done, without considering important material and social differences among individuals.

In this changing intellectual milieu, Richard Tawney argued that equality meant giving different individuals 'equality of consideration' rather than striving to achieve similarity in the natural endowments they were born with and uniformity in the welfare benefits they received. In Tawney's 'strategy of equality', government should endeavour to arrange resources so that each individual has an equal opportunity to utilize their physical and mental capabilities to the best of their ability: thus while people

> differ profoundly as individuals in capacity and character, they are equally entitled as human beings to consideration and respect, and that the wellbeing of a society is likely to be increased if it so plans its organisation that, whether their powers are great or small, all its members may be equally enabled to make the best of such powers as they possess.
> (1964, 46–7)

Like the Webbs in their opposition to the Charity Organization Society's attempt to intervene directly in individual character, Tawney believed that the focus of social intervention should not interfere with the individual's inner nature, their capacities, endowments and character. Rather, the focus is on the organization of environmental resources, 'to establish the largest possible measure of equality of environment, and circumstances and opportunity' (1964, 56), so that inequalities among individuals are lessened. Tawney's thinking works with an ontology that separates inner-character and outer-environment, focusing policy on the latter in the hope that the former will adapt through material nourishment and encouragement.

Within this ontology, Tawney places on society the moral responsibility for the welfare of its member, and defines equality in terms of this responsibility: society has a moral duty to accord each individual equality of respect whatever their different propensities. Terrill has contrasted this *qualitative* notion of equality with a *quantitative* equality which seeks uniform distribution of material assets among the population (1974, 123). The moral implications of his view of human nature imply not only that social services should be universally available to all – an established Fabian position since the Webbs – but that there is an onus on government to ensure that services are delivered in a way that accords equal respect and treatment to all. This theme of treating welfare recipients as morally worthy subjects whatever their social status is taken up in the postwar writings of Titmuss, and more recently in the speeches of leading spokespersons for New Labour (e.g. Smith 1996). It accords a further moral dimension to the philosophy of welfare universalism: not only are material goods to be distributed to people according to their needs, but this transaction should entail explicit moral consideration of respect for the recipient. This moral theme spells out the defining characteristic of ethical socialism. Tawney's argument about equality as equality of consideration signifies a shift in Social Democratic thought towards a greater sensitivity to social diversity and individual difference and their demands on policy. This theme, though present, was less perceptible in earlier writings of the Webbs, but became more dominant in the later generation of postwar Social Democrats like Crosland, Marshall and Titmuss. The hallmark of civilization is a just society geared to the common good of all whilst being sensitive to individual dignity. Far from equalitarianism inducing uniformity in individual achievements and levels of attainment, it would provide a basis for provisions geared to more specific needs once the universal minimum had been met. For,

> The more anxiously...a society endeavours to secure equality of consideration for all its members, the greater will be the differentiation of treatment which, when once their common human needs have been met, it accords to the special needs of different groups and individuals among them.
>
> (1964, 50)

This argument goes beyond the Webbsian and Beveridgean conception of the national minimum where once individuals' basic needs are met, the state can rest assured that it has fulfilled its duties, and individuals are then free to make their own arrangements for their different needs. The universalist argument, that began by directing society's resources to bringing everyone up to the national minimum, was now beginning to address the diversity of needs among individuals who possess an essential moral integrity despite these empirical differences. Common needs and different needs are no longer seen as distinct spheres of public and private welfare separated by the national minimum, but a totality structured into the universal needs shared by all and the particular needs that characterize different individuals. According to Tawney, public provision would be the main provider for this totality of need. This suggests a complex meta-account of human nature that conjoins common and different features among humankind within a public community of mutual support – an account, however, different from the basic needs model of human nature discussed above.

Tawney argued that the moral qualities of human nature meant that public services should aim for a more complete form of equality, one that allowed for individual flourishing within a framework of mutual welfare and co-operation. This involved 'the pooling of the [nation's] surplus resources by means of taxation, and the use of the funds thus obtained to make accessible to all, irrespective of their income, occupation, or social position, the conditions of civilization which, in the absence of such measures, can be enjoyed only by the rich' (1964, 122), so 'making the fullest possible provision for common needs' (*ibid.*). The idea of the state's distributing to everyone the surplus resources accruing to private profit implies that all should benefit from collective social services, a universalist policy aiming for social solidarity rather than protecting all from falling below the minimum. Indeed, Tawney recognized that there could be no '"clear principle of demarcation" [which] divides needs which may properly be supplied by collective action from those which individuals should be required to meet from their personal exertions' (124), and that the 'boundaries between the spheres of communal provision and private initiative differ widely both from decade to decade and from one country to another' (*ibid.*).

In articulating the principles that inform his 'strategy of equality', Tawney developed a notion of egalitarianism based on the idea of social enhancement rather than mere social uniformity at the minimum. In this he was suggesting that there is a creative economic process at work in welfare that raises the level of both individual and collective wellbeing. In practical terms this meant raising taxation progressively, spending public revenue on improving the environment, developing free social services, and creating supplementary sources of income in the form of social security (1964, 132). These policies would develop an economy geared to producing social priorities: namely, creating new channels of socially useful investment such as doctors and teachers; new forms of social capital in the form of parks, sewers, schools and libraries; interventions to regulate instabilities of economic demand; and resources for individuals in money and kind for increasing their opportunities and environment (133). For 'The standard of life of the great masses of the nation depends, not merely on the remuneration which they are paid for their labour, but on the social income which they receive as citizens' (*ibid.*) – an anticipation of the more recent argument for the social wage.

These equalitarian ideas imply a form of welfare policy which is more than individual compensation, national minimum protection or uniform redistribution. Tawney seeks to go beyond a strictly proportional (zero sum) logic of balancing the cost of resources against levels of need. Rather he views equalitarianism as a generative form of social investment that enhances collective and individual welfare according to a principle of extra-proportionality in augmenting and empowering human beings:

> In reality, of course, the greater part of the expenditure upon the social services is not a liability, but an investment, the dividends of which are not the less substantial because they are paid, not in cash, but in strengthened individual energies and an increased capacity for co-operative effort.
> (1964, 154)

Tawney was one of the first twentieth century thinkers to introduce the concept of 'equality of opportunity', which became a key principle of the post-1945 consensus between Tory and Labour governments. This concept can be understood as meaning that social investment not only creates new forms of collective wealth in the form of welfare provision, but also empowers individuals to achieve new levels of self-realization. He believed that 'it is possible to secure to all...not indeed equal culture or intellectual attainments, but equal opportunities of cultivating the powers with which Nature has endowed them' (1964, 141). In this argument Tawney was articulating a concept of what, since the 1980s, has been termed empowerment, whereby the development of individual autonomy is dependent in part on the provision of collective material welfare: for 'If, in short, freedom implies...the possession by individuals of a genuine, if partial, power of self-determination, then so far from being attenuated by measures conducive to the more general enjoyment of physical and mental vitality, it has gained in substance and reality as a result of them' (233).

Tawney would have dismissed the critique advanced by the nineteenth-century Charity Organization Society – and by the Radical Right of the late twentieth century – of the limited 'zero-sum' logic characterizing egalitarian policies. According to this view (e.g. Joseph and Sumption 1979, 23), in taking from the rich and giving to the poor, the Left ignores the extra-proportional augmentation of wealth that investment by the rich can secure – by, for example, encouraging the wealth accruing to the rich to 'trickle down' to the poor as well as contributing to overall economic growth. In effect, Tawney was applying the same logic – before Hayek used it in his critique of growing state intervention (1943) – of the extra-proportional gains of investment to lower income groups, rather than exclusively to the higher groups, and pointing to the diversity of wealth thereby generated. The Commission on Social Justice has more recently revisited this argument in its talk of promoting an 'active' welfare state to replace the 'passive' welfare state of Beveridge (Borrie 1994, 221) and in fostering an 'investor's' rather than 'leveller's' strategy which redistributes opportunities rather than income (95).

The purpose of state welfare lies not in imposing uniform measures of welfare resources on each individual, but in bringing individuals with different qualities into a common sphere of human encounter 'where community of environment and a common education and habit of life, have bred a common tradition of respect and consideration' (1964, 114). For Tawney, state resources had the potential to cultivate new forms of social interaction and reciprocity that would produce a greater equality of self-worth. What was important was to develop new social institutions that fostered opportunities for new forms of social interaction and collaboration. Terrill argues that 'Tawney carried the discussion of equality, in a novel way, from the plane of distributive justice to the plane of social relationships' (1974, 135).

Conclusion

The argument of the Webbs and Tawney about the ends of social policy and the meaning of social equality provide two different, though not mutually exclusive, conceptions of human need, the relationship between individual and society, and the means for fulfilling human nature. For the Webbs, needs are identified by the specific characteristics of humankind for which government guarantees both a sufficiently stable economy and minimum welfare provisions to ensure that basic needs are met. Beyond the minimum, individuals are free to meet their needs privately in the market. This concept of need entails the disaggregated concept of an inventory of discrete minimum needs. For each need for which the state accepts responsibility, there is a matching social right to welfare. It is this approach which informs Marshall's theory of citizenship developed in *Citizenship and Social Class*. For Marshall such a concept of rights implied a distinction between meeting rights at the minimum and achieving equality. Thus Marshall could argue that citizenship was 'the architect of legitimate inequalities' (1963, 73).

By contrast, for Tawney and subsequent ethical socialists like Titmuss, needs are conceived holistically. Here government is responsible for ensuring that each individual has the opportunity to meet his or her own needs and abilities and to contribute towards fulfilling each other's. Each individual is characterized by a unique pattern of abilities, the enhancement of which government provides through its collective social provisions and modes of investment. It is questionable whether the Marshallian concept of citizenship rights is appropriate for this concept of human nature.[4] Tawney believed that collective state provision would harbour mutual acts of welfare between individuals. However, he appeared to dismiss the idea current at the turn of the twentieth century (as it is again at the twenty-first century) that a plurality of welfare organizations – voluntary, self-help and commercial – is needed to contribute towards mutualism. Tawney seemed to believe that the mutualism provided largely by state welfare would be sufficient to meet most needs.

Given these different conceptions of need, the Webbs and Tawney advanced two different conceptions of the way individuals fulfil their needs in society, conceptions which display two different accounts of the relationship between individual and society based on their different views of the organic nature of society. For the Webbs, an organic relationship exists between each individual and society, and it is the totality of such relationships that comprises the social whole. These relationships were described in terms of *vertical* relations that joined each separate individual to the organic whole. Consequently, it was this conception of organicism that supported the Webbs' hierarchical approach to social policy. Their proposals for a comprehensive range of social services run by an elite of professional experts providing specialist provision for specific needs, were seen as the best way to achieve the common good to which each individual in need could turn.

By contrast, Tawney's view of the organic fusion of society lay in the network of *horizontal* relations between different individuals who were bound by relations of reciprocity, fellowship and community. Together the totality of relationships among individuals represented a different and less hierarchically organized conception of organic society. In this way Tawney probed more deeply than other Social Democrats the problem of economic equality and social relations:

> Satisfaction may be derived from the contemplation or enjoyment of a certain set of relations embracing all elements of an economy, instead of from the consumption of a physical entity, like boots. The enjoyment of economic equality...means the establishment of an indivisible set of relations between all human factors of production, in so far as they are recipients of final income.
>
> (1964, 126–7)

However, although these different views are here presented as ideal types of organic society, the vertical and horizontal conceptions are not mutually exclusive, and provide scope for considering alternative welfare arrangements that integrate provision for basic and mutual needs. The construction of the two conceptions suggests in outline how Social Democracy could in principle organize services for both types of needs: namely, that basic needs involve the provision of national minima for all as part of the vertical relationship between state and individual; and, with basic need protection in place, mutual needs involve the provision of welfare between individuals engaged in acts of fellowship and comradeship. However, the Webbs and Tawney saw welfare largely in state collectivist terms, which in hindsight can be seen to undermine the scope for mutual welfare. Without a clearer vision of what state provision could do for voluntary, mutual and self-help organizations, and what they could do for the common good, the Webbs and Tawney failed to develop a conception of welfare that included a role for the intermediary organizations of civil society; that is, for voluntary associations able to guide mutual relations between individuals and to represent classes of individuals in their negotiations with government. These issues continued to exercise the thought of the postwar generation of Social Democrats.

3
Equality and Difference in the Postwar Years

Introduction

The postwar years saw the establishment of the 'classic welfare state' (Digby 1989, 54) based largely on the Beveridge Plan for social security (1942), which represented the culmination of the Social Democratic philosophy of meeting universal human needs. What Beveridge achieved was the introduction of a comprehensive system of national insurance that provided national minimum provision for the range of different needs arising from disrupted earnings, namely basic pensions, sickness, unemployment, maternity, widows and industrial injuries benefits. Alongside this, other universal services for basic needs were established in health, family allowances and education. In implementing Beveridge, the 1945–51 Labour government established a welfare state responsible for providing minimum provision for basic needs. In so doing, it gave the fullest expression to the Social Democratic belief that the purpose of social policy was to contribute to human fulfilment by meeting basic needs.

Of course, the reality of welfare provision fell short of this universal ideal (see Glennerster 1995, 44). Some provisions continued to be selectively means-tested, based on the residual model of human nature, and universal services in health, education and pensions were limited on other selective grounds. National Insurance was more available for men than women and for the able-bodied than the disabled (41). Prescription charges were implemented in 1951 with exemptions subject to means-testing, and means-tested national assistance grew at the expense of universal national insurance (Timmins 1996, ch. 3). However, universalism was a powerful ideology in the postwar years for galvanizing public support for improving the level and scope of universal provisions in health and education. In addition, Beveridge's report on social security was strongly committed to a liberal view of individual responsibility, whereby individuals, once protected by the national minimum, would have 'room for voluntary action ... to provide more than the minimum for himself and his family' (1942, 7).

Beveridge also firmly believed that self-help could best be provided through mutual insurance organizations involving working people themselves. This philosophy of self-responsibility, which Beveridge set out in *Voluntary Action* (1948), drew on Social Democracy's mutualist approach to meeting human needs. However, at the time this text received less interest than his 1942 plan and subsequently had little impact on the statist conception of welfare and the national minimum established in the late 1940s and maintained until the 1980s.

In the fifty years since the implementation of Beveridge, fundamental changes to Britain's role in the transformed global economy have resulted in thoroughgoing reforms to the classic welfare state. Worsening economic cycles that defied Keynesian demand management, rising unemployment and fundamental restructuring of labour markets led to a series of fiscal crises in the welfare state, deepening poverty and widening inequalities in income and wealth. These developments have gradually reduced the effectiveness of the welfare state to offset the consequences of social change. Further, social factors, including growing numbers of pensioners and lone-parent families, new trends in disease and morbidity, and new medical technologies providing more effective and expensive treatment, have also overloaded the welfare state. Political change – including rising expectations, new opportunities to exit from state into private provision, and the rise of welfare activism among different sectors of the population – contributed to the gradual replacement of flat-rate benefits tied to the national minimum by earnings-related benefits and to the expansion of private and occupational pension schemes.

Throughout the postwar years, the basic needs conception of human nature embodied in the Beveridge welfare state held sway. At the same time, several reforms of the postwar social security system modified the structure of Beveridge. A distinguished line of Social Democratic thinkers – T.H. Marshall, Crosland, Titmuss, Townsend and Halsey – played an important role in re-thinking Beveridge, even though they kept faith with the basic need system of provisions that Beveridge had established. Only Titmuss developed a different line of thought that stemmed from Tawney and stressed the mutualist nature of humankind. More recently, communitarians have appealed to similar sentiments (Etzioni 1995; Blair 1995). Other writers such as Hadley and Hatch (1981) questioned the notion of a state monopoly of provision for basic need and stressed the importance of voluntary action within the mixed economy of welfare. However, this was from a position that kept faith with the Social Democratic commitment to meet common needs. In Chapters 5, 6 and 7, we will see that the Marxian notion of praxis and feminist notions of the recognition of difference are both based on a mutualist model of human nature, which shares similarities with the ideas of Green, Tawney and Titmuss.

From the 1940s to the end of the 1970s, the basic needs model represented the dominant conception of human nature in social policy. At the same time, arguments for a new social policy sensitive to social differences were heard. This chapter takes up the development of the basic needs model, introduced in the previous chapter, along lines which stress new notions of equality and difference. During this period, discussion of the mutualist conception of human nature was heard intermittently. It was a subordinate theme of Beveridge and a dominant one of Titmuss' late writings. It is presently gaining ground again with New Labour. The chapter covers a diverse and far from unified group of writers, including Beveridge, Crosland, Rawls, Titmuss and others. One important theme cuts through each of these writers, namely the need to discover a conception of welfare equalitarianism that accommodates some notion of social difference.

Equality as the national minimum: Sir William Beveridge

The 1942 Beveridge Report represented the fullest expression of the Social Democratic philosophy of basic needs, the culmination of liberal collectivism begun in the late nineteenth century (Cutler *et al.* 1986; cf. Glennerster 1995, 22). The implementation of the Report established a system of social welfare which, despite subsequent deviations from Beveridge's principles, held sway until the radical reforms of the 1980s and 1990s. This section describes the philosophy of human nature informing Beveridge's reforms.

In common with the basic needs model, Beveridge's conception of human nature divides need into two kinds, namely 'minimum needs' and needs above the minimum. On this division, he constructs an architecture of the rights and responsibilities held by the state and individual and the different methods of allocating welfare used by the state and the market. His liberal beliefs, however, committed him to a particular kind of collectivism, which saw social action – termed 'voluntary action' – as complementary rather than antagonistic to the market. Beveridge's own writings, especially the 1942 Report *Social Insurance and Allied Services*, were more practical than the writings of other members of the Liberal–Social Democratic tradition. However, this practical cast of mind in no way detracted from the role of the Report as an exemplar of the basic needs model of human nature. The elements of the Report's architecture deserve close study. We will discuss six elements that each reveals aspects of Beveridge's philosophy of human nature.

First, the division of human need into common basic needs and nonbasic needs is presented explicitly in his discussion of universal death grants and industrial assurance, although it underlies the whole architecture of his 1942 Report. Beveridge spoke of the 'essential universal needs' that all individuals possessed, and 'other needs' which are less 'uniform and less universal' (1942, 273). All individuals whether rich or poor should have rights to the former; whereas only some individuals had rights to the latter according to their command of market resources.

Secondly, for these two types of needs, two distinct types of social provisions were to be made available, namely collective and voluntary insurance, each expressing distinct attitudes about the freedom and responsibility of the individual and state. Collective national insurance was provided by the state and everyone in work paid a 'compulsory' flat rate contribution. 'Voluntary' insurance was the responsibility of individuals who chose to enrol in occupational 'industrial assurance' or in mutual assurance provisions provided by Friendly Societies and mutual assurance societies (273). The principle of national insurance meant in theory that all individuals would be protected from falling below the subsistence level of welfare, a level on which they could improve their welfare by their own efforts. This was expressed in the 1942 Report as 'giving in return for contributions benefits up to subsistence level, as of right and without means-test, so that individuals may build freely upon it' (7). Although Beveridge spoke of the national minimum in subsistence terms, he nonetheless pegged it at a slightly higher, and more eligible, level than means-tested national assistance.

Thirdly, underlying the structure of provision, Beveridge retained a set of incentives demarcating the division between work and welfare, which he had inherited from the Poor Law. Those falling below the national minimum because of interrupted earnings were subject to a residual conception of need that clashed with Beveridge's belief in basic needs. The dual provision of collective basic insurance and individual voluntary insurance was based on a particular view of incentives, namely the 1834 Poor Law Commission's view that state benefit levels should operate on the principle of 'less eligibility' (Checkland S.G. and E.O.A. 1974, 376). This incentive structure applied to the relationship between wages and benefits and between private and state insurance provision. In the first place, the state should ensure through the incentive structure of benefits and wages that welfare recipients were placed in a position of less advantage compared with the advantages enjoyed by the lowest paid independent labourer. The structure of incentives between work and welfare, provided by wages and benefits, determined that provision for basic needs would be set at a minimum rather than an adequate level. In this way, it supported incentives to encourage the able to seek waged work in the market. In the second place, this view of the role of public provision in the labour market further justified the maintenance of a clear differential between state and private insurance schemes. The subsistence level of state benefits provided an inducement to individuals to enter occupational or private schemes and receive these additional benefits on top of state provision. The principle of less eligibility has been gradually modified by the labour market restructuring of the last thirty years. It is presently being further modified by the Labour government's 'welfare to work' strategy with its new in-work benefits and national minimum wage to support those in low-waged jobs.

Fourthly, the distinction between voluntary individual and compulsory collective insurance gave rise to two different principles of equity, actuarial and equalitarian. The conventional actuarial principle of equity, that applies to insurance purchased in the market, means that the cost of insuring an individual against certain contingencies is determined by calculating his or her risk of experiencing, for example, injury in particular kinds of employment, illness related to particular life-styles, longevity and so forth. By contrast, collective insurance allows for the 'pooling of risks', whereby members pay compulsory contributions into a reserve fund from which they are entitled to claim benefits when they experience a range of needs-based 'risks' occasioned by unemployment, sickness, pregnancy, widowhood or retirement. National insurance is undergirded by a more powerful equalitarian principle governing all contributing members, with the effect that in Beveridge's version equal flat-rate benefits are paid to all individuals entitled to claim by having paid contributions of equal amount. In Beveridge's language, equal contributions and benefits 'implies both that [social insurance] is compulsory and that men stand together with their fellows. The term implies a pooling of risks' (13). Thus 'each individual should stand in on the same terms; none should claim to pay less because he is healthier or has more regular employment' (*ibid.*). The system of national insurance provided a platform on which voluntary, mutual or private welfare supplemented state provision for basic needs.

Beveridge thereby established the actuarial principle based on the market for private insurance alongside the system of national insurance based on the equalitarian principle. In theory, the actuarial principle adjusted payments to specific risks, and adjusted different packages of insurance cover to what the individual could afford. In what Beveridge termed 'voluntary insurance', individuals are responsible for paying for what they need above the minimum, which they would not do if this was provided by the state. In this sense the market principle of 'adjusting premiums to risks is of the essence...since without this individuals would not insure' (1942, 12). In turn this involved 'accumulating reserves for actuarial risks' (13). For Beveridge, 'Making provision for these higher standards is primarily the function of the individual, that is to say, it is a matter of free choice and voluntary insurance' (121). Individual needs above the basic were to be met in the market place. However, we will see later that Beveridge believed that the market could serve mutual purposes that supported reciprocity within the community. Indeed, throughout the Report, Beveridge (though a professed Liberal) articulated a Social Democratic notion of human nature comprising collective, mutual and individualist sentiments.

Fifthly, at the base of the two different principles of equity – equal benefits for equal contributions, and benefits and contributions adjusted to risks – are two different concepts of risk reflecting the different understandings of human contingencies that prevailed in the modern 'Fordist' regime that characterized production and welfare in the early postwar decades. These can be termed demographic and actuarial risks. The state's collectivist arrangements based on equality of treatment are concerned with risks that are common to all and arise as part of the human condition. As such they are risks or contingencies that befall all individuals at some point in their lives – e.g. birth, schooling, work, sickness, retirement, widowhood and death – and that can be calculated with some accuracy using available demographic data on birth, morbidity and mortality. These data enable analysts to plot the 'life cycle' of risks involved in human needing (see Falkingham and Hills 1995). According to the Keynesian theory of demand management, economic risks can also be calculated on the basis of studying normal economic cycles, anticipating their outcomes for economic and employment activity, and regulating such activity by means of demand-sided measures such as public welfare.

From a different perspective, however, private insurance companies would view such general demographic trends from the point of view of the investment risks their customers present. Each customer is classified according to age, gender, occupation, income, etc. to calculate in actuarial terms the cost of the risks that the insurance company would have to cover if particular contingencies such as sickness, retirement and death were to occur. Actuarial calculations of risk rely on the same demographic data as state social insurance. However, there is a crucial difference.

From the state's demographic perspective, the concept of 'risk' applies to contingencies that *all humans share* – and for this reason national insurance came to view these contingencies as needs rather than risks. However, the actuarial perspective stresses the risks of the insured individual rather than the population. From this perspective, these contingencies are risks in the sense that the investments of the insured *individual*s and of the insurance company and its shareholders are put at risk if calculations of future trends in claims are not soundly based. The two approaches reflect different views of need, namely the universal contingencies affecting all and the individual risks that create opportunities for self-interested gains and losses.

However, it is clear that both approaches adopt similar methods of work and depend on broadly similar kinds of data. Both use demographic data recording general trends in the population and employ statistical procedures for forecasting future trends in social need. The difference lies, however, in what Foucault termed the state's 'bio-political' governance of the population (1979, 139), where the state takes on some of the functions of the private domain of insurance firms and mutuals and socializes these for the welfare of the general population. In Britain and some other countries this bio-politics was secured on the basis of a national minimum for all and voluntary or private insurance for a much smaller group who wanted and could afford it.

Sixthly and finally, Beveridge's plan for social insurance envisaged two types of social institution each informed by a specific moral concern.

Beveridge's thinking here is especially relevant in pointing beyond the material concerns with meeting basic human needs to moral concerns about the mix of altruistic and self-serving motives in humankind. First, collective social insurance gave rise to a sense of social solidarity based on the fact that the cost of security was shared between three parties, namely the insured, employer and state (1942, 17). In Social Democratic literature this reflects the principle of solidarity between the 'social partners' of labour, employer and government. Separate but parallel to state insurance were the private and mutual insurance institutions that Beveridge believed would encourage the altruistic principle of voluntary action as well as profit maximization.

For Beveridge, the market had a capacity to support a new moral sentiment in humankind. This was different from the individualist principle of maximizing self-gain, because it was being harnessed by new forms of non-state collective endeavour within working class communities, namely co-operatives, Friendly Societies, and mutual aid societies. Since the nineteenth century these organizations have provided a range of different benefits for their members. In his book *Voluntary Action*, Beveridge described this as 'Voluntary Action for a public purpose – for social advance' (1948, 8). This institutional complex was based neither on the state's collectivist morality nor on a private market morality. Rather it was based on what can be termed a 'third way' which encouraged human qualities of enterprise and prudence in individuals who invested their savings in mutual organizations. This action would encourage altruistic support for the variety of hardships that can befall individuals. Beveridge described two motives that guided mutual endeavour. First, there was the motive for 'mutual aid', which arose from the community members' own need for security, and from their realization that others have the same needs and so must co-operate in building up a store of provisions in preparation for these contingencies (8–9) – a view reflecting T.H. Green's argument about the mutual recognition of human need. Secondly, there was the broader motive of philanthropy that Beveridge saw as guided by a sense of 'social conscience' affecting all members of society; for 'to have social conscience is to be unwilling to make a separate peace with the giant social evils of Want, Disease, Squalor, Ignorance, Idleness, escaping into personal prosperity oneself, whilst leaving one's fellows in their clutches' (9). In this, Beveridge held a view of the common good similar to that of the Webbs.

In sum, we can see in Beveridge's thinking how freedom and responsibility construct the human subject to accord with the different circumstances of the two types of need, basic and non-basic, which shape his architecture of national insurance. In maintaining the complex relationship between state and citizen, the state seeks a balance between two distinct constructions of human nature. On the one hand, the state aims to meet basic needs: 'to abolish want by ensuring that every citizen willing to serve according to his powers has at all times an income sufficient to meet his responsibilities' (1942, 165). On the other hand, it aims to provide the freedom of 'Management of one's own income' (12). On balance, the monopolistic pattern of postwar social services based on the national minimum has limited scope for individual autonomy and choice. The national minimum meant uniformity in welfare provision and placed responsibility for provisions for diverse needs outside the state and on the individual, and so, in the postwar years, beyond the reach of many people. Despite these disadvantages, Beveridge's architecture, which conjoined the principles of national insurance, voluntary insurance and mutual action, was based on a coherent meta-theory of human nature commensurate with the postwar years.

Equality as equal participation in human fulfilment: Anthony Crosland

For Crosland, the Beveridge welfare state was one of the main reasons for rising prosperity in the postwar years. This view was based on the welfare state's guarantee of securing basic human needs, which gave 'the most complete and explicit statement of the philosophy of the national minimum' (1963, 120). His optimism was sufficient to believe that the forces of social change – capital growth, prosperity and declining poverty – were moving in favour of increasing personal fulfilment, social diversity and freedom. Given these changes, Crosland saw that greater equality could be achieved by promoting more extensive opportunities for participating in education and economic prosperity (1963, 208). Government had merely to navigate society in the direction of greater prosperity. Instead of the Social Democratic belief, voiced by the Webbs and Tawney, that the fulfilment of human need was fundamentally a moral matter, Crosland proposed that the quest for personal fulfilment lay in a more impersonal direction, in unleashing the economic and technological forces that government could command. For Crosland saw policy in more mechanical and technological terms and less in terms of moral notions of human existence (see Clarke 1978, 65; Harris 1983, 180; Vincent and Plant 1984, 180; Plant 1996, 173).

In Crosland's vision of a tamed and 'humanized capitalism', resulting from the social and economic changes following the Second World War and advanced by the 1945–51 Labour government, socialism could be reconciled with capitalism. One aspect of Crosland's vision was that wide-ranging changes were reflected in the transformed consciousness of ordinary people. Economic progress and the humanization of capitalism removed the necessity for a social politics that struggled to fulfil human nature by improving social conditions; for 'A people enjoying full employment and social security has lost its dreams, and lost the need to struggle' (1963, 64). The need for a moral agenda that defeated the social evils of capitalism and advanced new ideals for humankind was replaced by a belief in the inevitability of economic advancement and by relying on the new technological skills of moderate government and judicious planning. Associated with the placation of human nature and the need for moderate government went a more cautious view of the present state of knowledge about human motivation. This suggested a degree of reluctance to further the socialist mission of transforming human potential through greater economic and social equality. As a reason for cautious reform, Crosland argued that, on the present state of knowledge, 'we cannot assert definitely what would be the effect either on personal contentment, attitudes to work, or the quality of our society, of a wholesale effort to suppress the motive of personal gain, or to elevate collective at the expense of individual relationships' (76). Crosland was cautious about the possibility of transforming human nature through social engineering. His revisionism arose as much from his belief that the enduring motivations of human nature (especially self-interest), however placated, had not fundamentally changed, as from his conviction that capitalism had indeed been tamed. With the benign forces of economic progress set to work, human nature itself adopts a pervasive mood of contentment. What Crosland said of postwar British capitalism in the 1950s, Galbraith has more recently claimed of American capitalism in the 1980s and 1990s in his *Culture of Contentment* (1992).

Crosland's optimistic belief that the Social Democratic aim of meeting basic needs had been substantially fulfilled led him to revise his attitude towards universalist social policies. If the problems of inequality and poverty were being solved, universal welfare became more a symbol of equality – 'the badge of citizenship' – than a concrete means to create equality. Consequently, charging for some social services was permissible as long as everyone enjoyed unimpeded access to welfare. Equality of opportunity in access to welfare permitted charging as long as it did not result in widening inequalities. The traditional opposition to private welfare by thinkers like Tawney and Titmuss was no longer necessary. Improved standards of living and freedom of choice permitted private welfare alongside public welfare. This would have a positive effect on state welfare; for 'as the gap is narrowed and facilities become genuinely comparable in quality, the mark of inferiority attaching to public services will disappear (1963, 86). Once this is achieved, 'It will then matter little whether or not occasional charges are imposed' (88). Consequently, universal free provision would no longer carry the significance it once did, and tests for charging – rather than means tests for access (Crosland's distinction) – could be allowed. The important point was 'that "universality" must follow *from* social equality, and cannot itself create it' (*ibid.*) – an argument fundamentally at odds with other postwar Fabian academics. Equality is about contributing to raising standards in the mixed economy of welfare to a level that state services should aim to emulate. *Contra* the tradition of state universalism from the Webbs onwards,

Crosland's revisionism is based on the belief that universal welfare is no longer necessary for achieving the realization of universal human nature. Rather than hankering after the old goals of Social Democratic policy, Crosland paints instead an utopian vision of the future which suggests new cultural rather than material goals for policies aiming to fulfil human nature:

> As our traditional objectives are gradually fulfilled, and society becomes more social-democratic, with the passing of the old injustices, we shall turn our attention increasingly to other, and in the long run more important, spheres – of personal freedom, happiness, and cultural endeavour: the cultivation of leisure, beauty, grace, gaiety, excitement, and of all the proper pursuits, whether elevated, vulgar or eccentric, which contribute to the varied fabric of a full private and family life.
>
> (353)

Once progress has been achieved, Crosland suggests that the goal of human fulfilment will be liberated from the 'old' collectivist moral agenda, associated with overcoming deprivation, and move onto a new agenda of personal aesthetic fulfilment, where what matters is beauty more than morality. Read in a more realistic sense, this vision suggests that Crosland was voicing an increasing concern about the welfare state's ability to respond to the growing diversity of needs that social and economic change had unleashed. The success of Social Democratic social policy led to its own-undermining, as new needs are created which it can no longer meet with the basic minimum. The fulfilment of common basic needs would lead inevitably to a new agenda for individual and family life – civic and collective life are not mentioned – involving a diversification of private and personal sensibilities. This concept of diversity and difference is undoubtedly at variance with the common needs tradition. In recent years, it has been championed by the Radical Right in its aspiration for a consumer society based on the market – as we will see in the following chapter – and by postmodernists in their celebration of the aesthetics of cultural difference against the ascetics of basic provision.

However, underlying Crosland's vision of human flourishing was a more conservative view of the inalterability of human motivation. This combination of desiring to unleash new human potential whilst respecting the enduring complexity of human nature and the centrality of self-interest lies at the heart of his appeal to New Labour today (e.g. Leonard 1999).

Equality as 'equality of outcome'

However, the 'rediscovery of poverty' in the 1960s, and the growing concern among academics and welfare activists about the failure of postwar welfare policies to overcome poverty and achieve a more equal society, went against the grain of Crosland's optimistic view of social progress. It further contributed to a quest for new ways of achieving greater equality, which were more sensitive to the different circumstances of the poor. Evidence that basic need was not being met and the national minimum not protecting the poor led policy-makers to rethink their philosophy of universal welfare. An important response involved strengthening the resolve to meet common needs by focusing resources on the particular circumstances affecting the deprived. Instead of relying on universal national minimum provisions to act as a catch-all for all individuals in need whatever their circumstances, policy began to target more closely the different circumstances causing disadvantage among different groups defined by race, gender and area-disadvantage. In this way social policy adopted a new method to meet basic needs. However, this was not based on universal provisions, but on selectively discriminating in favour of the poorest with the purpose of over-endowing groups and areas traditionally deprived of resources.

Egalitarian thinking in the early postwar years was dominated by the concept of 'equality of opportunity' as defined by Tawney and others. The 1960s however saw an intellectual movement among Social Democratic and Socialist academics and policy-makers seeking 'equality of achievement' or outcome. The new rhetoric spoke of addressing the manifestations of deprivation seen in lower school achievement, lone parenthood and higher unemployment. On the face of it, this appeared to depart radically from Tawney's and the Webbs' dictum that social intervention should be limited to modifying conditions producing inequality, and should not seek to intervene directly in personal capabilities and character to achieve what Tawney dismissed as 'equality of endowments'. Instead, the new approach appeared to seek to change the very characteristics of human nature, which Fabians believed beyond the reach of intervention, namely the physical and mental abilities of different individuals. However, on closer inspection, 'equality of outcomes' remained wedded to the same tradition as 'equality of opportunity' in seeking improvements in the *conditions* and not personal characteristics of the disadvantaged. The main difference between equality of opportunity and equality of achievement was a commitment, on grounds of equity, to redress the lack of resources shaping the circumstances that the most deprived faced in poor schooling, bad housing and under-resource health and social services. Additional resources were to be targeted at the poor to offset the deficit of resources contributing to their disadvantage. Although the approach was different, the principal aim of policy appeared the same as for earlier Social Democrats of bringing everyone up to the same level of basic needs-satisfaction. However, policy had shifted from extending the blanket of national minimum to cover everyone, to ensuring that the particular circumstances affecting deprived groups and inhibiting universal cover were removed. This involved adopting a new method for achieving equality of outcome, coined in the USA 'positive discrimination'.

In theory, positive discrimination sought to concentrate additional resources on particular deprived groups to give them an extra 'headstart' over those more advantaged. In effect, however, equality of results conformed to Tawney's philosophy of equality of opportunity, in that it sought to produce results by modifying the *environment* of resources available to particular groups. Thus Halsey stressed that 'equality of opportunity was without equality of conditions a sham' (1970, 11). In fact, policies for education and community development did not focus directly on specific social groups, but on deprived geographical areas where clusters of economically disadvantaged were said to be concentrated, and by giving these areas a 'discriminatory' boost.

In defining equality of outcome in education, Halsey argued that society achieves real equality:

> if the proportion of people from different social, economic and ethnic categories at all levels and in all types of education are (*sic*) more or less the same as the proportion of these people in the population at large. In other words the goals should not be the liberal one of equality of access, but equality of outcome for the median member of each identifiable non-educationally defined group, i.e. the *average* woman, negro or proletarian or rural dweller should have the same level of educational attainment as the average male, white, suburbanite.
>
> (1972, 8)

Equality of outcome or result meant achieving a comparable range of achievements between a specific disadvantaged group – such as an ethnic minority, women, lone parents and the disabled – and society as a whole. That is, the same pattern of distribution in society in educational qualifications, occupational status and ability to influence decisions should also be found in any one group defined by class, gender, race or disability. We can take Will Hutton's more recent '30:30:40 society' thesis as an example (1996a, 105; cf. Levitas 1998, p. 52). If the general employable population is divided into three groups of disadvantaged out of work, insecure on the margins of work, and the privileged in secure work, in the proportions of 30, 30 and 40 per cent respectively, the same proportions would be expected to apply to women, specific ethnic groups and other groups. A paradox therefore surrounds the equality of outcome strategy. On this reading, equality of outcome is in theory neutral on the issue of whether society should strive for greater equality or not. Thus the example shows that it is possible for equality to exist horizontally between different groups on the same social stratum (such as *middle class* blacks, lone mothers and working disabled), whilst society with its different social groups continues to be stratified by vertical inequalities. The principle of equality of outcome fails to engage with the structural constitution of inequality of whatever kind – income, wealth, power, privilege – leaving it untouched, and focuses instead on arbitrarily selected disadvantages such as ethnic minority membership, single parenthood or unemployed status.

Opponents of 'equality of outcome' on the Right often misrepresent equality of outcome as an extreme version of equalitarianism, believing those policies would seek the same uniform outcomes for all. However, as a matter of definition – as indeed of empirical outcomes – equality of achievement is as much to do with producing equality among the advantaged as it is among the disadvantaged. In the USA positive discrimination policies were pursued in the 1960s and 1970s more actively than in the UK. William Julius Wilson has shown that the increasing proportion of blacks achieving middle class occupation and suburban residential status by the 1980s occurred alongside the growing numbers caught in the increasingly deprived areas of inner-cities and experiencing higher rates of poverty, unemployment, out-of-wedlock births, female headed families, welfare dependency and criminality in 1980 than in 1970 (1987, 49–50). The narrowing gap between middle class blacks and whites in the USA was part of a pattern of disproportionately widening inequalities among blacks and among whites – an outcome conforming to the letter if not the spirit of equality of outcome as defined above by Halsey.

Critics on the Left, however, argued that the reality of positive discrimination by area was that deprived areas were merely subjected to new forms of selective policy by means of 'collectively' means-testing the poorest areas rather than the poorest individuals, which either way carried the danger of stigmatisation (e.g. Townsend 1979, 560–1). Moreover, as with means-testing generally, the areas that benefited did so at the expense of others that fell just outside the threshold of area deprivation. Consequently, Townsend argued that 'Areas or communities cannot be treated as autonomous or self-sufficient in terms of either economy or culture. Their functions and distribution of prosperity are in the main decided externally' (564). By comparison, Halsey's attempt in 1972 to render equality of achievement acceptable to the Right as well as the Left – as 'a dogma which might hold good on both political wings' – by proposing that 'Eventually an [Educational Priority Area] community must stand on its own feet like another and rejuvenate its world', suggests that area discrimination appeals to an individualist view of human motivation (1972, 12). In turn, it can be argued that this view is in accord with the residual view of minimum needs that underpins means-testing strategies generally.

Equality of outcomes is influenced by the liberal hypothesis found in writers from Rousseau to Rawls that, if inequalities of wealth and power had not created patterns of disadvantage between different social groups, there would then exist a 'natural' range of human abilities across different social groups. In this hypothetical 'original position' of nature, before individuals and groups exerted their differential abilities and powers for their own gains, abilities would be randomly allocated in the population.

Subsequently, however, the exercise of abilities and powers by the naturally advantaged has resulted in unnaturally disproportionate structures of advantage and inequality. Based on this implicit distinction between 'natural' and 'unnatural' advantage, Social Democrats and Liberals have been able to recommend policies of redistribution that *compensate* for 'unnatural' distributions of talents and basic goods. Positive discrimination of the most disadvantaged represents a way of meeting basic needs, but only on the basis that there is something inherently deficient in the disadvantaged individuals. This strategy incorporates into Social Democratic thinking different assumptions about human nature taken from the Right's view of the poor as deficient and needing policies that address this characteristic rather than meet the universal needs of all.

Equality as universal reciprocity: Richard Titmuss

Titmuss shared a concern with other Social Democratic thinkers about the failure of the postwar welfare state to meet basic needs. However, his approach was marked by its strong moral rather than technological approach to risk. Unlike Beveridge's view of the predictability of social and economic risks, and Crosland's deterministic view of risk prevention, Titmuss was committed to the ethical socialism of Tawney with its belief that human activity and fellowship were guided by a moral purpose in meeting needs and preventing risks. He re-asserted the moral ends of social policy and the material prerequisites for securing them in his debate in the 1960s with the neo-liberal economists of the Institute of Economic Affairs founded in 1957 (see Titmuss 1968, 115). Influenced by Hayek, the IEA questioned the authoritarian dangers of the welfare state from an individualist free-market standpoint – an argument examined in the following chapter. Towards the end of his life, Titmuss developed a powerful case for the mutualist model of human nature – which he termed the 'gift relationship' – as an important moral foundation of welfare. This argument developed the notion of human 'fellowship' found in the writings of T.H. Green and Tawney to complement the notion of basic human need.

Titmuss' account of the moral purpose of humankind is made by contrasting two models of social organization, the social and economic, which are distinguished by the intrinsic moral concerns guiding the former and their absence in the latter. The economic model is governed by bilateral exchange between two parties engaged in a *quid pro quo* for their separate but mutual advantages, and by an instrumental mode of rationality. However, Titmuss consistently argued that economic exchange between buyers and sellers can only meet individual needs that arise within the market and is entirely inappropriate for human needs in welfare institutions which cannot be reduced to a matter of exchange value. Moreover, economic transactions ignore – and may sometimes inflate – the social costs arising from externalities borne by groups rather than single persons. Titmuss referred to these costs as the 'diswelfares', 'diseconomies', 'stigma' or 'spoiled identities' occurring in modern industrial society. Consequently, market transactions fail to compensate individual victims who are powerless in the market place, or where the causation of their misfortunes cannot be identified, as in the case of environmental pollution and economic recession.

By contrast, social organizations accord a central place to moral concerns in social life, a model which he felt was normative for social policy generally. The social model is characterized by forms of exchange where there is no immediate or instrumental gain to be made by the recipient. Quoting the economist Kenneth Boulding's work, Titmuss argued that 'unilateral transfers...are justified by appeal to a status or legitimacy, identity, or community' and that 'it is the object of social policy to build the identity of a person around some community with which he is associated' (Boulding 1967, in Titmuss 1968, 21). For Titmuss, unilateral exchange occurs wherever 'the grant, or gift or unilateral transfer – whether it takes the form of cash, time, energy, satisfaction, blood or even life itself – is the distinguishing mark of the social' (1968, 22). The distinction between the social and economic was taken as definitive of social policy, which is concerned with 'types of moral transactions, embodying notions of gift-exchange, of reciprocal obligations, which have developed in modern societies in institutional forms to bring about and maintain social and community relations' (1968, 20–1). Undoubtedly, this definition is ambiguous in failing to clarify the distinction between unilateral exchange where nothing is given in return, and reciprocal exchange where material or symbolic goods are exchanged (Pruger 1973, 289, n3). Nonetheless, his stress on forms of exchange where instrumental relationships are subordinate to solidaristic relationships draws significantly on a view of human nature as governed by societal bonds and moral concern for others.

Titmuss was a pioneer in departing from the early Social Democratic view in social policy that saw society in the first half of the twentieth century as a predictable and regulatable order that permits, according to the Webbs, collective provision geared to prevention and treatment, and, according to Beveridge, state systems of compensation for largely foreseeable hardships arising from disrupted earnings. Although he did not seek to develop a theory of modern society that addressed the causes and consequences of social change and fragmentation – in the way in which more recent sociologists like Giddens (1994) and Beck (1992) have – he was aware of their impact on human need and of the unforeseeable contingencies of risk. Titmuss was one of the first postwar sociologists to address the contingencies of human need and the uncertainties of risk in modern society, in a way that draws lessons for policy and addresses issues of human nature. His normative lesson, in keeping with the Social Democratic tradition, is that only universal welfare provision can fully meet human needs and the unpredictable contingencies affecting the human condition. In this respect he continued a tradition in keeping with Beveridge.

In his last major work, *The Gift Relationship* (1970), Titmuss expounds the central importance of reciprocal relationships in welfare and society. This work constitutes a major statement in social policy of the view that human nature is realized and social solidarity sustained through everyday acts of reciprocity, involving both personal face-to-face reciprocity and impersonal, indirect and indeterminate forms of reciprocity, which together produce acts of 'creative altruism' in welfare (1970, 212). Impersonal, no less than interpersonal, giving expresses an important impulse in human nature that motivates acts of welfare:

> We are thus chiefly concerned with … 'stranger' relationships, with processes, institutions and structures which encourage or discourage the intensity and extensiveness of anonymous helpfulness in society; with ultra obligations; which derive from our own character and are not contractual in nature. (*ibid.*)

It is Titmuss' concern with social reciprocity that exemplifies what is presently termed the mutualist model of human nature. Here human nature is conceived as a quality realized not only in the individual but also in interpersonal relations between two or more individuals; for the identity of each is contingent on the other. The self and other constitute the basis of society; and society and its social forms (organizational, institutional, cultural, etc.) mediate this relationship. As with the organic and basic-needs models of human nature, the core of this idea identifies a particular form of moral sentiment in humankind; namely, the self's motivation to give help to others in times of need in the expectation that others would do the same for him, her or an unknown other in a similar situation at some indeterminate future time.

Titmuss' concept of the gift epitomizes a level of reciprocity that is not only fundamental to welfare but also essential to social bonding, the balance between rights and duties, and the viability of community. A core aspect of human nature is expressed in the propensity for 'anonymous helpfulness', motivating the state, voluntary and informal sectors of welfare. His example is the British National Health Service, and especially its voluntary blood donation system as it was in the 1960s; an exemplar of British social policy that 'encouraged sentiments of altruism, reciprocity and social duty' in 'measurable patterns of behaviour by social groups and classes' (1970, 225). Such institutions not only express, but nurture, organize and shape a 'deep human motive'. For example, 'the ways in which society organizes and structures its social institutions – and particularly its health and welfare systems – can encourage or discourage the altruistic in man' (*ibid.*).

Specifically, the NHS serves as an illustration of how social policy 'can help to actualize the social and moral potentialities of all citizens' (238).

Titmuss' cultural insights into the misnamed 'unilateral' type of exchange are of value in pointing to the normative values generated by state and voluntary welfare 'gifts'. His application of the concept to social policy shows how symbolic forms of value are produced through processes of deferred, displaced and sacrificial exchange which are of fundamental importance to universal human needs and social solidarity.

On the face of it, Titmuss' notion of 'unilateral exchange' appears to countenance a form of giving which does not entail reciprocity, and so posits a case which undermines a general theory of community based on social reciprocity, interaction, and the balance of rights and duties, as some critics have claimed (for a summary, see Page 1996, 102–7). However, he argues in terms of a deeper notion of reciprocity, which addresses mutual – rather than immediate and instrumental – forms of exchange characterized by their altruistic, indeterminate and future orientation, 'that will cause more good to exist in the universe than there would otherwise be' (Titmuss 1970, 238). This human motive is oriented to the 'universal stranger' and not just family, friends and defined social groups, and to 'common human needs' and not just the needs of particular social groups subject to stigma and discrimination. These motives of 'universality' are not described as abstract generalizations in human nature, but are expressed in empirical and context-specific terms. The statements of a large sample of blood donors reveal acts of altruism that are not 'complete, disinterested, spontaneous', but express specific feelings of obligation, approval and interest; 'some feeling of "inclusion" in society; and some awareness of need and the purpose of the gift' (238). What was seen as 'a good for the stranger in the here-and-now...could be a good for themselves indeterminately one day' (*ibid.*), because they or their kith and kin could be on the receiving end of blood and other welfare donations. This ethic of universal altruism was expressed in a range of concrete and specific situations of need in which respondents visualized themselves as both meeting the needs of others and receiving from others. The ethic implies a moral capacity to put oneself in the place of the other in need. Through the experience of discovering one's own needs in the other, the respondent donors were able to evoke an ethic of universal altruism: 'As individuals they were...taking part in the creation of a greater good transcending the good of self-love. *To love themselves they recognized the need to "love" strangers*' (239, stress added).

Moving from the concrete to the more universal, Titmuss argues that the human motive to enter into voluntary acts of reciprocity entails more than acts of immediate *quid pro quo* exchange. In Titmuss' humanistic philosophy, human interests are best served by universal love for others who are strangers and with whom there is no known contact other than through the gift itself. This expresses in idealistic terms what welfare institutions are: collective provisions to which members of the community contribute impersonally by paying taxes, according to their ability, and from which they receive according to their needs, and where professional and lay welfare workers give, often beyond the call of duty, unquantifiable gifts of welfare to those in need on the basis of a universal ethic. The ethic of giving in its personal and impersonal forms embraces not only the motivations of reciprocity and mutuality underlying the voluntary and informal welfare sectors, but also the motivation to exercise the rights and duties that underlie the relationship between citizenship and state. For example, seen in this light, impersonal tax payments and impersonal benefits are an extension and wider institutionalization of interpersonal exchange and giving. In this sense, universal welfare provided by state provisions for basic needs is an extension of more mutual forms of welfare. The challenge, therefore, is to make explicit reciprocal exchanges between state and citizen in a way that advances a notion of the common good implicit in the dominant models of welfare and human nature based on the state's obligations to meet basic needs. It is possible to see in Titmuss' discussion the beginnings of a rapprochement between the two different models of basic needs and mutual welfare, where the two come together to express a more unified conception of human nature and need. The possibility of rapprochement is a central theme in the second half of the book.

By centring welfare on the gift relationship, Titmuss helped to restore to Social Democratic thought the mutualist dimension that was barely present in writers wedded to the idea of basic human needs. He was an exception in advancing the ethic of mutuality found in co-operative forms of welfare, and in placing mutual aid firmly on the state's universal national minimum. Although these ideas are now seen in retrospect as part of the 'classic welfare state', they have not lost their relevance for social policy in late modernity (see Holman 1993). Ideas like the national minimum, mutuality and reciprocity are being redefined in ways that address continuing as well as new problems of welfare and poverty at the turn of the twenty-first century.

However, in another respect Titmuss' theoretical and analytical achievements, in clarifying the value choices involved in social and economic modes of exchange, amplify a problem at the core of his view of human nature, namely the problem of taking the division between the social and economic too far. Indeed at times it is difficult to know whether Titmuss is offering insights into generic forms of exchange which are prescriptive for all social and economic institutions, or whether he is focusing on welfare institutions alone. At its most extreme, parts of *The Gift Relationship* dissociate social from economic action in a way that is problematic for a unified conception of human nature. For, beyond the analysis of ideal types, Titmuss at times assumes that there are two kinds of action governed by either economic or social rationality. He implies that, when governed by economic criteria of exchange, action to meet need is a process without just or good outcomes. For meeting need requires welfare provisions that substitute for the ineffectiveness of the market. Though dismissive of economic reasoning, Titmuss' own conception of welfare as compensation for 'diswelfare' remains wedded to the same assumptions of value as conventional economics. However, at other times, he implies that human needing and social exchange are themselves transformed within a welfare state into a different order of human relationships and society. Like other Social Democratic writers, such as Robson (1976), Titmuss refers to 'welfare society' as a higher moral order for the welfare state (e.g. 1968, 124).

The fact is, however, that social goods are goods of exchange nonetheless and their allocation raises issues inescapably about the production of economic value. This fact has been most powerfully impressed on social policy in recent years by the spread of quasi-market thinking in welfare production and allocation. By adhering to a moral view critical of the capacity of economic exchange to address human needs, Titmuss – and other Social Democrats – failed to explore the different economic forms of exchange generated by the commodity form of capitalism. In particular, the process whereby commodity use-values for satisfying human needs are translated into exchange-values produced by the exchange of different goods in circulation were insights which Marxian analysis was to offer, as will be shown in Chapters 5 and 6. Nonetheless, his conception of equality as universal reciprocity is developed further by recent feminists in terms of the 'struggle for recognition' discussed in Chapter 7.

Equality as justice as fairness: John Rawls

The search for a conception of equality which claims to meet the basic needs of all individuals whilst advancing their different projects of fulfilment has remained elusive. The attraction of Rawls' *A Theory of Justice* (1972) for Social Democracy lies in its claim to provide principles of justice that lead to an equal distribution of liberties and resources whilst giving due regard to claims for more resources for some than for others (Runciman 1966; Weale 1981; Doyal and Gough 1991). His conception of justice as fairness has taken Social Democratic equalitarianism beyond the crude notion of justice as equal and uniform shares for all, and beyond the selective notion of favouring only the most disadvantaged, as in positive discrimination and the Right's selectivism. Further, Rawls' theory offers clear statements of principle capable of being applied to Western democratic institutions, and furnishes firmer foundations than previous theories for applying equalitarian principles to social policy. Today, some of Rawls' ideas can be found in circles close to the leadership of the Labour government and its Social Democratic project (e.g. Plant 1992; IPPR 1993; Borrie 1994; Barclay 1995; Brown 1999). At the same time these ideas sit uncomfortably alongside the communitarianism of New Labour.

This section argues that Rawls' account of human nature, equality and difference lies within the Social Democratic tradition with its concern to fulfil common basic needs, even though his account incorporates the principle of differential distribution from liberal individualism. However, we will argue that the application of Rawls' 'difference principle' must assume a further faculty of human nature, namely an ability for mutual understanding among differently advantaged individuals if they are to appreciate the benefits of differential distribution – benefits that cannot be appreciated from the position of individuals assessing their position in isolation from other individuals, as neo-liberals hold. The issue here is that Rawls assumes the existence of basic needs, but not mutual needs. Whereas, mutual need satisfaction and human interaction are necessary for Rawls' difference principle to work. Once again we see that Rawls represents a further example of the difficulty in Social Democratic thought of integrating basic needs and mutualist conceptions of human nature.

Rawls' principles of fairness are two-fold:

1. Each person is to have an equal right to the most extensive total system of equal basic liberties compatible with a similar system of liberty for all.
2. Social and economic inequalities are to be arranged so that they are both a) to the greatest benefit of the least advantaged...and b) attached to offices and positions open to all under conditions of fair equality of opportunity.

(1972, 302)

A fair distribution of resources should aim at equal liberties, opportunities and resources without advantaging any one group (Rawls' first 'equality' principle), unless rewarding one group improves the position of the least advantaged in the long term. It is the 'equal unless' proposition which defines Rawls' second principle, the 'difference principle', in permitting *just* forms of inequality. Equality represents the natural state of justice as fairness, namely, the state members of society would opt for if coming together for the first time under a 'veil of ignorance'. In this hypothetical 'original position' no one has prior knowledge of the others' capacities, roles and agendas. Under these conditions, Rawls contends, each member would agree to distribute primary goods equally and to maximize each person's equal right 'to the most extensive basic liberty compatible with a similar liberty of others' (60). For Rawls, primary goods are those that meet basic human needs for physical and psychological wellbeing, self-esteem and freedom of action or autonomy (62). Coming together in the original position, individuals would agree in principle to allocate 'human goods' to ensure that their needs are met. Still conforming with the tenets of this position, but becoming aware of differences among them, members might in time see advantages in rewarding some individuals – e.g. entrepreneurs, political leaders and social workers – more than others, because in principle their specific talents and efforts advantage the least fortunate, and in the long-run lessen tendencies to inequality, by creating more jobs, higher wages and more caring relationships.

Theories of justice address issues of human nature by predicating a conception of human needs and abilities, the fulfilment of which depends on achieving a particular pattern of distribution. Rawls' formulation of justice can be read in this way as an account of human nature, without privileging any one substantive view of human needs, motivations and abilities. We can approach Rawls' view of human nature by addressing the presence of comon basic needs, and the absence of mutual needs, in his theory of justice.

The appropriation of Rawls to the Social Democratic cause rests in large part on assuming that his conception of human nature posits a modicum of common needs shared by all. In other respects, too, Rawls follows a Liberal–Social Democratic programme of political thought. Implicit in Rawls' idea of a society based on justice as fairness is the idea of the 'common good', although this concept is not a central one. For example, the common good is thought of as 'certain general conditions that are to everyone's advantage' (1972, 246). This is implied by the sense that his principles of justice secure conditions of distribution that benefit the least advantaged as well as the most advantaged. Further, in order to contribute something to the common good, Rawls argues that the 'transfer' branch of government, involving welfare and social security, must provide a 'social minimum', which essentially 'takes needs into accounts and assigns them an appropriate weight with respect to other claims' on society (276), and guarantees 'an appropriate standard of life' (277). In this respect Rawls is articulating the institutional framework of a basic needs model of human nature which lies at the heart of Social Democratic thought.

However, at first sight, Rawls' support for the equalitarian moment in Social Democratic thought would appear to be undermined by his difference principle. The difference principle allows for degrees of inequality between the advantaged and disadvantaged that might deny meeting basic needs. This is why Rawls makes the first principle paramount, in that it *assumes* that each individual receives a modicum of primary goods, whatever degree of inequality is permitted by the second principle.

We can now go on to elucidate how an implicit notion of basic needs operates in Rawls' theory, and how the difference principle can only work if the faculty of mutual understanding is assumed. Based on the assumption of an original position, Rawls posits a view of personal character and need which is neutral in the sense of predicating no particular type of person with specific types of motivation. In broad terms he claims his 'principles of justice are not contingent upon existing desires or present conditions' (1972, 263). He calls this notion of goods and needs, with its lack of content, a thin theory of the good (395-8), in the sense that, as Sandel describes, 'it incorporates minimal and widely shared assumptions about the kinds of things likely to be useful to all particular conceptions of the good, and therefore likely to be shared by persons whatever their more specific desires' (1982, 25).

Given this, we are entitled to ask what would Rawls' theory, based on assuming individuals come together in the original position, require in order to apply it to the real world of differently endowed individuals. For the difference principle to work, different individuals in a real community must, we would argue, be capable of understanding three issues. First, they must be able to determine what would be a fair distribution of rewards. Secondly, this implies that they must have some knowledge of the range of needs there are amongst them, some of which are basic needs and some individually different. Thirdly, they must also be able to understand the constitutional means of reaching agreement on these matters of principle and substance. Specifically, on this last issue, advantaged and less advantaged individuals would have to be capable of reaching an agreement on what constitutes the range of needs among them, and how scarce resources should be distributed to meet these needs. For the advantaged would have to be prepared to gain their advantages knowing that in time the less fortunate thereby have some call on them; and the less fortunate would have to concede immediate benefits to the advantaged, though for their own benefit in the long-run. For both the advantaged and disadvantaged there is the expectation that they can take a wider and longer term view than their immediate interests dictate, that they can relate to a constitutional perspective in which they both play a part. Rawls recognizes that individuals belonging respectively to the advantaged and less advantaged will come to see that society is just when it successfully meets their differing interests (1972, 102-3). The difference principle thus implies a degree of mutual communication and intersubjective understanding between individuals with different needs and abilities. This understanding constitutes a 'thick' theory of need which provides a range of needs content, the kind of goods and services that satisfy these needs, and an ability to engage in discursive procedures that decide these substantive matters by applying formal procedures to specific circumstances.

Although Rawls' theory of justice operates as a meta-theory promulgating principles of distribution without privileging any one empirical account of human nature, some degree of intersubjective, mutual consensus formation over needs must be assumed when applying his theory to the real world. Consequently, it can be argued that individuals living in a given society will arrive at an understanding of what their universal and individual needs are. We can illustrate how this might work. The efforts of an advantaged individual *A* enable her to fulfil her needs by acquiring primary goods, such as income, wealth, property, travel abroad and theatre visits.

At the same time, by paying higher taxes and contributing to economic growth, she is able to advance the need fulfilment of the less advantaged individual *B* by widening the range of opportunities for him to acquire goods such as more jobs, income, health provision, education and subsidized arts. *A* acquires the first set of goods for herself alone and contributes to the second set of goods for the less advantaged individual *B*. Although *A* and *B* satisfy different needs and enjoy different goods, the implementation of the difference principle could only succeed if they as different persons, each with different as well as common needs, shared sufficient needs in common to enable them to see the mutual advantages the system of distribution offers.

This could work in three ways. First *A* shares some needs for primary goods with *B*, such as income and enjoyment of art. Secondly, whether needs are common or different, some of the second set enjoyed by *B* lead to his acquiring needs for new primary goods, such as better jobs, higher wages, better education and a broader appreciation of art, which enable him to acquire an enjoyment of property, travel and theatre, shared with *A*. Exposure to one set of goods and opportunities opens up channels to other goods and opportunities, such that in essence an entire world of opportunities is available to him. This might even apply to *A* as well in relation to aspects of *B*'s life-style. Thirdly, although *A* may not share needs for some goods enjoyed by *B*, she gains an indirect satisfaction from *B*'s enjoyment of these goods. For example, a sense of pleasure at *B*'s satisfaction and a greater sense of self-security resulting from the placation of *B*'s needs. In these cases, *A* is satisfied by a different but related order of 'meta' goods satisfying an altruistic or self-security need. For economic liberals, of course, there is a fourth way in which *B* can benefit from *A*'s efforts, but in this case *without* the two arriving at a shared understanding of their different and common needs. This is by means of the hidden hand of the market guiding *A* to invest her scarce resources and abilities in profitable pursuits which have beneficial spin-offs and which 'trickle down' to *B*. In this atomistic situation, neither *A* nor *B* need learn anything about their respective needs, interests and aspirations.

Each of these examples points to the existence not only of common needs, but of the enhancement of one's own satisfaction through encountering other individuals with their different means of need-satisfaction – an issue which touches on the importance of mutual human interaction in the enjoyment of primary goods. We will argue in Part II that both notions of human fulfilment – basic needs satisfaction and human interaction – are contingently related. Further, the advancement of each individual's satisfaction through the provision of primary goods for basic needs and the encounter with others' forms of satisfaction draws the individual into an encounter with a broader notion of the common good. More speculatively, they point to the totality of needs and primary goods that partial need-satisfaction and goods-acquisition hints at; that, in the process of meeting individual needs in a given local community, there arises the potential for a whole world of need-fulfilment. As we saw in discussing Titmuss, and as we will argue in Chapters 6 and 7, from an immediate, particular and local example of need-satisfaction there arises the possibility of universal need fulfilment.

For all the advances that his theory of justice secures in incorporating a just notion of differential rewards in an egalitarian system, the problem remains that Rawls' theory cannot safeguard against injustices without an *explicit* notion of basic needs. It is for this reason that Doyal and Gough argue for the addition of a basic needs clause to Rawls' difference principle, to the effect that 'inequalities will be tolerated to the extent that they benefit the least well off through leading to the provision of those goods and services necessary for the optimisation of basic need-satisfaction' (1991, 132). They argue in their theory of need that justice as fairness should entail three, not two, principles: (i) the right to basic need-satisfaction; (ii) the toleration of inequalities only if they contribute to the advantage of the least-fortunate; (iii) the existence of legal constraints on bringing about social inequalities (133–4). Doyal and Gough adumbrate a set of specific needs that are both universal to humankind and contextually sensitive to the different cultural practices that societies carry out in meeting need. At one level needs are spelt out in a form sufficiently abstract as to apply to different cultures, and at another 'intermediate' level they are sufficiently concrete to apply to real individuals in each culture. The provisions for meeting need – 'need-satisfiers' – will differ between different societies and cannot be formulated in theoretical terms (see 170). Recent policy deliberations by, for example, the Commission on Social Justice show how the basic needs principle can be used in social policy as part of an egalitarian principle of citizenship rights and a difference principle similar to that of Rawls (Borrie 1994) – as Chapter 7 explores later.

The level of abstractness in Rawls' theory has become an increasingly important issue for him in his more recent writings (1993) where he has sought to address the criticisms of communitarians (see Bell 1993; Mulhall and Swift 1996). In its simplest form, communitarians argue that notions of justice must be rooted in the norms of particular communities and cannot be derived from universal principles in the way that Rawls has attempted. In response Rawls has sought to defend the general – if no longer universal – relevance of his theory, and to rebut the relativism of his critics, by reference to the idea of an 'overlapping consensus' of different rational doctrines held by different social groups whose doctrines endorse from different perspectives a political conception of justice as fairness (1993, 134). Despite their political differences, each group according to this conception is able to acknowledge the others' right to their particular notions of justice, which despite differences converge at crucial points of understanding and toleration.

In developing his theory, Rawls has sought to address further the possibility of a theory of justice that addresses the rights and needs that are common to all and those that are held by different individuals and groups. However, this appeal can only be fully realized if one conjoins basic needs and mutualist assumptions.

Conclusion

Social Democratic thought is based on three inter-related models of human nature, the basic needs, mutualist and atomistic models. Continuity in the Social Democratic tradition is an important thread-guiding policy, despite fundamental changes in the twentieth century and especially in the last thirty years. It is this thread which some Social Democrats today lay claim to. Chapters 2 and 3 suggest that this tradition still has some relevance at the end of the twentieth century, despite the present plight of the welfare state and doubts about its future prospects under Social Democracy (e.g. Gray 1996, 1997 and 1998). This relevance lies in examining the separate conceptions of human nature and reconfiguring them in ways appropriate to the turn of the century.

The organic model was defined by Green and the Idealists in terms that expressed a dialectical relationship between the community and individual. The community acts for the common good of all in order to realize the 'character' of each individual, who in turn seeks to contribute towards the highest ideals that the community can aspire to. Individuals unable to fulfil their potential are supported by institutions which engender co-operation between the advantaged and less advantaged for the betterment of the whole community. Today, New Labour is reviving the rhetoric of the social organic model as part of its project of renewing its ethical Social Democratic roots, after nearly two decades when the language and expectations of an atomistic model of humankind prevailed.

The basic needs model describes human nature in terms of a clear, if sometimes arbitrarily fixed, demarcation of universal basic needs and individual needs. For the Webbs and Beveridge, state welfare was concerned to meet universal basic needs and organized in terms of a range of national minima. Beyond the minimum, an 'extension ladder' is available provided by charities supported by voluntary donations and dispensed by volunteers or paid professionals, by 'voluntary insurance' based on occupational or private insurance, or by 'mutual aid' based on community self-help and co-operatives. The demarcation of common and individual needs suggested the development of a secondary or meta-theory unifying the different assumptions about basic, mutual and atomistic human nature.

The mutualist model is based on solidaristic relations and institutions that promote co-operation and reciprocity among different individuals. Like the organic and basic needs models, mutualism goes back to the nineteenth-century Idealists. It can be argued that a new meta-theory of human nature is needed for the development of social policy in a context where the Radical Right's atomistic model has failed to capture the fullness of human nature and where Social Democracy's basic needs approach has failed to comprehend its diversity.

The concept of basic needs has provided the principal model of human nature for Social Democrats. Yet in the context of the social transformation of the last fifty years it has been vulnerable to various new ideas within Social Democracy. Crosland (along with T.H. Marshall (1963)) was one of the first to recognize that growing prosperity created a diversity of new needs that could no longer be satisfied by a uniform minimum. The question became two-fold: whether opportunities above the minimum would be sufficiently plentiful to satisfy these new needs, whilst allowing the minimum to remain as a safety net; or whether the uniformity of the minimum exercised a strangle-hold on all strata of society on and above the minimum. In the latter case, little thought was given in mainstream social policy to an alternative conception of social protection that appealed to a different notion of human nature, apart from the individualism of the Right, and even less to one that appealed to a meta-theory that addressed the complex aspirations that accompany social change. Positive discrimination provides one alternative. However, in retrospect, by means-testing the poorest communities, it posed little threat to the already advantaged of redistributing their assets. Only Rawls' conception of social justice offers the hope of integrating equalitarian and differential-treatment principles in a coherent way that could be applied to liberal social institutions. More than any other Social Democratic account of human nature, Rawls' account provides a meta-conception unifying both equalitarian and individually different conceptions of humankind. One weakness, however, lies in the lack of an explicit notion of basic needs that could prevent the poorest from falling into deeper poverty. Doyal and Gough have suggested that such a conception need not commit itself to a specific cultural notion of human nature. For, according to their theory of needs, a model of common human needs can be universal and at the same time applicable to different concrete circumstances without predetermining a particular set of cultural values. A second weakness, which Rawls shares with some Social Democrats, is the absence of a conception of mutual needs. We have suggested that mutuality and intersubjective understanding are necessary for realizing the principle of differential distribution alongside a principle of equalitarian distribution. Rawls does not address the question of integrating basic and mutual conceptions of human nature. Yet these two concerns have been and remain central to the Social Democratic tradition. We will examine how other traditions – the Radical Right, Marxism and Feminism – have tackled this programme.

The chapter has raised several questions that must be addressed in the context of other traditions of human nature in social policy. The basic needs model has been an important part of the welfare state in legitimating provision for common needs. But this provision in its postwar guise has suffered from being uniform and insensitive to the various interpretations of basic needs made by different social groups. Further, until the 1980s, wider interpretations of basic needs have been constrained by the state's hegemonic grasp of welfare services. Consequently, we must ask whether basic needs can continue to be provided in this way, whether welfare provisions should accept that it can no longer guarantee this type of fulfilment, or whether this aspect of human nature is best provided for by non-state provision. Further, as governments increasingly rely on non-state and quasi-state provision (such as NHS Trusts, and central and local government commissioning of non-governmental agencies), what kinds of human fulfilment are being provided for: the satisfaction of common needs, residual needs, individually different needs or mutual needs? What scope is there for the newly emerging welfare state of the last decade to satisfy these different types of needs in a socially inclusive way?

4
Human Nature and the Right

Introduction

The Radical Right's assault on the classic welfare state was intended as a key step in laying the foundations for a new political consensus replacing the Social Democratic compact which had dominated political life between 1945 and 1979. The new politics of the 1980s and 1990s not only gave rise to a different policy agenda, but also promoted a new vision of human nature based on the spirit of individualism, enterprise and consumerism. However, the realization in the 1990s that this project had not overcome the shortcomings of Social Democratic policy and had its own shortcomings, contributed to a deepening sense of disillusionment in the two major political agendas and cast doubt on their respective views of human nature. This chapter seeks to define the Radical Right's view of human nature, to explore the meta-theory that characterizes it, and to assess how far it has influenced social policy and what new directions policy might follow. In particular, it addresses the scope within the Right's view of human nature for fulfilling, what we have called, mutual human needs through market exchange based on voluntary association and competition among producers and on communal life among consumers. The term Radical Right is used to refer to the influence of neo-liberal economic thought, especially that of Hayek, on the Conservative Party in Britain and its satellite think tanks which influenced the policy agenda in the 1980s and 1990s. Essentially this creed stands for the liberation of human energy and enterprise by removing the shackles of state bureaucracy and regulation and by re-establishing the private market as the central institution for allocating goods to meet human need. This project involves not only deregulating various economic institutions – by opening financial, manufacturing and service industries to international competition – but also privatizing former state agencies involved in the provision of health, welfare, education, security, culture, communication, transport and the production of basic raw materials and components.

The human nature discourse of the Right

We begin by examining the Right's discourse on human nature as a set of propositions about the factual, motivational and normative content of human nature.

1   Human nature is based on the supply of innate natural abilities and needs found within a given group of individuals

The Right generally argue that a group of individuals – a community, nation or ethnic group – share a given stock of different abilities and basic needs. However, individuals differ in how effectively they harness these abilities to meet their needs. Conservatives among the Right see human nature and needs as unchanging and unalterable (Thorne 1990, 21). Liberals like Hayek – on whom this chapter focuses – by contrast, see human nature in terms that are more dynamic. Though sharing the same basic needs, individuals are born with different talents and go about meeting their needs in diverse ways. Consequently, a persistent theme in Hayek's work is the belief in the limitless possibilities of human fulfilment under circumstances of minimum state intervention. As early as in *The Road to Serfdom* he speaks of humankind's 'unbounded possibilities of improving their own lot' (1943, 13; also 1960, 86). Whether human nature is portrayed as bounded and unchanging or as unbounded and dynamic, these two views generate factual generalizations about motivation among humans in a state of nature. Within the range of motivations described, the dominance of self-interest is central, even if other motivations such as altruism and the selfless pursuit of knowledge also exist, as liberals such as Hayek and Friedman acknowledge. However, the idea that the state of nature consists in the raw unformed motivations of individuals in a state of anarchy – 'a battlefield of contending forces' (Thorne 1990, 27) – presents the Right with the problem of social order.

2   Human nature is dominated by self-interest

This is the driving force leading individuals to produce and consume for self-fulfilment. This theory of motivation, about how natural drives give rise to particular courses of action, argues that the pursuit of self-interest is best realized in market institutions, wherein numerous individuals can optimize their many different desires in an ordered way. The Friedmans voice a common theme on the Right that the market unwittingly contributes to optimizing each person's ends without their being necessarily conscious of it, that 'economic order can emerge as the unintended consequence of the actions of the many people, each seeking his own interest' (1980, 13–14). Specifically, the price system organizes the multitude of individual decisions to buy and sell by transmitting information, by providing incentives to individuals to lower costs and maximize returns, and by determining the distribution of goods (14). Hayek uses this account of self-interest as a way of explaining the West's unique historical progression towards greater economic freedom. For the West had 'the conscious realization that the spontaneous and uncontrolled efforts of individuals were capable of producing a complex order of economic activity' (1943, 11–12).

3   The Right sees human nature in essentially individualist terms

The agency for achieving human fulfilment is the individual. Though consisting of a generic set of properties, human nature essentially resides in each individual. The individual constitutes an agency that is a biologically and psychologically discrete subject and epistemically discrete object of knowledge. The individual subject is irredeemably driven by its biological or psychological drives to put itself before other subjects – or at least to give first regard to its closest kith and kin. This fact has important epistemic consequences, for individuals must accept what Norman Barry terms their 'constitutional ignorance' (1979, 9) of others' needs and interests. Hence, Hayek argues that 'the indisputable fact [is] that the limits of our powers of imagination make it impossible to include in our scale of values more than a sector of the needs of the whole society...since, strictly speaking, scales of value can exist only in individual minds' (Hayek 1943, 44). The individual is the prime agent for initiating action. This empirical claim carries explicit normative implications regarding the intrinsic freedom characterizing individual existence; for 'individuals should be allowed, within defined limits, to follow their own values and preferences rather than someone else's, that within these spheres the individual's system of ends should be supreme and not subject to any dictation by others' (*ibid.*). Because Hayek holds a view of the self predicated on its limited knowledge of others, he provides a constitutional defence of individualism, which is compatible with his general theory of human freedom and which places the sovereign self in a social context with other selves. On this basis, individual agency and action can be guided by rational choice and calculation but only within the limits of epistemic individualism.

4   Finally, humankind in the state of nature faces the problem of social order, of how to overcome the dangers of anarchy caused by different competing egos pursuing their own interests, and by arbitrary government imposing its will on individuals

The threat of anarchy leads to a set of normative propositions that are binding on individual action. Diversity in human motivation and capability, in needs and strengths, requires a system of order that nonetheless guarantees a modicum of individual freedom. The problem of order gives rise to a set of propositions about the discipline of markets, the rule of law, moral order and divine order that give shape, cohesion and direction to human endeavour. From factual generalizations about the real differences in talent, aspiration and application, the Right arrives at a set of basic normative 'presuppositions about the nature of individuals' (Novak 1991, 16), namely the need for market, juridical, moral and theological prescriptions for socializing raw human nature. We will discuss each in turn.

The *market* is for Hayek 'the best use of the forces of competition as a means of co-ordinating human efforts' (1943, 27). Though concerned about the normative purposes of human action and the dangers of anarchy, the Right frequently alludes to the moral neutrality of market forces (e.g. Willetts 1992, 86). Although the market is seen as superior to other institutions of exchange and decision-making, its operations are not committed to any one moral outcome or version of the good.

The *rule of law* supplants the dangers of arbitrary government with government bound by rules 'which make it possible to foresee with fair certainty how the authority will use its coercive powers in given circumstances, and to plan one's individual affairs on the basis of this knowledge' (Hayek 1943, 54). The rule of law, like market competition, works because it maintains a position of neutrality between different personal interests by being 'useful to yet unknown people, for purposes for which these people will decide to use them, and in circumstances which cannot be foreseen in detail' (56).

The Right generally recognizes that capitalism is not about the free market alone, and that it cannot 'thrive apart from a *moral* culture that nourishes its virtues and values' (Novak 1991, 56; see Green 1993, 1–3). Indeed Willetts, in the guise of rightist communitarianism, claims that 'Modern conservatism aims to reconcile free markets (which deliver freedom and prosperity) with a recognition of the importance of community (which sustains our values)' (1992, 92). Hayek, for example, recognizes the importance of moral rules of conduct that are 'a condition of freedom'. These rules lend a degree of certainty to human interaction so that individuals can 'show a regularity in their actions that is not the result of commands or coercion, often not even of any conscious adherence to known rules, but of firmly established habits and traditions' (1960, 62). The need for community and communal bonds to sustain human interaction and support is a subordinate theme in rightist discourse. We will examine later the viability of this mutualist theme for a society dominated by a market culture. Presently, we can observe that writers like David Marsland argue that the market is a precondition of any moral community (1996), and that others like Gray argue that it is dependent on a pre-existing public culture and morality (1992).

At base, it is the recognition of original sin and fallibility in human nature which gives rise to the Right's *theology* of social order. Hayek's recognition of the irremediable problem of human fallibility is the basis for his rejection of the rationalist case for developing institutions founded on rational principles which claim to remedy human evil and so overcome the problem of original sin. By contrast, Hayek believes in the evolution of institutions based on trial and error, on being tried and tested by tradition, rather than according to rational precepts. Such institutions provide the best environment for nurturing human goodness and minimize opportunities for human malevolence. Though not couched in theological terms, Hayek shares a view of original sin in common with others on the Right. The evolutionary and anti-rationalist tradition on human nature to which he belongs 'is here closer to the Christian tradition of the fallibility and sinfulness of man, while the perfectionism of the rationalist is in irreconcilable conflict with it' (1960, 61). The concern with human fallibility draws on a wider concern on the Right with the inescapable limitations of human nature and the inevitable contingencies of the human condition. Sir Keith Joseph shares with Hayek a fundamental critique of socialism as an example of the rationalist belief that humankind can escape human limitations. For the

> aspiration to be more than human lies behind the current obsession with security, the difficulty men now have in accepting risk, uncertainty, failure, disappointment. And the desire to escape from the human condition makes some ready to grasp at the inhumane vision offered by socialism.
>
> (1976, 71)

Against this escapist mentality, Joseph posits the values of the market, with the necessities of risk, work and competition, as the only realistic values for the individual in the face of contingent human existence. Novak sums up the Right's account of the moral prerequisites of social order as a 'respect for contingency and unintended consequences; a sense of sin; and a new and distinctive conception of community, the individual and the family' (1991, 29).

Human nature is therefore seen as in a permanent state of original sin and imperfection springing from the raw state of human motivation. Without self-discipline, human nature 'falls' into a state of anarchy, directionlessness and moral corruption, and falls prey to the designs of others. Whether theological or secular, the problem of original sin represents the dilemma at the heart of social and political thought of reconciling order and freedom. For many on the neo-liberal wing, the raw state of individual nature must be allowed to retain the spirit of freedom, diversity and pluralism, however much bound by the order of the market, the rule of law, morality or divinity. For the Conservative wing, however, the necessity of social order gives rise to the problem of controlling individual freedom whatever form it takes. The purpose of Conservative doctrines is to subsume individual freedom under an overarching order, whether based on divine or secular authority, the market or God.

Though the Right has often been criticized for lacking a sense of moral order and cohesion and favouring the moral neutrality of the market place, nonetheless the desire for order is found in each of these doctrines. For Hayek and others, the market order is grasped immanently in the everyday practices of market competition and voluntary co-operation guided by the 'hidden hand'. For a Christian liberal like Novak, it is located in a transcendent direction, which overshadows and gives meaning to what he describes as the otherwise 'empty shrine' of pluralist society 'which free consciences approach from a virtually infinite number of directions' (1991, 53). Novak stretches the bounds of metaphysical authority further than many others do on the Right. For 'at the core lies reference to God, the Almighty', as stated in the founding statements of the founders of the US Constitution (54). The role of symbols such as free speech and the free press is seen as a way of opening the individual to divine transcendence. Each safeguards the freedom of individuals in pluralist society. By imposing their own discipline, these freedoms enable the individual to learn 'that the common good transcends their own vision of the good' (*ibid*.). For Novak, the sacredness of the person under market capitalism is a reflection of divine authority (65). Because of this divine presence, the socializing influence of market institutions is not a matter of imposing social control. Instead, it is about inducing individuals to comply with norms and expectations that direct human action along sociable and productive lines, placing them in a position to consider the mutual advantages they share with others. This process of mutuality and consensus formation – of 'mutual consent' – subjects the self to the other's point of view and gives rise to a social institution 'that would reinforce imagination, sympathy, and a lively sense of being judged as if by an impartial spectator' (Novak and Preston 1994, 15). Again, a secondary theme is heard concerning the mutuality of human nature, which for Novak, as for Hayek, is contingent on and not separate from the primacy of market relations.

In sum, human fallibility affects all social institutions, including the market itself. For the sake of consistency, the Right recognizes that if individuals are prone to error then so are markets 'also vulnerable to corruption and defects' (Novak and Preston 1994, 15). Hence some neo-liberals (e.g. Barry 1987, 164) see the term *perfect market* as a misnomer.

Two views about human nature

At the heart of rightist thought lies a dilemma arising from two incongruous views of human nature. Several of the above characterizations of human nature form a set of logically coherent statements about the factual, motivational and normative features of human nature based on the initial premise that human action is dominated by self-interest. However, Hayek's unbounded view of human nature suggests that self-interest is not necessarily a dominant motivation, but exists alongside other motivations to produce a diverse range of drives in each individual, and a diverse combination of needs and talents among different individuals engaged in social co-operation. In Chapter 1, we described the former view as a primary account, which presents empirical, motivational and normative propositions as part of a logically coherent system of argument flowing from the axial principle of self-interest. The latter view, by contrast, typifies a secondary or meta-account in which some propositions are at odds with others, producing a tension in the overall argumentation (such as between altruism and egoism). The 'rogue' propositions either are relegated to a position of less importance, or pose a threat to the conceptual system leading to its overall revision.

In the practical context of politics and policy, new arguments about human nature are deployed in response to changing social, political and economic circumstances rather than for the sake of cogency and consistency alone. The versatility of secondary accounts of human nature makes them more adaptable to the task of furnishing the philosophical underpinnings of new approaches to policy. However, secondary accounts may appear increasingly inconsistent and present a dilemma that, in the face of rapid social change, requires new ways of thinking about human nature. The versatility of Radical Right philosophy, based in some cases on the contrary principles of self-interested individualism and the social unity of nationhood, authority and family (Hall 1983), has come to appear increasingly inconsistent in the 1990s. These two tendencies have grown apart and now define two distinct strands of Conservative Party policy: namely 'one nation' Toryism with its continuing commitment to state support for the vulnerable and insecure;[1] and market Toryism bent on furthering the market culture in welfare and the shift to residual state welfare.

The distinction between what Chapter 1 termed the primary and secondary accounts of the Right needs elaborating. The primary account of human nature describes a range of core self-directed motivations, interests and values defining human nature, such as self-interest, duty to one's kith, kin and kind over strangers, individual responsibility, and an individualist rationality. These values represent the core features of human nature over other-directed motivations such as altruism, service to others and collective solidarity. Self-interest is universal and invariant and prompts individualistic projects of social action that are best realized in the market.

The dominance of self-interest is seen in writers espousing either the importance of market competition or the cost/benefit calculus of individual rational or public choice theory – two separate but individualist schools of thought (see Green 1987). Sir Keith Joseph, an exponent of market reasoning, asserts that 'The motive is not goodwill … [It] is enlightened self-interest', and that competition is the key motive instilling in the seller consideration for the buyer. Consequently 'the self interest of the businessman is harnessed to the interest of his customer by competition' (1976, 59–60). In a similar vein, the Friedmans point to the primacy of individual initiative and voluntary co-operation in economic life (1980, 47).

Co-operation is justified on the grounds of advancing the different self-interests of the individuals involved, rather than other-regarding motivations, and motivating different individuals to co-operate in shared projects. Again, the spark of mutual social action is ignited by self-interest.

Charles Murray's work on the underclass represents an alternative individualist account that draws on a rational choice reading of human nature. His influential thesis attempts to reconstruct the rational choices motivating single unmarried mothers, the young job-shy and young criminals. A process of cultural diffusion unfolds in which these separate groups coalesce into the broader dependency culture of the underclass, producing 'values [that] are now contaminating the life of entire neighbourhoods' (1990, 4). Such rational choice is aided by 'the perverse incentives of welfare policy and the coddling of criminals' (25). Specifically, 'In the 1960s and 1970s social policy in Britain fundamentally changed...the rules of the game...for low-income young people. Behaviour changed along with the changes in the rules' (*ibid*.). For young criminals, 'committing a crime has been getting safer for more than three decades' (28). For young mothers, 'the sexual revolution of the 1960s markedly reduced stigma' (*ibid*.) and 'a series of changes in the benefit rates and collateral housing benefits lifted a large proportion of low-income young women above the threshold where having and keeping a baby became economically feasible' (30). The individual's rational choices are further compounded by the social proximity of the underclass, so that becoming pregnant, avoiding work or committing crime reinforce each other (31).

However, moving beyond primary theories based on self-interest, other writers present a secondary or meta-theory that characterizes humankind in manifold rather than singular terms. The raw nature of humankind is diverse in its motivation, interests and potentials. Hayek in particular talks of 'the boundless variety of human nature' (1960, 86). This manifold variety becomes the ground for the belief that the good society is one that advances liberty by means of the institution of the market to enable individuals to fulfil their different potentials. Thereby, the diversity of human nature and the cultural achievements of civilization are enriched. For Hayek, this means that individualism in liberal theory 'does not assume, as is often asserted, that man is egotistical or selfish, or ought to be' (1943, 44). In policy terms, 'There is no necessary connection between altruism and collective action or between egotism and individual action' (1973, 56). In other words, there is no logic that leads from a particular account of human nature to the enunciation of a particular project of intervention – hence the Right's claim about the value-neutrality of the market. For the Right, selfishness is endemic in human nature whatever the political regime. The market is favoured because it prevents unfettered selfishness by placing self-interested producers in a relationship of competition forcing them to keep prices to the customer at a minimum and to maximize profit margins through efficiency gains. Whilst harnessing self-interest for social ends, the market also encourages alternative ways of meeting need such as charity and mutual aid (Green 1987, 217). It is the unbounded view of human nature and diversity that remains attractive to erstwhile Hayekians and now liberal communitarians like John Gray (1992, 1996) and David Green (1993). Though rejecting the economic reductionism of Hayek, they continue to value the liberal principles of human diversity and tolerance that characterized his thought.

The existence of this influential secondary theory of human nature, seen in the writing of Hayek and his followers in the 1980s (e.g. Barry 1979; Gray 1986), suggests a model of human nature which is substantially broader and more complex than many critics and analysts have suggested. This theory proposes that human nature is made up of a boundless diversity of propensities, and that it cannot be characterized in terms of a narrow range of qualities governed by the dominant principle of self-interest. However, there are those on the Left who construe the Radical Right's view of human nature entirely in terms of self-interest. Stuart Hall's influential account of Thatcherism, for example, characterizes the neo-Liberal wing of rightist ideology – e.g. Hayek – by its 'aggressive themes' of 'self-interest, competitive individualism, anti-statism' (which combined with the themes of organic Toryism – nation, family, duty, authority, standards, traditionalism – to produce Thatcherism) (1983, 29; also Gamble 1979; King 1987, 10; Levitas 1986; Gamble 1988, 29). David Green criticizes Honderich's account of Conservatism for caricaturing the Right's view of individual liberty in terms that are unduly restrictive. He quotes Honderich as arguing that 'selfish human nature alone is what explains [Conservatives'] various and more important commitments concerning property and the market' (Green 1993, 24; Honderich 1990, 239).

However, in discourse that is more practical, the ideal typical distinction between primary and secondary theories of human nature is less clear cut. We can begin to see how accounts based on the different premises of singular self-interest or diverse motivation merge into each other. For many on the Right, whether espousing an unbounded view of motivational diversity or a more limited view, self-interest wins through in the real world. Either self-interest becomes the dominant motivation that reduces secondary accounts of unbounded human nature to primary accounts that are blind to its diversity; or, in primary accounts, it becomes the underlying motivation governing all motivation including other-directed ones.

As an example of the latter, the Friedmans' primary account of human motivation defines self-interest in very broad terms that suggest that it is a common feature underlying a diverse range of different motivations. For the term 'self-interest' means more than 'myopic selfishness'. Rather

> It is whatever it is that interests the participants, whatever they value. Whatever goals they pursue. The scientist seeking to advance the goals

of his discipline, the missionary seeking to convert infidels to the true faith, the philanthropist seeking to bring comfort to the needy – all are pursuing their interests.

(1980, 47)

However, the reductionism – not to say circularity – of this argument, in rendering scientific, evangelical and charitable motives akin to individual interest in personal gain, places this argument squarely among primary theories of human nature. If all these activities are self-interested, then everything is the same and there is no basis for differentiating between different types of human activity and values other than their value in maximizing self-interest.

By contrast, the human nature assumptions of neo-liberals holding an *unbounded* meta-theory are rendered more bounded when faced with the practical, moral and epistemic perplexities besetting politics and policy. For example, when examining various practical contingencies – specifically those of economic survival, human fallibility and ignorance – Hayek opts for a more delimited view of humankind. We will examine each of these three contingencies in turn.

First, the contingencies of economic life are advanced to justify the need for competitive individualism over altruism as the prime motivation for achieving individual betterment and advancing civilization. This is especially so when addressing the qualities needed under conditions of competition. Hayek consistently argues that 'effective competition is a better way of guiding human effort than any other' (1943, 27 *et passim*). Echoing a familiar criticism of the former Soviet Union, Gray argues that its collapse was brought about by the absence of 'incentives to work', specifically the 'benign incentives provided by the discipline of market competition' (1992, 6; also Lilley 1995, 12).

However, in a move also typical of the Right, Hayek proposes that competition, far from undermining social order, is conducive to co-operation among individuals and should not be understood in the narrow sense of individual self-interest. Competition in the face of state failure is the only way of co-ordinating economic activity and the division of labour; indeed 'It is the very complexity of the division of labour under modern conditions which makes competition the only method by which such co-ordination can be adequately brought about' (1943, 36).

Secondly, there are specific moral implications that arise from human fallibility and its threat to social and economic freedom, which require limits on human nature. Hayek's critique of collectivism acknowledges that, under collective regimes such as communism and fascism, human qualities that can only thrive in conditions of freedom are negated by other qualities such as dominance and tyranny. The ever-pressing danger of these evils raises for Hayek a constant threat against which human society must be ever vigilant. These evils deny individuals the freedom to follow their own destiny within the limits imposed by the rule of law. Freedom under the rule of law is a precondition for fulfilling human nature, which is no longer boundless but free and diverse only within legal limits. Despite an avowed permissiveness in encouraging diversity of achievement, Hayek recognizes that there must be normative limits placed on human conduct. In this respect, he arrives at a set of legal and moral preconditions for human flourishing, just as other writers on human needs have done, whether neo-liberal or socialist (e.g. Maslow 1970, 47; Doyal and Gough 1991, 86–90). The limits that Hayek's theory places on human nature derive from recognizing the dark side to humankind in its insurmountable state of fallibility.

There is a third reason that is more fundamental why the unbounded view of human nature is rendered more circumscribed in the real world of politics. For it is not possible to construct theories that assume an understanding of the total and unbounded breadth of human capability. Because of the 'constitutional ignorance' characterizing humankind, we are incapable of possessing a holistic account of the needs, strengths and values of all of humankind. At best we can know only the limited span of needs relevant to our experience and propose social values on this basis alone. Barry argues that in this thesis,

> man's limited knowledge is not merely an empirical problem, or a contingent fact about men which may be altered by some technological advance. It is a philosophical thesis about the form in which knowledge exists in the world and about the way in which the mind becomes aware of this knowledge.
>
> (1979, 10)

This epistemology has implications for our understanding of human nature. However diverse the human make-up, or, conversely, however uniform its characteristics, our understanding is at all times limited and fallible (in the epistemic as well as theological sense). Though unbound, diverse human potential cannot be realized by seeking to encompass the totality of needs and capabilities within a single theory or ideology.

Human nature, human ignorance and policy

At this point we can begin to explore the implications for policy of the Radical Right's view of human nature. In particular, the total complex of human needs consists of incommensurable properties that cannot be embraced by a unified ethical code of values for setting policy priorities. Indeed, 'the welfare and the happiness of millions cannot be measured on a single scale of less or more' (Hayek 1943, 42); to believe otherwise amounts to a *synoptic delusion*, namely, 'the fiction that all the relevant facts are known to one mind' (1973, 14). Inevitably for Hayek, social and economic policy must choose between the competing ends and needs of people (1943, 48). To believe otherwise is to commit what Gray terms the 'fallacy of conceptual realism' which denies the 'incommensurabilities among various goods contributing towards human welfare' (1992, 20). Whereas in fact needs are met despite their diversity, and welfare attained in a free society by dint of the largely *unknown* complex of exchanges between countless individuals following a variety of unrelated motives – of economic gain, civic duty, charity, and family and neighbourly obligation.

The impossibility of knowledge comprehending the totality of human nature forms the basis of his critique of policies designed according to holistic conceptions of human nature and needs; that is, policies governed by what he terms 'constructivist rationalism' (Hayek 1973, 8) based on the tradition of Cartesian rationalism. This tradition implies that the best way to achieve human fulfilment is to rationally design entire institutions to fulfil specific human purposes; for only then will human ends be secured (1973, 10). Instead he advances a more limited view of rationalism that draws on the tradition of British rather than Continental rationalists.[2] This limited view of what we can know of human nature implies the existence of tacit processes – or rules – guiding human practice. Social order is achieved as institutions and practices evolve and adapt over time, a largely unconscious process rather than one of design. In human evolution, the social practices that are preserved are those that best promote the survival and flourishing of society. This privileges rule following over purpose-seeking conduct, and habit, custom and tradition over human design and purpose (1973, 11). Thus Hayek can assert that 'our whole civilization in consequence rests, and must rest, on our *believing* much that we cannot *know* to be true in the Cartesian sense' (1973, 12).

For Hayek, human society and co-operation evolve because individuals have recourse to implicit understandings, or 'tacit knowledge', about the rules and conventions governing the range of activities from the routine to creative. Gray describes the core concept of 'tacit knowledge' as 'the vast fund of practical, local and traditional knowledge, embodied in dispositions and forms of life, and expressed in flair and intuition, that can never be formulated in rules of scientific method' (1992, 8).

In describing tacit knowledge, Hayek departs from the Kantian tradition whereby 'reason itself contains the standard for the critical examination of every use of it' (Kant 1909, 102), that is, by which pure reasoning provides the grounding for 'practical reasoning' and by which the former is given primacy over the latter. Instead Hayek posits the importance of tacit, but nonetheless rule-governed, knowledge in the evolution of social order, whereby 'spontaneous orders result from their elements obeying certain rules of conduct' (1973, 43). These are not the same as the rules of pure or theoretical reason, but exist pre-theoretically:

> the rules which govern the actions of the elements of such spontaneous orders need not be rules which are 'known' to these elements; it is sufficient that the elements actually behave in a manner which can be described by such rules. The concept of rules as we use it in this context therefore does not imply that such rules exist in articulated ('verbalized') forms, but only that it is possible to discover rules which the action of the individuals in fact follow. (*ibid.*)

This view of local and tacit knowledge is one that has become influential in recent years, namely that policy should be based on the decisions and discretion exercised by dispersed localities, rather than by centrally imposed powers applying legally rigid solutions (see Gamble 1996, 192). If policy cannot meet the totality of needs in society, it should focus on what specific local groups of individuals decide. Such a view suggests that the concept of legal rights, including welfare rights and social justice with their holistic assumptions of what is good for all, is problematic (Hayek 1976; see Gray 1992). Instead, social policies should enhance the welfare recipient's ability to control the way they manage their personal affairs. The Friedmans, for example, have long advocated a negative income tax which gives a single means-tested cash-payment paid through the tax system and covering a variety of different needs, to be spent as the recipient chooses (1980, 120–21). Similarly, the Right – and some on the Left – propose vouchers that empower individuals with choice in obtaining health care (e.g. Green 1988, 1995), nursery provision and schooling – as in the now aborted Tory government's nursery voucher scheme that would have been implemented in 1997.

Hayek is opposing his view of practical reasoning and tacit knowledge to the Idealist tradition beginning with Kant and present in the Victorian Idealists, New Liberals and Social Democrats, who argued that practical policies should be governed by notions of a higher ideal such as the 'common good' of all. Rather, there can be no totalistic view of human nature and its needs, and no basis for arriving at a conception of common ends or the 'common good'. Individuals must choose between competing ends. At best the market provides the information to enable individuals to exercise choice on rational grounds (by comparing the relative costs and benefits).

However, from a critical perspective it can be argued that both market liberalism and idealism, whether in their classic or modern forms, share an elitist approach towards policy that derives from a certain kind of hidden knowledge. For idealists, the order of the common good is achieved by the morally superior individual. For Hayek, spontaneous order is achieved when gifted and enterprising individuals exploit their tacit knowledge and subject themselves to the mystery of the market order.

Complexity and 'unbounded' human nature

In the light of this discussion, Hayek's claim to hold an unbounded theory of human nature, embracing self- and other-interested motivation, looks problematic. This has implications for his and indeed the Right's view of social policy generally. To what extent is he able to reconcile a dominant notion of individual self-interest in meeting need with a notion of civilized concern for the common needs of all, exemplifying the altruistic side of human nature? In keeping faith with his unbounded view of human needs and capacities, Hayek would have to reconcile the two opposing motivations of self-interest and altruism. However, it is difficult to see how this can be done. As we shall see, on the one hand, the Radical Right has fostered a market ideology that reduces human needs to calculations of individual opportunity costs and benefits, a model of 'economic man'. On the other hand, the Right retains at least a minimal notion of state welfare[3] – governed by poor law principles, means-testing and targeting – by which it takes responsibility for the minimum basic needs of the poorest.

On the face of it, these two concepts of individual self-interest and collective responsibility for minimum needs contradict each other, and so present a problem for the secondary account of human diversity Hayek seeks to provide. The idea of collective responsibility for need is inadmissible because of the sovereignty of the individual in the market place. This problem can be compared with the Social Democratic position where the premise of universal basic needs is combined with the notion of freedom for individuals to meet needs other than basic needs as they think best in the market. For Social Democrats, the problem of this secondary account is reconciled by drawing a dividing line, namely the national minimum, between common basic needs met by the state and individually different needs above the minimum met by the individual alone. The collective obligation to meet basic needs is thereby combined with individual obligations to meet non-basic needs above the minimum. For the Radical Right, the relationship between common needs and individual needs is reversed giving priority to the individual's freedom and responsibility in the market over society's collective obligation to meet need through welfare provisions. One way of reconciling this dilemma is to see the needs of those requiring state help as containing special inabilities or incapacities additional to their common needs. These needs therefore require particular forms of support to help them to fulfil their obligations and expectations in the same way as others. In some cases this involves attaching tests or conditions, in addition to needs criteria, to benefits so that government can monitor the behaviour of the poorest who are assumed to face specific problems. An example is where actively-seeking work conditions apply to job seekers allowance and income support claimants to motivate job search – an approach now actively developed in the Labour government's welfare to work strategy. Here the residual minimum – rather than national minimum – serves as a dividing line conjoining welfare dependants and the self-reliant into an apparent unity.

The Right's down-grading of the significance of common basic needs is part and parcel of its criticisms of two key features of the Social Democrat welfare state: namely, the government's commitment to meet basic needs; and mutual action between different individuals to meet needs. However, these criticisms are not without contradiction. We now explore the extent to which the pro-individualist and pro-collectivist arguments of the Right, and specifically of Hayek, represent the horns of a dilemma. We will also explore the possibility that the Right can reconcile this dilemma by appealing to a notion of mutual action that satisfies the needs involved in market transactions. For such a view would extend the Right's conception of human nature beyond a limited atomistic one to a more cogent secondary conception. However, first, we will prepare the way by clarifying the anti-welfare sentiment in Hayek's individualism.

1 Economic reductionism

The anti-welfare sentiment is expressed in the paradigmatic way Hayek reduces the individual's concerns about meeting need to concerns about economic gains and losses, and limits collective state responsibility to upholding the rule of law in economic matters. The economic is the most important sphere of human concern, more fundamental than other spheres such as politics and morals. On the primacy of the economic, Hayek argues that

> Economic control [by the state] is not merely control of a sector of human life that can be separated from the rest; it is the control of the means for all our ends. And whoever has sole control of the means must also determine which ends are to be served, and which values are to be rated higher and which lower, in short what men should strive for.
> (1943, 68–9)

This represents a position which is radically different from the Social Democratic tradition from the Webbs to Titmuss where social morality is given pre-eminence over the economic sphere and is used to override the materialist values of the market place. For Hayek the market order stands above the political and moral order.

Hayek's view of the market is justified by appealing to his epistemic individualism. If individuals are best placed to understand their immediate situation, then the state should only regulate the general framework of the rule of law within which individuals are free to pursue their own economic advantages. For this reason, the rule of law exists primarily to safeguard economic freedom. In public policy, the 'state should confine itself to establishing rules applying to general types of situations, and should allow the individual freedom in everything which depends on the circumstances of time and place, because only the individuals...can fully know these circumstances...and must be able to predict actions of the state which may affect these plans' (1943, 56). In contrast, where the state can see the effects of its policies on particular people, it is forced to take sides and make decisions that deny people freedom of choice. The state then becomes a 'moral institution', where the specific meaning of moral is intervention programmed towards specific ends. According to Hayek, here morality assumes the conceit of synoptic knowledge.

2 Common basic needs and the Right

Based on his view of the rule of law, Hayek is able to acknowledge the need for limited state intervention, as long as in law the state treats all 'economic parties' even-handedly. Hayek recommends a basic level of welfare provision that gives voice to his pro-welfare sentiments. According to this argument, social minima, health and safety legislation, limited hours of work, which compensate for unforeseen disasters in the economy or nature, are 'fully compatible with the preservation of competition' (1943, 28). The key questions for Hayek are two-fold: 'whether in particular instances the advantages gained are greater than the social costs which they impose'; and whether 'the organisation of these services is not designed in such a way as to make competition ineffective over wide fields' (*ibid.*). It is these objectives that the rule of law is meant to secure.

Hayek defines the national minimum in welfare in subsistence terms, that is, by defining the most basic needs for survival, which are taken as an absolute datum that applies to all people in terms of their residual needs. In 1943 he recognized the need for 'security against severe physical privation, the certainty of a given minimum subsistence for all' (1943, 89). Similarly, nearly two decades later, Hayek argued that 'There are common needs that can be satisfied only by collective action and which can be thus provided for without restricting individual liberty' (1960, 257; see Gamble 1996, 49). Hayek explicitly recognizes universal though minimum needs which can be provided only collectively, despite the diversity of needs the market meets. It is precisely this conception that the national minimum has assumed since first propounded by late nineteenth-century New Liberals and Social Democrats. Here Hayek comes closer than elsewhere to accepting a national minimum solution for the problem of reconciling common and individually different needs – as distinct from the Right's favoured solution of relying on market diversity for the majority and means-tested residual provision for the poorest. We will see later the extent to which former rightists now accept this viewpoint.

Hayek's notion of insecurity informs his recognition that government should provide some form of minimum protection against the exigencies of the market that create poverty:

> There is no reason why in a society that has reached the general level of wealth which ours has attained, the first kind of security should not be guaranteed to all without endangering general freedom...there can be no doubt that some minimum of food, shelter, and clothing, sufficient to preserve health and the capacity to work, can be assured to everybody.... Nor is there any reason why the state should not assist the individual in providing for those common hazards of life against which, because of their uncertainty, few individuals can make adequate provision.
>
> (1943, 89–90; also 1960, 257–8)

Where these involve 'genuinely insurable risks', there is a case for comprehensive state social insurance (1943, 90). This argument leads to a position similar to Beveridgean national insurance which became the hallmark of Social Democratic welfare and the postwar consensus between Left and Right until the mid-1970s. The idea of providing provisions 'outside of and supplementary to the market' (*ibid*.) further underscores the extent to which Hayek shared with Social Democrats a view about the need for an 'extension ladder' above the minimum.

We have seen in the first part of this section that Hayek's epistemic individualism leads to an economic view of human motivation that appears to exclude forms of motivation involved in nourishing collective bonds and strengthening the common good. Yet the radical implications of individualism are substantially weakened by his notion of basic needs that entitles everyone in principle to minimum welfare provision. This concession represents a significant slippage in his philosophy of human nature from atomistic individualism to common basic needs, for which the state carries ultimate responsibility. This dilemma in his secondary account is never resolved except insofar as basic needs are defined in residual terms of subsistence, which are meant to preserve the sovereignty of the individual's freedom in the market with the minimum of state interference. The development of New Right social policy in the 1980s and 1990s shows how far this dilemma has been resolved in the direction of a competitive individualism framed within the collective structures of the public sector (the 'internal market'), and moving increasingly to devolve basic needs provision on to the private and voluntary sectors. However, before we examine these developments we will consider finally whether market practices as understood by the Right constitute a form of mutual praxis that provides a further means – in addition to common basic needs – of moving beyond an atomistic conception of human nature towards a more complex meta-theory.

3 Markets as mutual praxis

Despite the individualism of rightist thought, it could be argued that market transactions between buyers and sellers implies a basic motivation for humans to co-operate in producing for needs, a view which *cannot* be reduced to an atomistic conception of human nature. David Willetts, for example, refers to the 'fundamental human instincts', that Adam Smith identified, to 'truck, barter and exchange' (1992, 80), instincts for activities that are far from atomistic. We can see in the notion of bartering a form of 'communicative' action between buyers and sellers who must seek each other out, negotiate a sale and reach agreement over its terms – an intersubjective and mutualist model of human nature. According to Habermas' notion of communicative action, different parties reach understanding on the basis of an expectation that each one has of the other that his or her claims are open to rational verification by the other (e.g. 1979, 63), without recourse to force or fraud. On this basis, market exchange involves each party coming to an agreement about each other's needs, namely, the buyer's need for a specific commodity and the seller's need for fair payment in return for supplying the commodity. Habermas' intuition is that rational understanding is a co-production between two actors.

However, it is precisely the assumption of dominant self-interest in market exchange that problematizes this mutualist conception. Consequently, the intersubjective relations involved are seen as driven by instrumental motives between single individuals (or collective entities such as firms) whose moments of agreement are at best transitory. Habermas, in the *Theory of Communicative Action*, describes how in late capitalism the media of power and money impose forms of rationality that have engulfed and 'colonized the life world', destroying the very basis for intersubjective trust, agreement and co-operation (1987, 318). As we will see, post-Hayekians like John Gray have sought to re-accommodate non-instrumental modes of conduct in their account of human motivation.

Yet there is a further aspect of the Right's view of market transactions that lends itself to a mutualist interpretation. Hayek's privileging of the 'tacit knowledge' of entrepreneurs over the scientific knowledge of experts assumes an important role for intersubjectivity and pre-theoretical practical reasoning in market relationships. For Hayek, the concept of tacit knowledge implies a praxis notion of 'knowledge in use', whereby 'man acted before he thought and did not understand before he acted' (1973, 18). Drawing on his anti-Cartesianism, Hayek argues that mind is not an independently existing entity separate from nature, which objectively observes nature and rationally designs human institutions to improve the human condition. Rather, minds work by seeking to adapt 'to natural and social surroundings and have developed in constant interaction with the institutions which determine the structure of society' (1973, 17). What the human spirit aspires towards is contingent on what it has already achieved in harnessing the forces of nature and cultivating civilized culture. In this praxis-based theory of human knowledge and action, one can see what seems to be a degree of common ground with the early Marx's notion of praxis as 'sensuous knowledge'.

However, despite the appeal of some writers on the Right to notions of market transaction understood in terms of communicative competence and praxis,[4] which ground human motivation in social rather than exclusively individual self-interest, there are fundamental problems. These arise from the individualist conception of personal agency that undermines such an interpretation. For example, commodities are produced to satisfy subjective wants not common needs, so that universal need-satisfaction is met at best indirectly and incompletely as a bi-product of meeting personal wants. Further, although this argument retains a notion of reciprocal action which extends the scope of human purpose beyond individual self-interest and presupposes 'voluntary co-operation' (as Friedman and others argue), it remains limited by the incorrect assumption of epistemic individualism. Individuals know only what they share with co-producers, and only come together to co-operate on a 'voluntary' basis because they have identified with the same self-interests. The assumption is that entrepreneurs have no other reason to co-operate in reciprocal and communicative action once this project has been accomplished. Wainwright (1994) has recently sought to reconstruct Hayek's notion of tacit knowledge along social lines that nonetheless accept that totalistic views of human needs are 'synoptic delusions'. She retains a socialized view of political agency exploiting tacit knowledge in satisfying needs. This view is based on different levels of collective action which have the capacity to re-group into larger alliances, and which cannot be reduced to individualistic conceptions of agency. Mutual interaction between individuals has the unbounded capacity to generate increasingly complex levels of social organization that are insufficiently theorized in the atomistic terms of the Right (see Gamble 1996, 192).

In summary, despite signs of slippage in Hayek's pro-market liberalism towards acknowledging the need for minimum state welfare, and his recognition of forms of mutual action directed at meeting needs, these welfarist leanings are significantly undermined by his epistemic individualism and his view of the primacy of market competition.

The policy impact of the Right

So far we have examined notions of human nature held by thinkers who have influenced the political Right in recent years. The 1980s and 1990s saw fundamental changes in social policy and public institutions where theory was put into practice on a grand scale, with the express intent of stimulating previously dormant human qualities of enterprise, competitiveness and productivity. The reforms of the last two decades can be understood as much as a programme of freeing the human subject from long-held habits and 'perverse incentives' as an economic strategy of de-regulation.

In this section we examine the different accounts of human nature that have influenced recent developments in social policy. However, this examination does not reveal a coherent meta-theory of human nature. For we find that these accounts are not all of a piece and that there are contradictions between them. These policies involve restructuring public welfare institutions along market lines based on a competitive individualist view of human motivation. This is a primary theory based on a dominant motivation. At the same time, the use of a rhetoric of empowering individuals in the market suggests that greater competition can unleash a diverse range of talents – caring, volunteering and altruism as well as self-interest – consonant with an unbounded conception of human nature. Here, the construction of human nature appears to embrace a more complex view of motivation than self-interest alone.

In the first half of the 1980s, the Tories undertook large-scale programmes of selling off council housing and public utilities, implementing compulsory competitive tendering in public services, and converting many government services into independent agencies for supplying benefits, passports, driving licences and so forth. By the late 1980s and 1990s, the government had extended and refined the policy of privatization by introducing various private sector techniques throughout the public sector, such as competitive market pricing, human resources management and total quality management. These spawned further innovations in the public sector such as internal markets, quality assurance and citizens charters. Consequently, new conceptions of the human subject based on competitive individualism and individual rational choice replaced the traditional notion of the individual with universal basic needs served by public services. Citizens became consumers and public servants became commissioning and provider managers. The traditional model of public service was reshaped to mimic the market (Klein 1996). Large organizations such as National Health Service hospitals and front-line services such as general practice (GP) and local authority social workers were re-organized into purchasers and providers of services – buyers and sellers subject to the forces of demand and supply (see Le Grand and Bartlett 1993). Providers had to compete with each other for the purchaser's custom, and purchasers shop around for the best value and most appropriate care packages that service-providers could deliver. On the provider side of the market, hospitals and community health care services took on trust status, operating as quasi-autonomous agents in hiring staff and in designing, pricing and delivering treatment packages sold to district health authorities, local authorities, GP teams and private employers and insurance companies. On the purchasing side, health care practitioners, such as GP fundholders and health districts negotiated with trusts over the price and package of care. Each fund-holder, for example, received a *per capita* grant to purchase services for patients (see Butler 1993; Cutler and Waine 1994). Once agreement between purchaser and provider on the appropriate package of care was reached, it was formalized into a contract with specifications of price, quantity and quality standards, and with recourse to legal remedy if breached.

The introduction of quasi-markets and managerialism fundamentally changed welfare provision and delivery, and contributed to the formation of what Clarke and Newman term the 'managerial state' (1997). Introducing market prices to all public services provided purchasing managers with information for comparing the value-for-money that different providers offered. This in turn was meant to enlarge the freedom of choice open to managers. Associated with the dissemination of price information to purchasers, the Tory government's citizens charters gave users the right to information to enable them to exercise critical choice in selecting services, an idea broadly following public-choice theory. For example, in the NHS, information has been available in the form of leagues tables based on indicators of hospital performance in patient care, together with the publication of National Audit Commission reports on specific aspects of health care. A similar approach has been adopted in primary, secondary and higher education (and in 1999 in local authority social sercvices). Providers for their part were meant to respond to the new incentives of the quasi-market by improving quality and choice for the user. Informed by this new information, the public was empowered to exercise more competent choices and judicious demand which in turn should attract a higher quality of supply.

However, the new rationales for meeting need – quasi-markets, human resource management, public choice and quality management – rested on quite different and often contradictory notions of human nature. Some of these rationales, far from empowering the individual, represented a diminished view of human fulfilment.

First, human resources techniques in the public sector have sought to extract new levels of staff commitment by devolving responsibilities for decision-making onto individual agencies. Finance and policy implementation have been devolved to the lowest feasible level and smallest unit of provision giving local managers a greater degree of autonomy. Each decentred unit, whether an independent agency or part of a larger organization, competes with other units, internally and externally, to secure the best outcome for themselves. In some local authorities, for example, one department, such as the social services, purchases blocks of provision such as nursery places for children with special educational needs from the education department within the same authority. In addition, it can contract-in from the private sector if necessary. In principle, central government outlines overall policy parameters, including the standards to be achieved and the overall budgets to work within. In turn, each unit is expected to redraft policy into local policy statements outlining the standards and goals to be achieved by the unit (see Lawson and Taylor-Gooby 1993, 4 *et passim*). These standards and their performance are then assessed by central inspection and regulatory agencies. The implications of this human resources management strategy are justified in terms of empowering individual users, providers and purchasers to fulfil their responsibilities, potentials and needs. At the same time, this individual empowerment and in-group solidarity has been associated with a competitive ethic producing a culture of insecurity among employees which is detrimental to their own need-satisfaction and the satisfaction of their users.

Secondly, this fundamental shift in public policy rested on the lessons of public-choice theory that responsibility for service provision should lie as far as possible with the individual provider. Rational-choice motivates consumers to maximize satisfaction and providers to maximize their performance (see Dunleavy 1991, 3). By restructuring the complex of incentives to maximize individual self-interest, public choice theory seeks to promote the provider organization's goal-maximizing activity. However, this public-choice inflection appeals to a utilitarian ethic that is out of kilter with the Hayekian market ethic. For public choice is about the individual maximizing his or her utility according to a scale of values that it is assumed all individuals hold. This is at variance with Hayek's notion that markets enable individuals to define their own wants and desires for themselves. It contradicts his arguments about the incommensurability of different human utilities and needs and the impossibility of a community arriving at a single unified ethic (see Gray 1992, 20).

A third area of innovation has been the new concept of quality that informs total-quality management in the public sector, as exemplified by the citizens' charters introduced in the early 1990s. The concept of quality is based on a particular notion of human need. However, unlike earlier conceptions of need, which reflected explicit and publicly defined political goals to improve human welfare, the new concept of quality relies on a notion of needs without any preconceived content. For in the economic market, the content of needs is decided entirely on contingent grounds according to whatever consumers want and whatever producers can produce. Defining need becomes an exercise in circular reasoning. For example, according to the International Standard ISO 8402 Quality Vocabulary, the definition of 'quality' prevailing in the discourse of 'total-quality management' is 'the totality of features and characteristics of a product or service that bear on its ability to satisfy stated or implied needs' (quoted in Bergman and Klefsjo 1994, 16). On the one hand, according to this rationale, the producer supplies the consumer with whatever it wants; on the other, whatever the consumer states it needs, the market will provide; a circularity of undefined and amorphous needs and satisfactions. The structure of this argument is similar to the Friedmans' statement commented on earlier that individual self-interest 'is whatever it is that interests the participants, whatever they value' (1980, 27). In public sector managerialism, a highly plastic notion of human nature and its needs has prevailed, in which human qualities can no longer be differentiated and human values no longer appraised. These assumptions have supported the most fundamental changes in Britain and elsewhere of the last fifty years in the organization and culture of work. The assumption of amorphous human nature represents the culmination of the neo-liberal individualism that Hayek propounded earlier in the twentieth century, and a particular way of constructing a theory of unbounded human nature. The problem of articulating a theory of human nature with diverse and – as we have seen – contradictory content is overcome once the content is emptied of any reference to substantive human needs.

Finally, new managerialism was based on a view of human motivation which is distinctly at odds with a Hayekian view of individual motivation and freedom. For as Cutler and Waine argue, managerialism represents a prescriptive approach to the market, manipulating market mechanisms to accord with government parameters, especially politically determined budgets and policies (1994, 21). Devolved units, which competed against each other in internal markets – e.g. locally managed schools, nursing home providers, GP fund-holders – operated within the strict financial limits and regulatory frameworks set ultimately by central government.[5] This was a far cry from the freedom of entrepreneurial innovation. Further, the consumer of welfare services, far from exercising sovereignty in the market place, at best relied on the purchasing power of the proxies exercised by their GPs, local authority social workers and other local purchasers of service.

The new culture has supplanted a public sector ethos that was advanced at the beginning of the twentieth century by the Webbs and others and was based on serving citizens whose concrete needs – for minimum income, health care, education, housing and so forth – formed the basis of rights to a national minimum of welfare and a democratic involvement in the advancement of welfare policy. The conception of needs of the Radical Right and managerialism has replaced a tradition associated with Social Democracy where needs were collectively defined. Though the notion of universal welfare was far from fully implemented, its status as an ideal remained the basis for collective projects.

In sum, in the 1990s the new utilitarianism has been supported by the hollowed out notions of 'need' and 'total quality' used in public sector managerialism and quality management. The two conceptual innovations in need and utility have been inserted into a more traditional neo-liberal view of human motivation based on a belief in the importance of individual 'incentives', 'enterprise' and 'efficiency' and framed within the precepts of the rule of law that apply to contracts between purchasers and providers. The traditional connotations associated with need and quality in the public sector have been re-valorized into the substantive model of human nature of the Right based on individual self-interest. It can be argued that these reforms have done little to develop the communitarian impulse in rightist thought that seeks to overcome the atomistic consequences of unimpeded market competition and to strengthen the mutual bonds between individuals.

Beyond Hayek: the alternatives of libertarian radicalism or pragmatism

In the post-Thatcher era, a growing number of Right intellectuals came to question the limited aims of Tory policies that emerged after 1979, especially the narrow conceptions of individual, economic and market freedoms that shaped social policy in the 1980s and 1990s (e.g. Gray 1992; Anderson 1993; Green 1993). These doubts were exacerbated by several developments that proved beyond government control: namely, growing inequality and poverty; the restructuring of international capitalism, industrial restructuring and labour redeployment with its attendant social costs, and the fragmentation of poor communities.

Willetts, for example, acknowledges tellingly that 'the most deeply felt criticism of Conservative policy in the 1980s was that somehow the commercialism unleashed was destroying the sense of community' (1992, 78). In advancing what he calls 'communal liberalism', Green comments on the shortcomings of market liberalism, arguing that '"more goods" do not make a good society and its capacity to create "more goods" is not alone what makes capitalism superior to communism' (1993, 1). Rather, 'It is the realm of "activity in common", which is at once voluntary and guided by a sense of duty to other people and to the social system on which liberty rests' (1993, 3), which must be involved in new ways to re-energize 'civil society' (1993, 4). In an appeal to the philosophy of the 'social market', Gray has likewise distanced himself from the pure Hayekian tradition of market liberalism – 'an amoral appeal to the prosperity that market institutions deliver' – and now advocates the contribution of market institutions 'to individual wellbeing via their enabling individuals to live autonomously in a form of life containing valuable options furnished by a common stock of inherently public goods' (1992, 2).

One response on the Right to this general criticism has been a revival of communitarian liberalism (see Gray 1996, 15–17; 1997, 329) which recognizes the positive role of government in generating mutual and enterprising forms of local welfare (e.g. Gray 1992). The communitarian impulse in some strands of rightist thought draws on this belief in the mutual resources of human nature; that is, in the ability of different individuals to respond to each others' needs and to co-operate voluntarily in producing to satisfy needs. The other response has been to further reduce government involvement by shifting welfare responsibilities more decisively onto the individual and family. The most controversial example of this view was Charles Murray's famous 'thought experiments' in *Losing Ground* (1984, ch. 17). This posed the possibility for US social policy of removing benefits from unmarried mothers, ending open access to high school grades, and removing all race relations legislation introduced after 1965. Some of these ideas gained credibility in the US in the mid-1990s with the passing of welfare legislation that seriously limits federal provision. In Britain, right-wing think tanks and writers (e.g. Bell *et al.* 1994; Marsland 1996), prominent Tories and government ministers like Michael Portillo (see Timmins 1995, 513–4), and finally the Conservative government itself in one of its last policy pronouncements, contemplated the privatization of pensions with only means-tested benefits for the poor. This followed a raft of reforms in which responsibility for national insurance benefits for sickness, unemployment and maternity had been passed from government to employers.

Each of the two responses rests on a particular view of individual and collective motivation. The new and more aggressive competitive individualism argues that for welfare reform, 'no solution will be fully satisfactory...unless it runs with the grain of human nature, and uses the power of incentives and market structures instead of ignoring or trying to suppress them' (Bell *et al.* 1994, 14). In this light, the welfare state's bureaucratic structures are seen to 'strangle the natural, spontaneous developing co-operative institutions on which freedom depends – the family, the market, the legal system, and the local community' (5).

By contrast, a more pragmatic liberalism is now being followed by former neo-liberals. We will focus on this development because it exemplifies sentiments in rightist thought which seek to articulate a theory reflecting the diversity of human nature; whereas the former approach continues to advocate traditional rightist theories based in singular self-interest. At the core of Gray's revision of Hayek is a view of human nature comprising three elements: autonomy, satiable human needs, and a public culture receptive to the beneficial effects of 'the rich diversity of options provided by a good community' (1992, 1). On the surface these elements appear consonant with the long-term influence of the Enlightenment tradition on Liberal thought. However, in several respects Gray is inspired by a post-Enlightenment attitude, especially in his disavowal of universal reasoning in favour of a kind of relativism in tune with intellectual currents influencing both the Right and Left today.

For Gray, first, autonomy stands as the precondition for human fulfilment, namely 'the capacity for rational deliberation and choice, the absence of coercion by others and the possession of the resources needed for a life that is at least partly self-directed' (1992, 26). However, Gray lends a contextual inflexion to his definition, in that autonomy is a quality of life typically found in Western societies: 'It is an essential element of the good life for people situated in our historical context as inheritors of a particular, individualist form of life'. Consequently 'No inhabitant of a modern pluralistic, mobile and discursive society can fare well without at least a modicum of the capacities and resources needed for autonomy' (*ibid.*). Reflecting parts of Hayek's critique of social justice (1976, ch. 9), Gray argues that the conditions governing autonomy are largely culturally specific and cannot be rendered in the universal language of human rights (1992, 26).

Secondly, following Raz (1986), Gray posits the idea that human nature consists of *satiable needs*, i.e. basic needs that can be satisfied by determinate amounts of provision. He argues that 'Most basic needs have the property of satiability, which means that once they are met, the content of the welfare claim which guarantees their satisfaction is exhausted' (1992, 66). Although an individual's needs may be inexhaustible, Gray argues, it is still possible to determine for a particular need a level of satisfaction which if met leaves the individual in an improved state of welfare by *diminishing* need (38), and which, more importantly, allows individuals a degree of autonomy to further meet their required levels of need themselves. It follows that 'reasoned public discourse can occur as to the content of basic needs, which invokes the shared norms and common life of the society' (67). The lack of scientific determinations in defining basic needs does not deny discussion of their content any more than it denies discussion of other indeterminate areas of human interest. Nor is the incommensurability of basic needs a problem, for the fact that a common level of satiation can be reached does not deny that individuals will achieve their own additional levels of satisfaction. The diversity of experience of satisfaction implied here predisposes state welfare to furnish benefits in cash rather than in kind, on the basis that, for example, monetized vouchers enable greater choice to be exercised.

Gray's notion of satiable needs represents a new gloss on the long tradition that saw the welfare state as supplying resources that meet minimum standards of basic need, a view shared by writers as different as Beveridge and Hayek. However, Gray gives new powers to the welfare state, in that meeting satiable needs implies an 'enabling welfare state' equipped to go well beyond subsistence claims in meeting basic needs including the need for autonomy (1992, 31). However problematic the distinction Gray makes between satiable and basic needs, satiable needs are not by definition the same as subsistence needs. This poses the problem of how precisely Gray would distinguish between subsistence, satiable and basic needs.

The notion of fixed levels of satiable need implies that the welfare state can meet needs without being committed to equalitarian policies that aim to redistribute resources. What is important is the wellbeing of the holders of welfare benefits, not any distributional principle (1992, 36). Gray argues that the distributional objectives of some welfare states end up by upsetting human needs, especially those that arise from the integrity of family life, 'where the good fortune of being born into a happy, civilized family is one that may prove decisive as to one's life chances' (37). Nonetheless, Gray is arguing for a more enhanced welfare state than many on the liberal Right argue. Such a welfare state is committed to selective welfare, except where universal provision supports autonomy and satiable needs (39).

However, can autonomy be a *satiable* need in the sense Gray defines? Doyal and Gough would agree with Gray that autonomy is a basic need of the highest order, and that societies should seek to achieve the highest degree of fulfilment possible, what they term 'optimum' satisfaction (1991, 111). However, higher levels of satisfaction are possible as higher levels and kinds of need are invoked, such as new forms of individual and 'critical' autonomy (68–9) – a view in keeping with Marx's theory of human nature discussed in Chapter 5. Contrary to Gray's position, they argue that there are no pre-determined levels of need, and that there can be no determinate ceiling placed on what the state should do to satisfy need. However, Doyal and Gough would agree with Gray that the determination of appropriate levels of satisfaction is a matter of rational consensus formation between many individuals (e.g. 126).

The problem here is that it is difficult to rationally discern a level of need-satisfaction that concurs with Gray's notion of satiable need-satisfaction. This level would have to be a compromise between the desire for collective or aggregate satisfaction and the resources available for collective need-satisfaction. The market is one means of achieving this compromise; democratic decision-making another. These two procedures achieve different levels of optimum satisfaction. However, they would not necessarily produce the same outcomes as Gray's satiable needs-satisfaction. The latter implies a definition of basic need-satisfaction that is less than optimum fulfilment. However, how in practice would we know the difference between this and a market optimum, national minimum or residual minimum? For markets and political decision-making do not have procedures for discerning levels of satiable needs. In the long run the process of reaching higher forms of need satisfaction is dependent on societal development and the means of consensus-formation, and involves the discovery of new needs and new technologies.

Turning finally to the third element of Gray's notion of human nature, the need for a rich public culture, we find here a contradiction between Gray's materially limited view of the welfare state and his support for an enriched public culture. This culture is a pluralistic one that supports the manifold fulfilment of human potential in achieving the good life, 'in which autonomous individuals have a rich array of options and amenities to choose from' (1992, 74). Such a culture recognizes the contingencies of human existence and the obligation on humans to seek to meet each others needs. Thus, a basic need is 'one whose satisfaction is essential to the possibility of a worthwhile life, and whose frustration renders impossible the living of a good life' (63). A public culture must therefore be underwritten by the state at least at a minimum level. In material terms welfare can be devolved substantially onto private individuals, social groups and charities. However, Gray (in a way reminiscent of Tawney's discussion of public goods) lists a large number of provisions, which are part of the public culture, whose responsibility rests on the state, including universal health care and pensions, and, in addition, environmental provision, transport, cultural and arts policy, science policy, family policy, currency stability and monetary policy.[6] For these institutions, 'The market is not free-standing or self-justifying, but part of a larger nexus of institutions, sharing with them a justification in terms of the contribution it makes to human wellbeing' (81).

In Gray's revision of Hayek, the hierarchical relationship between the market and other institutions is democratized. The market along with other institutions becomes subordinate to the values of individual fulfilment and is no longer the dominant order within which fulfilment is possible. Individual need-satisfaction and autonomy depend above all on a strong public culture 'in which choice and responsibility go together, and is realisable only as a common good' (1996, 17). Gray further argues that 'The central application of the communitarian liberal view to public policy is that market freedoms have instrumental values only' (*ibid.*). Gray's view of public policy is an anti-Enlightenment one that is meant to supersede the grand political ideologies of modernity. What emerges is a view of human nature as diversely constructed out of different self-interests, other-interests and mutualist sentiments that together are capable of articulating common levels of satiable needs and individual levels of autonomy and fulfilment. However, whilst this complex conception abandons primary and singular conceptions of human nature familiar to the Right, its internal contradictions undermine its status as a coherent meta-account of a diverse human nature. Human diversity is registered but not comprehended.

Conclusion

Rightist political thought since Hayek has arrived at a crossroads. In one direction lies scope for expanding public policy based on a new compact between government and civil society to secure a broader mix of market, voluntaristic and state provision for human need. Gray's project appeals to an enlarged notion of human nature: a broader range of basic needs, an enlarged notion of individual autonomy, and an enriched public culture encouraging the broadening and diversification of human need and a morality of mutual respect and obligation. In the other direction lie further limits on public policy and a widening gap between government and the market: the displacement of welfare onto private markets, a shift grounded on a strictly limited notion of self-interest. Although needs are diverse and varied, their satisfaction and enrichment becomes less a matter for public debate and more for private action within the market place or the quasi-markets of semi-autonomous government agencies.

The two directions represent different approaches to human nature reasoning. Gray attempts to articulate an enlarged notion of human nature embracing different propensities. Murray and others by contrast offer a concept of human nature that further diminishes the human propensities for which a public culture should be responsible. It is a notion that is clearly rendered into a primary account of motivation geared to individual self-interest. However, although Gray seeks to broaden the Hayekian project of providing a secondary or meta-account of human nature, he fails – as did Hayek – to articulate the precise connections and logic that integrate this extended range of human propensities. Whereas Hayek saw this meta-principle as operating through the spontaneous order of the market place, Gray argues for an enlarged and integrated domain of public, market and civil institutions. However, it is in no way clear what meta-principles work to secure this integration. Indeed his relativism and 'incredulity' towards Enlightenment meta-concepts has the effect of suppressing such questions.

We have suggested that the recent communitarian turn on the Right can appeal neither to a full conception of need nor to a national minimum conception of the kind advanced by Social Democrats, without abandoning the essentially atomistic account of human nature that the Right holds. It is only by abandoning this account that writers like Gray are able to propose a fuller notion of need than the residual notion traditionally ascribed by the Right to poor law and means-tested social provisions. As a consequence, the concept of satiable needs turns out in practice to be indistinguishable from the Social Democratic notion of need; namely, a notion that government is responsible for ensuring that a wide range of needs are met by government services, community organizations and markets. Indeed a further way forward for some of the erstwhile Right has been to extend their political alliances and ideological discourse in the direction of the type of Social Democracy represented by New Labour.

Part II

Critical Perspectives on Human Nature

Part I examined several theories of human nature shaping the two influential political traditions in social policy in the twentieth century, namely Social Democracy and the Radical Right. However, we have seen that the welfare programmes advanced by the two traditions have in recent decades faced serious problems which undermine their respective visions of human fulfilment. Recurrent fiscal crises and encroaching global insecurity have undermined the idea that by improving economic prosperity government can raise the quality of national minimum provision and provide greater scope for mutual provision among individuals and groups.

In Part II we examine two broad theories – Marxism and feminism – which exert a less direct influence on social policy, but which have nonetheless had some impact on academics and social movements. Marxism presents a theory of human nature that is radically different from Social Democracy's. In view of the problematic relationships that exists between basic needs and mutualist models of human nature in Social Democratic and Radical Right thought, especially in the context of recent decades of fundamental social change, Marxism offers a fresh way of viewing this relationship. We will examine what this way offers social policy. Feminism has challenged the idea that there is a universal human nature characterized by common basic needs shared by all. It argues that in reality welfare policy gives priority to the needs of men over women. Some elements within feminism have argued that universal common needs can only be identified if different social groups engage in a struggle for recognition that entails taking seriously each others' point of view. In this way these groups seek to reach an immanent universalist view of human fulfilment and needs. This approach offers new insights for the mutualist tradition in welfare.

5
Marx and Human Nature

Introduction

Interest in Marx's theory of human nature and need has grown at a time when, in the 1980s and 1990s, his political and intellectual influence waned. However, at the same time the exhaustion of the postwar philosophies of Social Democracy and the New Right suggests that it is all the more important to examine other traditions which offer different accounts of human nature. Seen from a broader and more philosophical perspective, Marx's philosophy offers insights that contribute to a greater understanding of modern problems in social policy, such as the question of human need and the analysis of social and economic processes hindering or advancing need-fulfilment. One central question, therefore, is what precisely has this theory to offer social policy over others, such as Social Democracy's, which have exercised a stronger influence in the twentieth century? This question is the main concern this chapter and the next.

This chapter concentrates on Marx's early works, in particular the 1844 *Economic and Philosophical Manuscripts*, the 1844 *Excerpts from James Mill's 'Elements of Political Economy'* and, with Engels, *The German Ideology* (written in 1845–46). This corpus offers a concept of human nature based on 'praxis' that provides one of the most compelling accounts in the history of social theory of the mutual dimension of human nature. Though not part of mainstream social policy, this account nonetheless contributes towards a renewed understanding of the intersubjective nature of human needs found in the Social Democratic tradition and revived in communitarian liberalism. Praxis refers to the practical work of individuals in harnessing the material of human, organic and inorganic nature in meeting their needs (for a full elaboration see Bernstein 1972, Part I). It implies individuals with different abilities and needs co-operating in producing goods and thereby coming to recognize their shared humanity.

In his later works on historical materialism (in particular *Grundrisse* and *Capital*), Marx examines the processes of producing for need embodied in the development of the means and relations of production, representing the productive forces shaping history. His focus on human nature and fulfilment broadens to take into account material structures shaping production and consumption and determining the modes of life and consciousness governing individual existence. In this respect, Marx's historical materialism, together with his earlier work, provides an account of the formation of needs and their means of satisfaction that is significantly different from Social Democracy's account.

The nature of human co-operation is shaped by productive processes which under capitalism involve the owners of the means of production extracting part of the value produced by workers for their own profit. This results in the exploitation of workers and their alienation from the fruits of their labour. Consequently, the scope for human co-operation is limited by conflict between the two classes. These class relations constitute capitalist relations of production. Existing productive forces and relations not only impose material limits on the means available for need-fulfilment, but also limit the horizons of knowledge and experience governing need satisfaction. Workers' aspirations are limited by the education, science and culture they are exposed to – insofar as these are under the control of the ruling classes. Productive forces thus contribute to ideological relations between different social classes. However, human nature also has the capacity to overcome these limits and achieve new levels of fulfilment through political struggle and the creation of new technologies of production. Consequently, impelled by the need to realize its potential, humankind struggles to harness productive forces to create new means and relations of production. This eventually leads to the demise of the capitalist mode and the inauguration of a socialist mode of production which produces 'a fresh confirmation of human powers and fresh enrichment of human nature' (Marx 1975b, 358). Marx portrays human nature as in a state of becoming, punctuated by different stages of history formed by the development of the mode of production. For Marx, 'The entire movement of history is...the comprehended and known movement of its becoming' (1975b, 348).

However, inherent in Marx's account of human nature are problems about the standards he employs for appraising human fulfilment. For the notion of perpetual human development and change, whatever the periodic limits humankind faces on the way, cannot provide the basis for an eternal and immutable standard required for assessing such fulfilment. By contrast, the concept of praxis implies that only immanent criteria or standards of value are available to co-participants who share in the practical labours of producing for need, and who arrive at standards derived from confronting their pressing needs and reaching for new means of satisfaction. In time, immanent criteria of value are institutionalized and take on the appearance of external standards – but always standards that are grounded in, and are not independent of, human practice. On this interpretation there can be no appeal to criteria derived from an external or eternal source. What then does Marx's theory of praxis offer for understanding need fulfilment; and what insights can this offer social policy as a means of fulfilling human need?

Marx's account of human fulfilment differs from Social Democracy's in posing a contrast between what is required in meeting basic needs and what in meeting truly 'human' or 'radical needs' (1975a, 277, 252). One important implication of this contrast is that Marx's ideas subject the universal basic needs model of Social Democracy to critique, and opens the way for a different notion of universal need. This contrast is explored in this and the next chapter in terms of the primary and secondary models of human nature found in Social Democracy, Marx and Marxism, and in Chapter 7 on two types of universalism described as transcendent and immanent. Specifically, this chapter asks two questions of Marx's theory of human nature. First, what does it contribute towards an enriched understanding of basic needs that are truly human needs? Secondly, what does it offer in developing a theory of mutual needs based on social interaction between individuals and between human and non-human nature? Having established the provenance of his theory of human nature as a standard of human fulfilment, we will be in a position in the next chapter to clarify Marx's conception of human needs, and the development in the theory of need provided by recent Marxists.

The human nature discourse of Marx

Marx's theory of human nature offers a set of propositions addressing respectively the empirical, motivational and normative properties of human nature – a framework of analysis adopted in previous chapters. The following exposition of Marx's theory examines each proposition in turn. First, the empirical features of Marx's theory derive from his account of natural human needs.

1 Human nature is an integral part of the totality of the natural world, namely the human species, animal species and organic and inorganic nature

Needs can only be satisfied by the resources gained from this totality; not merely from human nature, but from organic and inorganic nature as well For Marx, being in a state of need means that the subject is inescapably dependent on the totality of nature – a relationship between humankind and nature that casts human nature as an extension of nature, such that 'Nature is man's *inorganic body*' (1975b, 328).[1] This exemplifies one of many naturalistic propositions in his account of human nature. That humans *consciously* organize their life for the purpose of needs-satisfaction constitutes the distinctive feature of the human *mode of life*. This insight gives rise to a set of motivational propositions about the characteristic mode of human action that we will elaborate later. In *The German Ideology*, Marx and Engels affirm that 'The first historical act is thus the production of the means to satisfy these needs, the production of material life itself' (1976, 42). Needs therefore provide the individual with his or her orientation to the object world and their distinctive mode of life within it, namely their characteristic way of organizing social life. Marx and Engels attest to the essential connectedness of needing individuals to their needed world, a naturalism that invests human life with purpose and direction, for 'in the real world...where individuals have needs, they thereby already have a *vocation* and *task*' (289). This refers to the important role of praxis in guiding human knowledge and action in the natural world, to which we return. Peter Dickens, in his reading of these passages from the early Marx, stresses the dialectical process involved in praxis, namely that by acting to change nature, humans in turn change themselves (1992, 44–5 and ch. 3).

2 Human nature is essentially unbounded

Marx sets no limits on the horizons of human need and ingenuity in meeting need. However, within history the realization of human nature is limited by the means and relations of production existing within a given mode of production. Despite this, individuals can catch a glimpse of their shared potential to transcend these limits and satisfy their needs beyond the present level of satisfaction. The need to utilize the manifold resources of nature presents a challenge for human ingenuity and industry. In rising to this challenge, universal human nature comes to be reflected in the diversity of nature. Consequently, 'because man is more universal than animals, so too is the area of inorganic life from which he lives more *universal*' (1975b, 327). Individuals comprehend the plenitude of nature as a wealth of objects available both for their immediate satisfaction and for constructing the means of producing for universal needs. This reflects the universal perspective that Marx sees as characteristic of human life; that is, 'that universality that makes the whole of nature his *inorganic* body; (1) as a direct means of life and (2) as the matter, the object and the tool of his life activity' (328).

From the above naturalistic propositions about human nature in Marx's early writings, we can construct a set of propositions about the motivations characterizing the human mode of life, which show how human needs are reflected in the intentions and desires motivating social action.

3 The characteristic means by which humankind relates to nature is labour

Indeed humankind's dependence on nature means that 'The worker can create nothing without *nature*, without the *sensuous external world*. It is the material in which his labour realizes itself, in which it is active and from which and by means of which it produces' (Marx 1975b, 325). From the beginning of history humankind relates to external nature by means of labour, for 'life involves before everything else eating and drinking, housing and clothing and various other things' (Marx and Engels 1976, 42). For Marx, labour means extending the powers of humankind into the natural world, to work on its raw material and produce for need. The extension of human powers thus entails 'objectifying' the human subject into the object world and leaving its mark there. In this way Marx can claim that 'The object of labour is therefore the *objectification of the species life of man*' (1975b, 329). For what is characteristic of human nature, and less visible in animal nature, is its ability to humanize the external world by extending its need-fulfilling practices into non-human nature.

4 The nature of human life is understood by the concept of praxis, the need-satisfying process in which different individuals co-operate in applying their labour to the object world

Here Marx goes further in describing human life. According to this view, human life involves positing a *direct* relationship between the human subject and the objects of nature. The relationships involve a direct experience with the '*sensuous* external world' of human and non-human nature that satisfies need (1975b, 325). This communion of the senses with the external world therefore posits an exchange of 'free mental and physical energy' (326), which in satisfying need contributes to fulfilling an individual's potential – hence Marx's reference to humankind's 'continuing dialogue' with nature as the prerequisite of survival and flourishing.

Praxis therefore implies two processes: (i) the intention to satisfy need and the realization of intention as need is satisfied; and (ii) the development of conscious reflection on the causation entailed in this process. The process of needs-fulfilment becomes praxis when, because a need is met through realizing an intention, the individual reflects on his or her action (including unsuccessful action) and begins to construct the rudiments of theoretical knowledge. Such insights raise the level of consciousness. However, the process does not take place in a consciousness dissociated from sense experience, but is grounded in the sensuous practical experience of satisfying need which alone initiates conscious insights into ways of handling need (see Doyal and Harris 1983).

5 The integral relationship humankind has to nature, including other humans, means that the human mode of life is of necessity grounded in material forms of exchange and undertaken in socially organized forms of labour

Human fulfilment is realized socially so that personal fulfilment is contingent on social fulfilment. In his sixth thesis on Feuerbach, Marx proposes that the essence of human nature lies in the social nature of human existence; this essence 'is no abstraction inherent in each single individual.

In its reality it is the ensemble of the social relations' (Marx 1976, 4; see Geras 1983). Given that *human* existence is irreducibly *social*, Marx can generalize that 'the *social* character is the general character of the whole movement [of human history]' and that 'The *human* essence of nature exists only for *social* man; for only here does nature exist for him as a *bond* with other men...as the vital element of human reality' (1975b, 349). Human ends and needs are conceived according to the social relations and means of production available to humankind at a particular stage of its evolution. Not only are needs satisfied through these socialized modes of existence, but the social significance of need is determined by these modes as well.

6 The true value of goods produced from nature lies in their use as sensuous objects for human consumption and for developing the tools and skills involved in producing goods and services

Marx formulates this insight in his early work, for example the *Manuscripts* (1975b, 362), and develops it fully in *Capital*, in his essential distinction between use- and exchange-value (1967, 36–7), i.e. between the value of commodities that satisfy need and their value in exchange with other commodities in the capitalist system of production.

7 It is the practical thrust of human activity – i.e. its 'industry' – which drives the development of human knowledge, rather than philosophy or abstract reasoning

Thereby science and technology are the means of harnessing nature's resources to satisfy need and transform human life. By expending collective labour on exploiting nature for human fulfilment, industry ultimately reveals the true essence of humankind. Marx describes industry as 'the *real* historical relationship to nature, and hence of natural science, to man. If it is then conceived as the exoteric revelation of man's *essential powers*, the *human* essence of nature or the *natural* essence of man can also be understood' (1975b, 355). It is only by means of the relationship of humankind to nature, wrought by the labours of industry and formative of history, that true human nature can be discovered:

> Nature as it comes into being in human history – in the act of creation of human history – is the *true* nature of man; hence nature as it comes into being through industry, though in an *estranged* form, is true *anthropological* nature. (*ibid.*)

8 Marx develops a normative account of human nature

This is seen, first, in the way he contrasts the conditions of alienation and deprivation under capitalism with an account of what human nature would be like if fulfilled as far as possible by capitalism's means of production. (Marx acknowledges capitalism's superiority in satisfying human needs over previous modes in the *Grundrisse* (1973, 409–10).) This can be seen by comparing the deprivation of the many with the satisfaction and fulfilment of the privileged few:

> The production which these productive forces could provide was insufficient for the whole of society and made development possible only if some persons satisfied their needs at the expense of others, and therefore some – the minority – obtained the monopoly of development, while others – the majority – owing to the constant struggle to satisfy their most essential needs, were for the time being (i.e. until the creation of new revolutionary productive forces) excluded from any development.
> (Marx and Engels 1976, 431–2)

This contrast is then used to suggest an ideal society where inequality and deprivation are absent, an antithesis of the reality of existing society. We can describe this process of arriving at normative conclusions by the term *counterfactual*. The antithesis serves as the first of two standards for critically evaluating society.

However, the idea of antagonistic classes co-operating in allocating goods and values strictly according to need rather than profit would imply a fundamental transformation of the social relations of capitalism. For Marx, fundamental conflict arises as the forces of production – i.e. the drive for new ways of meeting need – come into conflict with existing social relations of production organized around the means of production. These social relations are the relations between the classes of owners and workers, whose uneasy relationship can eventually explode into outright class antagonism. Out of this struggle, the productive forces bring forth new means and relations capable of meeting human needs more fully. Marx uses not only the notion of the fulfilment of human nature as an ethical standard for appraising existing social relations. He also seeks to conceptualize the fulfilment of human nature beyond these relations in new transformed social relations, so employing human nature in a *dialectical*, as well as counterfactual, manner. This represents a second standard for evaluating society.

However, different interpretations of Marx's normative critique of capitalism vary in the way they construct normative standards that apply to existing society, as we will see below. For some Marxists (e.g. Geras 1983), the potential fulfilment of human needs possible within the capitalist mode of production constitutes a transhistorical standard for evaluating the quality of existence reached by humankind within that mode and subsequent modes. Other Marxists (e.g. Markus 1978) by contrast adopt a teleological perspective that sees fulfilment as only possible once all forms of exploitation have been overcome and the conditions causing alienation transcended. In this view the standard of human fulfilment represents a standard (at best, an imaginary one) applied retrospectively to all known societies whatever their historical conditions.

9 Humankind's incarnate form

Marx's needs-oriented philosophy of praxis means that knowledge of 'sensuous certainty' gives rise to a particular kind of theory characteristic of *human kind's incarnate or embodied form*. 'Embodied' knowledge is grounded in an experience of real needs.[2] However, the experiences of human alienation and deprivation under capitalism deny individuals the opportunity to experience complete and embodied communion of the senses in the way that Marx's concept of praxis implies. Cut off from the fruits of their labour, individuals have at best only a partial knowledge of their needs and means of satisfaction. Consequently, Marx must rely on more speculative approaches for describing need-fulfilment than is possible by means of the *counterfactual* juxtaposition of unequal needs-satisfaction with an imagined state of more equal satisfaction under existing productive means. This requires a more rigorous notion of the *dialectical* transcendence of unequal satisfaction to achieve full satisfaction by the creation of new productive means and social relations.

These two approaches to normative critique give rise to two senses of fulfilled needs understood according to Marx's notion of praxis which we will call 'concrete' sensuous fulfilment and 'ideal' sensuous fulfilment respectively. First, needs are identified which are fulfilled for some but not for the majority of individuals. For the labouring classes, their sensuous needs are identified from the certainty of the bourgeois classes' greater satisfaction. Marx contends, for example, that the conditions of capitalist exploitation have achieved the means of satisfying need alongside increasing deprivation, whereby the 'multiplication of needs and the means of fulfilling them gives rise to a lack of needs and of means' (1975b, 360). The means and relations of production might be marginally adjusted – by way of welfare, wage and taxation – to increase the availability of resources to those in greatest need. This implies a just distribution that remedies present levels of inequality and exploitation, but only to a degree compatible with the prevailing mode. It is this counterfactual sense of need fulfilment which is conveyed by the Social Democratic notion of distributive justice – Rawls' 'difference principle' comes to mind here. The second sense of fulfilment goes beyond the first. Here needs are understood not as they are, but as they might become under a future mode of production. In the first sense, knowledge of existing needs and means derives from an experience of needs and means made possible by the existing mode of production. In the second, knowledge based on a counterfactual *and* dialectical reading of sense certainty provides an intimation of unfulfilled needs that goes beyond existing needs and states of satisfaction to express those potential needs whose fulfilment can only arise under a transformed mode of production. Just as new forces of production intimate the need for new relations of production, so they will generate new needs with new challenges to produce goods for their satisfaction. In contrasting the realization of human nature under conditions of private property (i.e. the capitalist mode of production) and of communism, Marx contrasts 'one sided' with 'total' satisfaction of need:

> The sensuous appropriation of human essences and human life, of objective man and human *works* by and for man, should not be understood only in the sense of *direct*, one-sided *consumption*, of *possession*, of *having*. Man appropriates his integral essence in an integral way, as a total man.
>
> (1975b, 351)

Marx seeks to capture the embodied experience of this 'total' fulfilment in concrete terms (whose sensuous language betrays the fact that this exposition remains essentially metaphoric and suggestive):

> All his *human* relations to the world – seeing, hearing, smelling, tasting, feeling, thinking, contemplating, sensing, wanting, acting, loving – in short all the organs of his individuality, like the organs which are directly communal in form, are in their *objective* approach or in their *approach to the object* the appropriation of that object. (*ibid.*)

Throughout his early writings, Marx suggests the scope of human nature by means of a series of opposite metaphors contrasting a limited and full conception of human nature, for example, 'one-sided' and 'many-sided' needs, animal and human needs, organic and inorganic life, material and spiritual life, and so forth. However, this metaphorical style of argument is inadequate for the task of characterizing fully human needs that are realized through practical struggles or praxis. At best it depicts ideal characterizations of human nature – hence the author's rather clumsy phrase 'ideal sensuous fulfilment' used presently. The question remains, however, as to what Marx meant by truly 'human' needs, and what this notion might offer social policy.

Marx and the limitations of Social Democratic welfare

Marx provides a secondary or meta-theory of human nature (embracing synchronic and diachronic dimensions of human development). This is an advance on primary accounts that understand human nature by means of the logic governing the capitalist mode of production alone (a synchronic dimension). Such accounts are typical of the Social Democratic arguments of writers that social policy should meet common basic needs. Here the capitalist means of production, which have the potential to realize needs universally, are in fact socially organized to meet the needs of the few rather than the many. What this account fails to do is to explain the contradiction in which an economic system, with the capacity to meet the needs of all, and to do so more fully than previous systems, is in fact constrained by social or class relations to meet the needs of the few more than the many. By contrast, Marx's meta-theory of human nature supports a fuller critique than those available to the Social Democratic tradition. Marx is able to open up a critical exposition of capitalism's ability to distribute goods on the basis of need. We can apply this critique to the Social Democratic concepts of basic needs and mutually fulfilled needs (e.g. Titmuss' 'gift relation'). Further, we can pursue our objective of understanding more fully Marx's contribution to enriched notions of basic and mutual needs, and describe the relationship between the two.

Marx begins his critique of basic needs with an attack on Adam Smith and the classical political economists' notion of basic need. For Marx this notion represents 'the absolute minimum necessary; just enough for [an individual] to exist not as a human being but as a worker and for him to propagate not humanity but the slave class of the workers' (1975b, 287). It is this tradition which influenced the concept of poverty developed by late nineteenth-century researchers such as Booth and Rowntree, and which influenced the ideas of the Webbs and Beveridge and postwar national-minimum policies discussed in Chapter 3. Marx describes in derisory terms a conception of human satisfaction which embodies the idea of humankind as 'a stomach' (285), with 'minimum bodily needs', reduced to the 'paltriest minimum necessary to maintain his physical existence', and relegated to become no more than a 'servant of the flesh' (290), or a 'prisoner of crude practical needs' (353).

The problem with the concept of basic need in defining welfare provision is that it rests on an assumption of distributive justice limited by the existing mode of capitalist production. For Marxists, the broadly Liberal notion of meeting basic needs assumes a pattern of distribution whereby only part of the surplus value extracted from the total value of goods produced by labour is allocated to labour. In fact the bulk of this surplus accrues as profit to the owners of production. The quality and quantity of welfare for basic needs – whether poor law, means-tested or national minimum – is determined by the level of the surplus, part of which is taxed to finance public and charitable welfare. Seen in this way, welfare for basic needs is dependent on the general health of the economic system. It is a form of social amelioration whose very substance is based on the exploitation of the class producing the surplus by the class profiting from the surplus. In this sense, the idea of meeting basic needs reinforces the alienation of labour from the products it produces for need. Welfare based on surplus value reflects the relations of exploitation and alienation and therefore cannot address truly human needs.

Secondly, Marx develops a notion of mutual needs that surpasses the ideas of Social Democrats like Titmuss, discussed in Chapter 3. One of the most explicit formulations of a mutualist account of human nature in Marx is found in *Excerpts from James Mill's 'Elements of Political Economy'* (1975c). Here he provides one of several contrasts between human fulfilment under private property and under communism. Under private property, prior to the introduction of exchange, 'Man produces only to have something for himself. The object of his production is the objectification of his immediate selfish needs', whereby the 'limits of his needs is the limit of his production' (274). Even when surplus is produced and economic exchange occurs between individuals, this 'does not mean any advance beyond selfish needs' (*ibid.*), for the products exchanged by two individuals 'are not united for each other by the bonds of *human nature*' (275), but becomes merely a 'source of acquisition' (274). The development of the capitalist means of production is insufficient, despite its ability to harness new creative energies, to transform human-beinghood, because capitalist social relations are still tied to *individual* need-satisfaction and self-interest.

By contrast, for Marx, the antithesis of private property and wage labour would be the emancipation of human nature where people 'produced as human beings, and each individual *doubly affirmed* himself and his neighbour in his production' (1975c, 277). Marx describes this double affirmation in phenomenological terms that resemble Titmuss' account of the 'gift relationship' described in Chapter 3, using a similar analysis (but arriving at a different conclusion) to Hegel's 'struggle for recognition' described in *The Phenomenology of Spirit* (1977, 111–19).

(1) In my *production* I would have objectified the *specific character* of my *individuality* and for that reason I would have enjoyed the *expression* of my own individual *life* during my activity and also, in contemplating the object, I would experience an individual pleasure, I would experience my personality as an *objective sensuously perceptible* power *beyond all shadow of doubt*. (2) In your use or enjoyment of my product I would have the *immediate* satisfaction and knowledge that in my labour I had gratified a *human* need, i.e. that I had objectified *human nature* and hence had procured an object corresponding to the needs of another *human being*. (3) I would have acted for you as the *mediator* between you and the species, thus I would be acknowledged by you as the complement of your own being, as an essential part of yourself. I would thus know myself to be confirmed in your thoughts and your love. (4) In the individual expression of my own life I would have brought about the immediate expression of your life, and so in my individual activity

I would have directly *confirmed* and *realized* my authentic nature, my *human, communal nature*. Our production would be as many mirrors from which our natures would shine forth.

(1975c, 277–7)

Here Marx provides an exposition of standards for human fulfilment, which is substantially, and conceptually more developed than the concepts of basic needs and mutually fulfilled needs in the Social Democratic tradition. In (1) above, Marx describes the individual's experience of satisfying specific aspects of his or her need met by producing goods from the resources of the object world. In (2) this individual has the satisfaction of knowing that his or her labour produces goods that contribute to satisfying another person's needs; in social policy terms, by co-operative mutual support. In (3) and (4), by mediating between the needs of the other person and the object world, this individual further enables the other to achieve fulfilment not only of his or her basic needs, but fulfilment through recognition of his or her humanity and so through mutual needs. Hence, the individual is recognized in turn for his or her humanity. At this stage, basic needs and mutual recognition complement each other and progressively enhance each others fulfilment – like many mirrors from which our natures shine forth – in furthering the historical process of collective self-realization and transformation. We will see shortly that for Marx basic and mutual needs are implicated in each other.

Both Titmuss and Marx use notions of human relationships – 'gift relations' and 'communal' relations – to expose the limitations of capitalist production for need. Titmuss' account of the gift of welfare appeals to qualities of human existence that surpass limited forms of 'bilateral' economic exchange in contributing to greater fulfilment than satisfying mere individual want. However, welfare capitalism is governed by two irreconcilable principles – bilateral and unilateral exchange – which are both constituted within the terms of the productive relations of capitalism based on individual need-satisfaction and equivalence in exchange. Economic exchange is in essence two parties giving something for something where the value of the exchange is based on clear norms of equivalence in terms of money, goods or contributory benefits. However, unilateral exchange or the welfare gift is more ambiguous. On the one hand, it is dependent on the bilateral exchanges of capitalism insofar as what is given is dependent on surplus value – i.e. charity or welfare benefits. On the other, it lies outside a strict, monetized calculation of equivalence, where the elements of a benefit or service are beyond measurement, as in measuring improved quality of life, basic needs met, security and peace of mind. In this light, the wider reciprocities Titmuss invokes in terms of care for the 'universal stranger' and the 'gift of life', displaced in time and social distance, are even more problematic.

By contrast, Marx's broader meta-analysis suggests that human nature can be fulfilled socially by economic means that transcend the existing mode of production to achieve new levels of fulfilment based on relations of mutual and socially co-operative interaction. Marx describes the fulfilment of the self and other through exchange under communal forms of existence: namely, the experience of giving and producing that enables people to objectify their powers through seeking the fulfilment of others; the gratification of knowing the other's satisfaction in having his or her needs met; the sense of self-value gained in confirming the other's human identity; and the confirmation of one's self gained from the realization of the other. In Marx's account of human nature, basic needs take on a human dimension only in the context of mutual co-operation and recognition: basic and mutual needs together form human needs.

6
Marxism, Human Nature and Need

Introduction

In the last chapter, we saw that Marx provides a conception of human nature that posits a standard of need-satisfaction for humans to aspire towards. In his later writings on historical materialism, this conception is framed within an empirical account of the development of society and its economic infrastructure. This account posits the material means of production that under certain conditions impede human development, but that under others support its fulfilment. Throughout his work, Marx examines two notions of need: minimum basic needs which the owners of production meet through systems of wage-labour and welfare so that workers can reproduce their labour power; and truly 'human needs'.

Marx thereby develops a secondary or meta-account of 'human' or 'radical' needs (1975a, 252). This is an account of human development in which fulfilment is reached when exploitation and alienation are overcome and relationships among humans and between humans and non-humans are conducted in truly human terms. According to his conception of praxis, human nature is realized immanently in the struggle to fulfil human needs and overcome the limitations of the present mode. Marx posits a view of human nature located in humankind's transhistorical capacity to realize its needs, despite whatever material and social impediments it encounters under a particular productive mode. However, it is questionable whether this transhistorical account of human nature can provide an eternal standard of need-fulfilment that traverses different periods of history.

The precise meaning of human fulfilment has been one of the major issues of Marxist theory since the 1970s. This is the main concern of this chapter. 'Human needs' represents a standard of fulfilment different from basic needs and important in determining the goals of social policy. Marx's account of human nature provides normative criteria for evaluating the productive means, including social policies, for meeting needs. Several questions therefore need to be addressed concerning whether modern

Marxism can determine the content of truly human needs; and whether the normative criteria contained in this concept can be rendered sufficiently clear. Moreover, in response to the emergence of a politics of difference associated with feminism and new social movements, a further question arises as to whether these criteria are sensitive to recently politicized forms of difference in human nature emerging around issues of gender, race, disability and sexuality, without imposing a common conception of normality. This issue is taken up again in Chapter 7. Can Marxism acknowledge the difference between basic needs which are common to human nature whilst being sensitive to higher needs that define the specific concerns of particular social movements (Hewitt 1996)? Clearly, Marx's notion of human needs is made to do a lot of work. We therefore need to understand clearly what this concept means.

The different interpretations of Marx's notion of human fulfilment can be placed on a spectrum ranging from those writers who see human nature as conceptualized by various contradictions, and others who view it more holistically. At one end we find Althusser's reading of Marx's 'epistemological break' and his outright repudiation of Marx's notion of human nature as 'ideology', and with it the rejection of a normative model of human fulfilment. Althusser characterizes this as part of Marx's early works before the 'break' and incompatible with the subsequent birth of the scientific Marxism of historical materialism (1969, 34). Several other writers, though questioning the fundamental nature of Althusser's break, have identified other critical breaks in the development of Marx's concept of human nature. Soper, for example, identifies irreconcilable tensions between Marx's cognitive and normative discourses on human nature (discussed below in section (a)). Benton addresses the tensions between the historical processes of humanizing nature and naturalizing humanity, which unfold in the historical development of human powers (b). Both these and other writers recognize, *pace* Althusser, the importance of human nature in Marx's work. Geras (c), in particular, advances a transhistorical notion of human nature, which can prescribe standards for assessing human conditions of need fulfilment. We will endeavour to apply the ideas of Benton and Geras to social policy (d). At the other end of the spectrum from these dualistic interpretations, there are the more holistic readings of Marx by Markus and Heller (e), from the Budapest School, who see no major contradiction between Marx's cognitive or explanatory account of human history and his normative standards for appraising human conditions. In the discussion we will focus on the exegesis that followed in Althusser's wake and which, though in some cases influenced by Althusser's work, has sought to give more significance to Marx's theory of human nature. For many of these writers, Althusser's anti-ontological reading removes the possibility of addressing normative criteria and methods of criticizing the capitalist mode of production. They contend that this critique cannot be undertaken without reference to a notion of human fulfilment from which human relationships based on exploitation and alienation can be exposed as inhumane. Human emancipation and fulfilment implies a notion of human nature.

(a) The normative and cognitive discourses in Marx's theory of human nature: Kate Soper

The renewed interest in Marx's theory of human nature rests on a general recognition that the critical thrust of his analysis of capitalism must rely on a standard of the kind of human fulfilment which capitalism thwarts. Some writers, however, recognize that his vision of human nature is far from coherent because it reflects the lapses and discontinuities characterizing the complex development of his thought over several decades. Soper, for example, recognizes what she terms a 'normative discourse' on need (which criticizes capitalism's inability to meet the needs of all individuals) set alongside, but not clearly delineated from, a 'cognitive discourse' (seeking to explain capitalism's development), which is 'inconsistent with' the former. Of the two discourses, the cognitive appears 'to preclude any judgement about the pattern of consumption and the historic needs to which, as the latest form of the development of the productive forces, it has given rise, while the other [the normative discourse] directly condemns the pattern of consumption associated with capitalism' (1981, 94, also 134). However, a cognitive theory of labour addressing the needs of workers must rest on a normative standard of consumption needed to realize fulfilment. It is precisely this normative discourse on human needs and consumption that draws its ethical criteria from Marx's account of human nature. Without addressing questions about the nature of needs in Marx's philosophical anthropology, how is his understanding of human consumption to be grasped (34, 91, 99 *et passim*)? It is indeed this kind of questioning that demonstrates the humanistic underpinnings to Marx's concerns about the limits and failings in capitalism's endeavour to secure the full development of human needs. For

> were this line of attack not underpinned by some form of humanism, it would have no rationale at all. For why...should it matter, if not for humanistic reasons, that capitalist relations of distribution restrict the effective demand of the masses? (96)

Further, Marx's theory of human nature can be seen to support *explanatory* moments of the cognitive discourse. If the cognitive discourse is a theory about productive forces, there has to be an account of what *human purpose* is fulfilled by these forces, namely the fulfilment of truly human needs. In other words, Marx must provide a teleological justification for the existence of productive forces, which makes explicit the reason why these forces exist as a matter of concern for human life and not merely as an impersonal juggernaut driving technological change.

To explore the immanent and purpose-driven nature of human action – i.e. praxis – it was necessary for Marx to deepen the analysis beyond an account of the economic transformation of the forces of production, and to focus on what Soper terms the 'existential' nature of the transformation in human nature which the normative discourse attempts. Thus Soper argues that the 'theory of personality' suggested in the *Grundrisse*, about the interchange between man and the objective conditions for the formation of self, entails 'apparently antithetical accounts of need' (1981, 137). In this account the worker is portrayed, on the one hand, as subject to the limitations of capitalist relations of production and need-satisfaction, and, on the other, as experiencing an opening up of its human universality. Soper concludes that the antitheses in Marx's theory of personality give way to a positive evaluation of the human transformation made possible through the medium of capitalism. This theory of personality

> has to be seen precisely as the theory that supports and confirms the discourse about the all-sided development that an all-sided and non-specific extension of self in one's objectifications of the self makes possible. (*ibid.*)

Capitalism is but one moment in the process of universalizing human nature and reaching higher levels of fulfilment. In this respect Soper quotes Marx's discussion in the *Grundrisse* to the effect that, 'When the limited bourgeois form is stripped away, what is wealth other than the universality of individual needs, capacities, pleasures, productive forces, etc. created through universal exchange? The full development of human mastery over the forces of nature, those of so-called nature as well as of humanity's own nature?' (Marx 1973, 487–8). Marx's analysis of higher needs can be seen as uncovering deeper levels of human nature, whilst at the same time revealing greater degrees of interchange between human and 'inorganic' nature.

However, against this optimistic analysis of human development, Soper acknowledges that the tensions and contradictions in Marx's theory of human nature call for a deeper understanding of the human condition, namely of the existence of natural limits to human fulfilment. Freud's dualist account of human nature, for example, points to these limits, and suggests that there are limits in achieving, let alone determining, higher needs.

Modern social policy lacks a standard that serves as a norm for assessing human fulfilment beyond the scope of present society. In Soper's language, it possesses 'universal' standards based on the paltry notion of basic needs, but lacks a 'transhistorical' standard that guides the formation of social policy through the profound changes characterizing late capitalism. (However, we will see shortly that Geras suggests that Marx does offer transhistorical standards.) In capitalist society as presently constituted, social policy is torn between, on the one hand, a limited view of human fulfilment tied to basic needs and, on the other, a notion of human needs understood as the needs of society. The latter involves normative notions of the functional requirements of society that need to be met in order for society to survive, requirements which individual members must conform to, such as the conventions of family life and work discipline. As Gough has shown this leads social policy to translate the needs of the individual into the needs of capitalist society (1979, 151). Further, as we argued in Chapter 1, the pragmatic turn in social policy and politics in the 1990s, following the wide-sweeping reforms of the late 1980s and early 1990s, and the fundamental transformation of society over the last quarter of a century, has issued in a relatively modest programme of social policy far removed from the more visionary programme of postwar reform. This itself narrows the scope of normative standards for assessing social development.

(b) Marx on the humanization and naturalization of need: Ted Benton

Benton addresses a different dualist tension in Marx's work, found in the 1844 *Manuscripts*, in his accounts of the human project of civilizing nature and the broader process of humankind coming to terms with nature. On the one hand, Marx develops an understanding of humankind as integral to nature; and, on the other, of humankind engaged in the exploitation of nature for its own fulfilment. For Benton, the two processes of naturalizing human nature and humanizing non-human nature are at odds with each other. The latter, seen for example in Marx's contrast between conscious human fulfilment and instinctive animal satisfaction – of man's superiority over beast – clearly privileges human needs over the needs of the totality of nature of which humankind is but one part. Marx's view is a dualist one that sees human beings as morally and ontologically different from non-human beings, and, as Benton argues,

> suggests a denial of the complexity and diversity of the emotional, psychological and social lives of other animals. Such a denial renders merely rhetorical Marx's characterisation of history as 'nature developing into man'.
>
> (1988, 12)

Benton seeks a restructuring of Marx's argument along lines which strengthen the naturalistic concerns in his work and which re-order the relationship between human, organic and inorganic nature, without reducing cultural phenomena and human needs to naturalistic phenomena (13). This enhanced view of human needs helps to identify new social standards of human fulfilment that apply to capitalist society and its welfare provisions (14). Restructuring Marx's argument requires identifying a common core of needs shared by human and non-human animals, and differentiating the specific *modes of life* of particular species. For example, humans have specific *ways* of satisfying needs which are different from the ways of other species that nonetheless share the same needs. On this reading, Marx can be seen as

> making a distinction not so much between practices which satisfy different needs as between different modes of satisfaction of common needs. The satisfaction of aesthetic and cognitive needs does not *require* the performance of further practices, over and above the practices through which physical needs are met. In a fully human, or 'true' practice of production, physical needs would be met in a *way* that was aesthetically and cognitively satisfying. (*ibid*.)

A human mode of life shapes the specific way in which humankind experiences, identifies and satisfies its physical needs (*ibid*.). Indeed the mere satisfaction of physical need in humans – e.g. hunger – without the cultural salience given it by the human mode of satisfying need could be construed as pathological in lacking those qualities that characterize human life. Eating food 'from hand to mouth' would be taken as unnatural for humans who normally satisfy their needs by cultural means whether consuming chips from grease-proof paper or on a silver platter. Marx and Engels capture the distinctively human mode of satisfying need:

> [the] mode of production must not be considered simply as being the reproduction of the physical existence of the individuals. Rather it is a definite form of activity of these individuals, a definite form of expressing their life, a definite *mode of life* on their part. As individuals express their life, so they are. What they are, therefore, coincides with their production.
>
> (1976, 31)

Specifically human needs have a material basis – shared with other species – that is distinguished by the way humans deploy resources for needs in culturally distinctive ways. Higher needs are an expression of this distinctly human mode of life.

Benton's account of the relationship between the common needs of human and animal nature and the need-satisfaction that informs a particular species' mode of life is analogous to Doyal and Gough's universalist account of need (1991). Here the need-satisfying practices of a specific human culture are construed as a particular way of satisfying universal needs that all humans share. These practices are the expression of the way of life that informs a particular cultural community, 'Since there is no escape from the rules and discourses of one's form of life' (43). These different cultural practices satisfy what Doyal and Gough call 'intermediate needs' common to all cultures (e.g. food and water, protective housing, safe environment, health care, etc.), but satisfied through culturally specific means whose satisfaction meets universal human needs for survival and autonomy. A parallel can be drawn between, on the one hand, Benton's view of the need-satisfying practices characterizing a particular species' mode of life that give specific species-expression to the core needs common to different species, and Doyal and Gough's account of the distinct need-satisfying practices of a particular culture that nonetheless express the universal needs that characterize all of humankind. The implications of this type of argument for the content of need is that by examining universal needs within a particular culture, one also addresses the specific cultural standards and technologies of need-satisfaction that contextualize the content of universal needs.

The question of the content of needs cannot be separated from the question of the structure of need. Benton's conception of the mode of life characterizing a particular species raises several issues for social policy about the structure of need, and so about the parameters defining its content. The argument that the human-species' mode of life depends on a particular structure of the means of needs-satisfaction suggests a particular agenda for social policy in formulating needs. If the human mode of life is distinguished by the particular *human* way physical needs are met, namely in a way that enriches cognitive and aesthetic need-satisfaction as well as physical needs, then this structure of need is normative for social policy in two senses. First, meeting basic needs – e.g. food, warmth, shelter and health – is no longer sufficient. Higher needs must become part of an enhanced agenda for social policy – an insight that has guided policy since Maslow first formulated his hierarchy of needs in the 1940s (see 1970). However, this must be sought in ways that Benton warns should avoid dualist opposition between lower and higher needs (1988, 12 *et passim*). Secondly, the way social provisions meet basic needs must be organized to enrich rather than negate the cognitive and aesthetic appetites that distinguish humankind. The concept of 'enrichment' in work and welfare has been explicitly part of social policy's agenda for some time, being concerned with the 'quality of life' in health, community care and other areas, and with the ability of the poor to participate in a community's life-style (Townsend 1979, 249). However, the absence of such concerns in government social policy calls into question not only the adequacy of official policy, but also the failure to recognize the limits placed on human fulfilment through focusing exclusively on basic needs and failing to design provisions that acknowledge the hierarchy of need-satisfaction characterizing human life. For Benton, the historical process of realizing humankind's potential gives rise to new and enriched understandings of the human mode of life, and to new standards for gauging the gap between human deprivation and fulfilment.

(c) A permanent standard of human nature: Norman Geras

In contrast with Soper's and Benton's view of the contradictory developments in Marx's theory of human nature, Geras argues that the concept of human nature retains its meaning as an abiding standard throughout the intricate developments and tensions in Marx's thought. However, on the core issue of the need for a notion of human nature in Marx's work, Geras agrees with the other writers, that his theoretical achievements would not have been possible without it. For example, even in a late text such as *Capital* (1967), the concept of human nature serves as a basis for a Marxist ethics. Geras contends that this text 'is a moral indictment resting on a conception of essential human needs, an ethical standpoint, in other words, in which a view of human nature is involved' (1983, 84). More specifically, he goes on to argue that human nature acts as a kind of theoretical bedrock to the structure of Marx's thought amidst propositions dealing with the diversity and contradictions characterizing the human condition:

> if diversity in the character of human beings is in large measure set down by Marx to historical variation in their social relations of production, the very fact that they entertain this sort of relations, the fact that they produce and that they have a history, he explains in turn by some of their *general and constant*, intrinsic, constitutional characteristics; in short by their human nature.
>
> (1983, 67, stress added)

Geras argues repeatedly that Marx's account of human nature contains needs that are universal and permanent throughout humankind and human history. He talks of Marx's 'schedule of general human needs' (72), based on 'the supposition of a common human nature from beginning to end' (79). Even when Marx emphasizes the historical variability of human nature, 'he still conceives the variation as falling within some limits and those not just the limits of a bare subsistence' (72). No doubt Geras is correct in noting Marx's reference in the 1844 *Manuscripts*, as we saw above, to universal and permanent human nature. However, it is precisely the idea that the needs characterizing human nature are *general and constant* that is so problematic. It can be argued that what Geras does is advance a notion of human nature and needs that is constant and general in substance and not just in form. As Benton argues human nature can be characterized in terms of universal common needs and capabilities that are given *substantively* differing forms under different human modes of life. Universal needs are expressed in different ways in terms of the different levels and kinds of higher need-satisfaction achieved in different cultures, historical periods and conditions of production. However, Geras' conception of human immutability and generality, is at the expense of a more dialectical understanding of human development. This alternative understanding would allow for the variability and development of human needs in the context of historical change. At the same time it would sustain a concept of need that acts as a theoretical bedrock, or 'limit concept', throughout the currents of change and mutability characterizing human development. One could ask, for example, what range of variability in human needs does the notion of 'permanent needs' permit? Conversely, are there natural limits to the scope and development of human nature which Marx's account would acknowledge?

Geras' characterization of the scope of human needs is, therefore, overly unilinear and one-dimensional. However, other commentators have sought to classify needs in terms of a transformative and radicalizing perspective as humankind moves from one productive mode to another (e.g. Heller and Soper; see also Springborg 1981, 105). Referring to *The German Ideology*, Geras argues that 'the enduring imperative of essential human needs' (1983, 70) entails a single unitary 'schedule of general human needs', namely needs 'for other human beings, for sexual relations, for food, water, clothing, shelter, rest and, more generally, for circumstances that are conducive to physical health' (1983, 72). To this he adds 'the need of people for a breadth and diversity of pursuit and hence of personal development' (*ibid*.), referring to Marx's notion of many-sided human activity. This single schema of needs embraces both basic needs for mere survival and needs implicated in human emancipation (i.e. higher needs), so that the latter are with the former part of the same order of needs; for 'The same needs that figure in elaborating the...first premise of all history figure equally as preconditions of human liberation' (*ibid*.). Here Geras appears to concur with Benton's discussion of the hierarchy of human needs. Nevertheless, Geras does not discuss Marx's view of needs that are necessary for liberation. In appearing to endorse a basic needs approach, he ignores several important conceptualizations of human nature that Marx provides: namely his distinction in the *Manuscripts* and elsewhere between actual and potential needs (see Benton 1988, 5–6), his dialectical analysis of need, and his account of the generation of new needs and their realization made possible by the transformative conditions of historical development. Geras' authority for this reading is the claim in *The German Ideology*, 'that men must be in a position to live in order to make history' (Marx and Engels 1976, 41); that is that, however diverse and enriched the scope of human fulfilment, these achievements must first be based on a viable mode of existence. On this basis, Marx could recognize the existence of an innate human nature which manifests itself in 'universal and permanent needs' (Geras 1983, 69). Geras thus reduces Marx's concept of need to a single, albeit diverse and developmental, schedule.

Geras' notion of a permanent normative standard of human nature stands apart from and in judgement of a historicized notion of need. In this he brings Marx's notion of human nature and need closer to a Social

Democratic view, namely one based on a standard of basic need fulfilment which gains incrementally higher and more diverse levels of satisfaction as society grows in prosperity. In Chapter 3, for example, we saw that Crosland offered the prospect of a future Britain achieving new forms and higher levels of need, including new types of aesthetic and cognitive satisfaction, commensurate with the growing prosperity of a humanized capitalism. Of course, the Social Democratic notion of melioristic social reform would not map on to a Marxist view of human nature born to labour and struggle in striving to meet its needs. The point for Marx was that in engaging in struggle, labour comes face to face with the awesome possibility that it is capable of transforming the means and relations of production. Geras' notion of a permanent and unhistoricized human nature cannot embrace the idea of labour constructing new social relations and means of production beyond the present stage reached by capitalist society. His notion is limited to the context of the current mode of production.

Yet of equal importance, Geras underlines the priority Marx gives to the organization of material resources necessary for the physical needs of human existence that has conditioned human life for centuries; for

> The first premise of all human history is, of course, the existence of living individuals. Thus the first fact to be established is the physical organisation of these individuals and their consequent relation to the rest of nature.
>
> (Marx and Engels 1976, 31; quoted in Geras 1983, 66)

Two consequences flow from defining human life as involving before everything else basic needs satisfaction. First, whatever form social relations of production take, whatever purposes they fulfil in meeting needs, whatever needs are met and by whatever means, physical needs must be met first and foremost. Meeting physical needs stands as the fundamental desideratum of all human existence throughout time. Secondly, meeting physical needs is the precondition for meeting higher needs. In this sense, there is a part of human nature that is permanent and unchanging whatever circumstances shape it, namely provision for physical needs. In this, Geras reflects an important impulse since Maslow's conception of need (see 1970, 47), that the satisfaction of lower needs is a precondition for higher need-satisfaction. By the same token, meeting basic needs is the first task of social policy before all else. Yet this unchanging material premise of human nature can be met in different ways, and, as Benton suggests, must entail meeting higher levels of need that with physical need constitute the human mode of life. The primacy attached to meeting physical need does not pre-empt variations unfolding in the constitution of human needs. Once economic production and social policy have secured physical satisfaction, the development of different need-satisfying activities implies that the constitution of human needs and capacities changes. However, despite these changes, there is always a particular stratum of basic need for physical survival that remains unchanging. Therefore, whether or not one accepts Geras' overall reading, he rightly stresses the basic desideratum of Marx about how we are to understand human nature – whether it is seen as a variable or unchanging entity. In this sense, the traditional Social Democratic commitment to a national (and nowadays international) basic minimum in social policy remains the essential precondition for all other levels of need-satisfaction secured by individuals with or without state help.

(d) Fully human needs and social policy: an example

An example of how a distinctly human mode of life could influence policy is seen in the area of provision for disability. Despite the comprehensive reforms following the Beveridge Report (1942), provision for disability remained an undeveloped area for many years. However, in recent decades provision in cash and kind has undergone substantial reform. This involves provisions for people with physical, mental and learning disabilities, such as non-means-tested disability living allowances, carers allowances and mobility benefits, together with means-tested benefits such as income support, with specific additions for the disabled and their carers, and housing benefit. Alongside financial provision has gone benefits in kind in the form of accommodation, day care, domiciliary and 'special needs' provision in education, training, therapy and community care. In broad terms, disability provision has moved significantly away from the dominance of institutional provision in the 1950s and 1960s, based in the main on an impoverished conception of basic needs and a failure to extend universal national minimum provision to disability. Provision is now based on a more extensive notion of basic needs for income, food, shelter and mobility, and increasingly provision for social integration, education and work.

The introduction of new commissioning arrangements for care provisions provided by independent agencies such as voluntary and self-help organizations has opened up opportunities for an enriched conception of the needs of disabled individuals. For example, organizations like the National Autistic Society (NAS) seek to promote what is termed 'supported living' homes for able autistic individuals, such as those suffering from Asperger's Syndrome (Lowndes 1994, 13). This initiative is based on constructing a package of public provisions for basic need in cash and kind as a way of meeting the physical *and* higher needs for accommodation, so encouraging independent living in a more fully human way. By interpreting the accommodation needs of such individuals as entailing therapeutic and other supportive needs, organizations like the NAS have defined the housing costs covered by housing benefit as involving a wider range of need other than mere shelter. In providing for the physical needs for shelter, nourishment and warmth, the programme is also contributing towards individual choice about where and with whom one lives, how living arrangements are organized (decorations, furnishings, spatial habitat), and how one accesses neighbourhood resources (shopping, transport, social centres). In meeting physical needs the programme engages with a range of higher needs – cognitive, aesthetic, emotional and social – which enhances the individual's autonomy and control, and recognizes the different levels of need-satisfaction entailed in a human mode of life. Such an innovative use of housing benefit is an indication of how social policy can address those higher needs that are intrinsically part of basic need satisfaction. We will return to this issue and the recent reform of supported living arrangements in Chapter 8.

(e) A holistic ontology: George Markus and Agnes Heller

We have referred to Soper, Benton and Geras' approaches to deriving normative standards from the contradictions and tensions in Marx's theory of human nature. These standards serve as guides for the transition from a capitalist to a socialist society that meets human needs more fully. By contrast, Markus and Heller hold out the hope of retrieving a more holistic ontology from Marx. This ontology or theory of human nature presents humankind as an evolving force in the dialectical struggle both within humankind itself and with nature. Through the development of human nature, there unfold inherent and evolving standards of fulfilment that enable humankind to critically assess the problems of capitalism and to work towards new social forms more geared to fulfilment. Unlike Soper's and Geras' accounts, normative standards are not seen as permanent and transhistorical, but evolve as part of the transformative development of human potential through social praxis and struggle. Markus offers the possibility of uniting the two antagonistic traditions in Marxist scholarship, of philosophical anthropology and historical materialism. More specifically he offers the possibility of reconciling normative and cognitive discourses and the concerns of humankind and nature – the two tensions that Soper and Benton address. His holistic ontology is based on Marx's own premise that humankind is a finite part of nature and so bound by the laws of a 'materialist naturalism'. Humans exist with nature by securing the external objects of their needs. However, unlike animal life, such exchange is characterized by a creativity seeking to exploit natural resources for the betterment of human life. Thus, Marx's starting point entails a conception of human praxis in constant interaction with nature, which is the basis of socio-historical development and furnishes standards of human fulfilment. It is Marx's notion of the inseparable linkages between humankind and nature, fashioned into a human mode of life by the praxis of labour, which furnishes the premises for a holistic ontology.

Markus contends that this ontology provides the basis for four universal features of human nature – or 'species character' (Honneth and Joas

1988, 38) – namely, work, consciousness, sociality and historical development. These features constitute the permanent *formal* features of human nature, which undergo development in their substantive detail under different social and economic conditions. Work, consciousness and sociality change as needs and capabilities develop in relation to the historical evolution of human modes of life and production. These characteristics of human nature help to define the distinctive qualities of humankind's mode of life. In formal terms, humankind is distinguished first by its capacity for work, whereby individuals utilize the raw materials of nature as tools to secure the objects of external nature that satisfy need. For Markus, the praxis of human labour is from first to last needs-directed in that 'every human action presupposes the existence of some want determining the on-going activity' (1978, 10). These activities entail the development of physical and intellectual skills. For the process of human interaction with nature is inextricably one of mediation by means of instruments, skilled technologies and intellectual representations (language, science, art, etc.). Whilst denying humans immediate and direct encounter with nature (unlike animals), these skills nonetheless have the overwhelming advantage of infinitely expanding the horizons of human ingenuity. These horizons lend historical shape to praxis: human activity and need-satisfaction are conceived within a time-span which marks the achievements of human fulfilment and which gives rise to a conception of the historicity of needs (*ibid.*, also Heller 1976, 24).

Secondly, humankind is characterized by the formation of *consciousness* that governs the purposive activities of work and social life. For consciousness enables humankind to see itself, its external world and its relations with the world, from a perspective that extends beyond its immediate needs and so has the potential for embracing a more comprehensive viewpoint. Thirdly, this ever-widening perspective is encountered and acted on by individuals in the context of *social* relations with each other, such that the perspective is irreducibly one of a social consciousness. The individual's awareness of her social relations with the external world is already doubly couched: first, in terms of the individual in relation to others whose otherness intimates an external reality she must learn to contend with through mutual recognition; and secondly, in terms of the social 'we' embedded in the external world without which she cannot live. Fourthly, Markus argues that in the context of *history*, humankind is in the process of generalizing these universal features, both in the sense of global systems of economic organization and cultural practice, and, at least in principle, in the sense of realizing the fulfilment of universal human nature as a potential for greater need-satisfaction. For

> the life of every and each individual becomes dependent on the activity of a growing circle of other individuals with whom he no more stands in personal contact and communication, but at the same time each

individual thereby acquires – at least *in principio* – the possibility to make use not only of human experiences, of objective and subjective wealth accumulated in his particular community, but of those accumulated by the whole [of] mankind.

(1978, 24)

A consequence of Markus' holistic conception of human nature is that the process of universalizing human nature entails the correlative possibility of enlarging the scope of individual autonomy; for 'the universalization and individualization of man constitutes in this sense a single integral process, even if its unity...is realized during a whole great epoch of history only through constant, deep antinomies' (*ibid.*).

Heller shares with Markus a belief in the overall unity of Marx's human ontology, between its cognitive and normative moments. Like Markus, she seeks to discover an integrity in the complex conceptual apparatus Marx employs in describing the antinomies of human nature and need. She further seeks to shed more light on the meaning of the notion of truly 'human needs' and its place within his overall theoretical structure. Marx constructs a schema of oppositions between different types of need, which generate tensions symptomatic of the transformative processes shaping the human struggle to satisfy need. Heller's method of reconstructing Marx's theory is to describe different schedules of need – in contrast to Geras' unitary schedule – prior to explicating the type of theoretical suppositions that underlie each schedule and the practical possibilities each poses for human life.

Marx classifies needs generally on the basis of their objectification, that is according to the objects that are needed and the associated activities of production which extend and objectify human powers (Heller 1976, 28). In explicating the meaning of 'radical needs', Heller explores three antinomies, namely 'material' versus 'spiritual' needs, 'natural' versus 'socially produced' needs, and 'necessary' versus 'spiritual' needs. Marx is seen to formulate each antinomy in terms of concepts integral to his theorization of the value forms of capitalist production, specifically surplus value, labour time, and the counterfactual values posed by universal human needs. Heller contends that

> The idea that radical needs are in some sense central to labour runs like a thread through Marx's work: either because surplus labour (performed for its own sake) becomes need; or because of the increase in free time, which gives rise to radical needs (and to the need for still more free time); or because the need for universality which, having arisen in the form of mass production, cannot be satisfied within capitalism.
>
> (1976, 90–1)

Each of the three antinomies reflects Marx's central preoccupation with the labour process and the production of value. We will examine briefly

Heller's understanding of how Marx derives normative standards of fulfilment from his theory of human nature and contrast this with Geras' understanding.

In the first antinomy, between the needs for material and spiritual goods, Marx describes a simple opposition. The need for material goods includes needs for social life and for satisfying labour. Heller stresses that this constitutes more than a basic needs approach; for 'The satisfaction of material needs is not only the basic condition of human existence, the expansion of material needs is at the same time a sign of the "enrichment" of man' (1976, 28). Like Benton, she is reflecting Marx's own depiction of a distinctly human mode of life where physical needs are only satisfied by means of higher needs satisfaction.

In the second antinomy between 'natural' and 'socially produced' needs, Marx takes the analysis further. On one level natural needs are sometimes described as 'biological', 'material' or 'physical', whilst social needs refer to the construction of needs through the process of capitalist production and its impact on consumption patterns. Both types of need are thus contingent on the primary pursuit of economic activity, that is the generation of use- and exchange-values, and the maintenance of the labour process. Both provide standards in considering the impact of capitalism on humankind. However, at a deeper level, Marx finds that capitalism generates an infinite variety of material needs, but only rewards the labourer sufficient to satisfy his basic needs to reproduce his labour power, the 'simple maintenance of human life' (Heller 1976, 31).

With the third antinomy between 'necessary' and 'spiritual' needs, Heller argues that Marx reached a different conclusion from that reached when viewing material needs. A moral imperative enters the analysis of causal processes of human behaviour. Material needs are part of the realm of necessity subject to the laws of production: 'necessary needs are the needs that are constantly growing out of material production' (1976, 34). But under the transformed conditions of a society of 'associated producers', material needs, which in one sense remain the same, come into line with moral and spiritual needs that cannot be purchased, and so are not commodified, but involve the individual in his or her free labour time (34). These are needs characteristic of the 'realm of freedom' (*ibid.*). In this context the law of value characteristic of capitalism is superseded by 'need' as a category of value (38), that is, the free development of human 'wealth', of all the many-sided activities that constitute the free individual. Heller shares with Geras and Benton the view that the evolution of the human mode of life requires a type of need-satisfaction that increasingly meets physical and higher needs. Individuals can then exercise greater autonomy and freedom of choice over how their needs are satisfied. In this sense greater autonomy implies also scope for diverse social groups to exercise freedom of choice and pursue their different projects. It is these notions of autonomy and diversity that are sought in the example of 'supported living' examined earlier.

If Geras construes Marx's concept of human essence in permanent and unchanging terms, then, in contrast, Marx (according to Honneth and Joas's treatment of Markus' exposition (1988, 39)) 'historicizes the concept of "human essence" without divesting it of its biological points of reference' (*ibid.*), especially with respect to physical needs. At base, all the writers discussed presently agree, despite their different readings of Marx, that the historical development of human nature is dependent on satisfying the physical needs of human existence by means of nature's resources. The development of human needs involves provision for physical existence *and* for evolving human modes of life. However, by contrast, Markus and Heller provide a developmental concept of human nature which, in focusing on interaction between human essence and nature, sees physical needs as themselves transformed in the unfolding of history. This is a concept of dialectical development firmly grounded in the naturalistic context of human life, a context that serves to orientate human development.

Markus in particular provides a third model of the relationship between physical and higher needs characteristic of the human mode of life, in addition to those of Benton and Geras. We have seen that Geras construes physical and higher needs as part of a single register of human needs, and that Benton sees higher need-satisfaction as a hierarchical and truly human expression of the satisfaction of physical needs. By comparison, Markus identifies more explicitly the dialectical unfolding between physical and higher needs as humankind externalizes its powers in appropriating natural resources for need-satisfaction to achieve more fully the humanization of nature and the naturalization of humanity. In particular, this dialectical construction of needs fulfilment shows that physical needs are no longer construed as constant but undergo change as higher need-fulfilment develops with new technologies of production and social relations of co-operation.

Productive means and resources are developed in order to advance human fulfilment through externalizing human powers on to nature and though internalizing nature's regularities into human existence, through the applications of science and technology. This explanatory framework raises questions of the role of social policy as a technology aimed at satisfying needs and advancing human fulfilment. Just as Geras and Benton's notion of need-satisfying modes of life raises specifically critical questions of social policy under capitalism, so Markus and Heller provide a more historicized account of the evolution of society into one giving primacy to need fulfilment. This is a vision in which social policy is conceived as a practice that sees the satisfaction of physical needs in terms of evolving higher capacities that contribute to greater degrees of human autonomy and freedom. Though Marxists generally do not focus on the practical and detailed nature of policies for need, their analyses, at least in the writers presently surveyed, point to the particular kinds of social tensions, contradictions and transformation that must be addressed if needs are to be more fully met.

Conclusion

Social Democracy provides theories of basic needs and mutuality as two separate models of human nature. Marx's theory, by contrast, provides a mutualist account of praxis that can give rise to an understanding of the process of satisfying needs. At the same time, the praxis of meeting needs and realizing human potential is predicated on satisfying basic physical needs first. The satisfaction of physical needs is a prerequisite for meeting higher needs for social interaction and mutuality. The two accounts are irreducibly part of the same theory of need. For Marx, praxis is therefore characterized by the specific way the human-species goes about meeting needs and developing its mode of life. The two notions of basic needs and interactive praxis are integrated into a meta-theory of human nature. We will return to this contrast with Social Democracy below.

The chapter has ranged over several interpretations of Marx's theory of human nature, gauging areas of agreement and difference among recent commentators. Many of the commentators agree that the concept of human nature provides an important limit concept that serves, so to speak, as a counterfactual measure of the complex and dynamic processes of change that humankind has undergone throughout history. This is a counterfactual measure in three senses. First, it provides a *normative* standard that specifies the content for defining the notion of fulfilment and need satisfaction.[1] This standard unfolds into two moments described in Chapter 5: namely the counterfactual one that addresses what needs would be like if fully met within the existing mode of production; and the dialectical one that addresses what new needs and forms of satisfaction would be like as the forces of production bring forth a new mode, implied by Marx's contrast between one-sided needs and many-sided satisfaction. Many-sided fulfilment is understood by reference to existing levels of satisfaction that could be more fully experienced if a new mode of production were attained. Heller, for example, makes much the same point as Soper and Geras, that 'In order to be able to analyse the economic categories of capitalism as categories of alienated need ... it is necessary to create the positive category of a system of non-alienated needs' (1976, 27; Geras 1983, 62; see also Springborg 1981, 109). Secondly, Geras argues that human nature serves an *explanatory* role in providing a model of continuity against which can be seen the continual flux of social and economic transformation. Thirdly, Marx's notion of human nature provides a sense of human *purpose* motivating social life to reach higher levels of fulfilment, a dialectical construction of the normative standard of human fulfilment (Soper 1981). This is an important teleological function for understanding a species whose characteristic activity entails setting, seeking and achieving goals. Bernstein points to the explanatory significance of this particular notion of teleology:

> Marx's materialism is essentially teleological, not in the sense that teleology commits us to the fantastic notion that a final cause precedes in time an actual event and somehow directs it, but in the empirical sense of teleology where we want to distinguish goal-directed activity from the mechanical regularity of matter in motion.
>
> (1972, 42–3)

In these respects, the theoretical richness of Marx's concept of human needs stands in contrast to the limited theoretical assumptions that underlie the Social Democratic notion of basic needs.

These commentators recognize the importance of Marx's theory in providing normative, explanatory and purposive bearings for his overall project of historical materialism. The theory of human nature enables Marx to integrate these three aspects of understanding in a way that overcomes the fact-value split. Thus Soper acknowledges its explanatory role in underpinning a cognitive theory that, in seeking to explain the development of capitalist society from a critical standpoint, is forced to address the form society should take if it is to meet truly human needs, and to determine the nature of society succeeding capitalism. This requires a conceptual and metaphysical framework from which to direct speculation beyond the empirical study of social reality, with its present level of need-satisfaction and deprivation, to an ideal end-state where needs are satisfied and human relations achieve new levels of co-operation. This represents a movement from present reality to future possibility. Marx's concept of human nature provides a set of ontological properties that are logically presupposed when speculating about the future shape of individual and social existence under a post-capitalist mode of production. These properties give to speculation (a necessary activity in thinking about the direction of the present into the future) a discipline and direction in moving beyond the empirical study of existing society to address the productive means, social relations and new levels of need-satisfaction in a future society.

This logical framework is especially important in considering the implications of Marx's theory of human nature for social policy. For here much of Marx and Marxist theory is pitched at a level of generality and abstraction that fails to engage with everyday issues of need and social policy, and discourages the derivation of policy prescriptions from explanatory and normative propositions. However, the value for social policy of the analyses considered presently lies in furnishing a logical framework that can guide speculation about policies addressing social problems. Geras, for example, posits the material preconditions that Marx ascribes to human existence, and Benton the manifold levels of need-satisfaction that meeting physical needs necessarily entails in human life. Further, the concept of praxis confers a degree of specificity on the particular need-satisfying practices and productive processes individuals and groups engage in. Need-satisfaction becomes the central concern of human existence and fulfilment. Seen in this light, Marx is addressing issues that are central to social policy.

Earlier we asked what does Marx's account of human nature offer social policy that is an advance on other accounts of human nature. The time has come to address this question.

The broadly termed mutualist model of human nature, introduced in the discussion of Social Democracy, draws on the same sources as did Marx, that is, Hegel's struggle for recognition (see Bernstein 1972, Part I), and shares an affinity with Marx's notion of praxis. Praxis adds the following propositions to the Social Democratic model. First, in Marx's hands, the idea of mutuality is couched explicitly in terms of the subject's engagement with the object world of organic, inorganic and human nature. This is a world in which the subject is intrinsically a part, despite the experience of alienation and the appearance of ideological forms of mystification. Praxis is not just one aspect of human nature, and the source of altruistic sentiments, as it has been for Social Democrats. It is also the fundamental means of realizing sociality and co-operation and achieving need-satisfaction, and at the same time of striving to overcome alienation and mystification in order to rediscover humanity's inalienable dignity and its true relation with nature. Praxis is thus the basis for achieving a human mode of life.

Secondly, Marx's notion of praxis provides the basis for a theory of knowledge which grounds the individual's struggle to satisfy needs in the wider societal and historical context of the capitalist productive mode. Being part of the objective world, individual subjects must engage with it at the level of sensuous labour and struggle in order to arrive at cognitive understanding: sensuous experience precedes consciousness and cognition. Labour reflects the essence of human nature in being the form of action through which human needs are satisfied and self-realization achieved. The knowledge that emerges from praxis is an expression of human essence revealed in the needs of individuals engaged in co-operative work. The satisfaction of needs gives rise to both self- (and social) knowledge. By engaging in the intentional activity that characterizes labour in shaping the natural world to its needs, the individual thereby discovers the content of its needs and the objective means of satisfaction. The intentional gap opened up between subject and object, between needs and means of satisfaction, is formative for the subject's knowledge of itself and its object world. Marx's account of human nature accords centre-place to the capacities of individuals to transcend this gap by transforming the social and material structures constituting human and non-human nature in their projects of need-fulfilment. Such action can only be prosecuted intersubjectively. In this sense, Honneth and Joas contend, in their discussion of Markus, that work makes

> the regularities of nature into the guiding principles of [man's] activity. At the same time as the possibilities of satisfying his needs increase through his action upon nature, the pretensions of the human being's needs also become greater; the appropriation of nature follows a spiral consisting of the satisfaction of needs made possible through particular labour processes and of the expansion of needs produced by the satisfaction of needs.
>
> (1988, 37–8)

It is not only mutual co-operation between self and other that defines praxis; praxis is also grounded in work on, in and through nature. Indeed, 'The human species therefore gains access to nature for itself only through praxis' (20).

Thirdly, praxis is emancipatory, a view frequently overlooked in state social policy. In their discussion of Marx, Honneth and Joas contend that 'In the very same labour process in which it increased its knowledge of … [the] natural environment … the human species also expands its needs and capabilities' (1988, 21).

However, Honneth and Joas point to what they see as a serious limitation in Marx's view of praxis; namely, that in limiting praxis to labour Marx was unable to discover the importance of communicative action between co-participants who collaborate in producing for need. Marx, Honneth and Joas argue, 'was so little aware of the categorical limits of his concept of labour that he was unable seriously to investigate a domain of social interaction' (1988, 23; see also Honneth 1995, 147–8). By contrast, their critical examination of Marx's and Marxist accounts of human nature seeks to advance a social theoretical understanding grounded in a fuller notion of praxis; that is, one in which intersubjectivity is both the precondition of sensuous certainty about the objective world and the precondition for consensually based validity (1988, 16). For there can be no appeal to an external source of validity that is not grounded in intersubjectively shared understanding. For Marx, and for Honneth and Joas, knowledge of the world is derived from different individuals co-operating in need-satisfaction. However, the argument can be taken further. For, if the individual's interest in need-satisfaction is shared with co-workers collaborating in production, this implies that the criteria for validating knowledge of the subjective and objective world is consensually formed. Not only must the truth status of knowledge be tested in terms of its ability to contribute towards fulfilling human needs, but also this testing must be conducted communicatively between individuals co-operating in producing goods for needs; they must justify their assessment of knowledge to each other and reach agreement. Marx's theory of human-nature-as-praxis therefore entails implicitly a consensual theory of truth with 'practical-critical' force (Marx 1976, 3). If there is a link between a consensual theory and the pre-structured nature of the object world, as Markus suggests, then consensus is not necessarily based on convention but has objective validity.

Social policy is no exception in giving expression to a consensually based truth between self and other. If social policy is about policies to meet basic and higher needs, then it could be argued that its contribution to consensually grounded truth represents the fulfilment of the highest of human needs. This approach is present in embryo in the Social Democratic tradition, in work on consensual measures of poverty (e.g. Mack and Lansley 1985) and on citizens' forums on community needs and service appraisal (see Walker 1987; Stewart *et al.* 1994).

The fact that the praxis of meeting basic needs is contingent on communicative action between co-participants is, however, only one side of praxis. The other equally indispensable side is the necessity to meet basic needs themselves, without which communication cannot take place. The argument of Honneth and Joas, in their critical assessment of Marx's notion of praxis as labour, and Geras' argument about the primacy of physical wellbeing in developing a fully human mode of life, represent different though related positions on human nature as a standard of fulfilment. Physical need-satisfaction is the prerequisite for effective communicative understanding, a higher basic need essential to achieving human autonomy. At the same time, communicative understanding is the means whereby a human mode of life is socially achieved, so that humans can achieve individual and collective fulfilment. The recent revisiting of the politics of recognition by feminists (e.g. Benhabib 1992), critical theorists (e.g. Honneth 1995) and communitarians (e.g. Taylor 1992) represents an important attempt to explore further the dimensions of praxis whose purpose is to reach communicative agreement. However, the primary significance of the prerequisite of basic needs satisfaction for all forms of human activity cannot be overlooked.

Marx provides an enriched account of human nature and needs, compared with other accounts examined presently, in which basic needs and higher needs are integrated into a single theory. In the next chapter, we examine further the relationship between these levels of need in the work of feminists who pose the question of difference, rather than commonality, as central to human nature and social policy.

7
Feminism, the Politics of Recognition and Social Policy

Introduction

Unlike previous accounts of human nature in social policy, each expressing a distinct tradition within modern political thought, feminism draws on a range of different traditions and offers a variety of different views of human nature. Despite its abiding concern to advance the woman's viewpoint and challenge patriarchal domination, feminist theory is not a unified perspective. It draws on Marxism and Liberalism and, under the banner of 'radical feminism', has trailed new perspectives drawn from disparate traditions. The chapter touches on a range of feminist theories of human nature, namely Liberal, Social Democratic, biological fundamentalist, deconstructionist, Marxist and psychoanalytic feminism. However, given this scope, it concentrates on feminist theories that reflect the two influential models of human nature in the twentieth century, namely common basic needs and human mutuality found in Liberal, Social Democratic and Marxist thought.

In the last chapter, we saw that basic needs and mutual needs represent universal accounts of human nature, in that we all share common basic needs and higher needs for mutual fulfilment through social co-operation and reciprocity. However, although liberal and socialist feminists draw on universal notions of human nature, derived from the Enlightenment belief in common needs, human rights and equality, feminism itself finds these universalist theories wanting in a way that challenges to the core the notion of universal human nature. Feminists criticize the failure of these creeds to deliver equal rights, entitlements and citizenship in the form of social policies for particular subaltern groups of whom women are the largest. In the last thirty years feminism has delivered one of the most challenging critiques of social policy in a Beveridge welfare state supposedly based on universal values (Williams 1989). The welfare state, for example, is taken to task for the lack of inclusivity that taints its promise of universal citizenship (Lister 1990), for being blind to the needs and circumstances of women in the private domestic sphere (e.g. Millar and Glendenning 1989), and for constructing an overly public conception of citizenship which values the public deeds of men over the private labours of women (Pateman 1989). At base, it has devalued the vital contribution that private informal caring makes to the quality of welfare and to the economy in general.

Contemporary feminism has been at the forefront of movements engaged in prosecuting a 'politics of difference', in which subaltern groups have demanded recognition of their distinct identities and needs that have been overlooked by mainstream politics. Among these demands have been calls for child care provisions to enable women to pursue education and careers and for provisions advancing wider choice over reproductive practices and health care. At the root of these demands lies a concern to discover a form of life more amenable than patriarchal forms to women's needs and abilities. A politics of difference poses major questions on the nature of women's needs and on the existence of a generic human nature shared by men and women.

At first glance, the politics of difference suggests a type of a welfare politics that departs from the traditional concerns of modern democratic politics. It casts suspicion on principles of equality, universality of need and policies seeking redistribution, compensation and inclusion and other principles of social justice. It dismisses the methods of reasoning devised by liberal theorists adopting attitudes of value neutrality (Ackerman 1980, 11), placed under a 'veil of ignorance' (Rawls 1972, 12), attitudes which rely on constructing disembodied subjects in place of subjects with real needs and identities (see Benhabib 1992). By contrast, the politics of difference involves minority groups discovering an essential difference in their identity that liberal political theory and welfare policy committed to universalism and value neutrality cannot acknowledge. Consequently, as Habermas has observed, 'the new conflicts are not ignited by distributional problems but by questions having to do with the grammar of forms of life' (1987, 392). These conflicts cut across issues of distributional justice among 'equivalent' subjects and call for recognition of formerly invisible subjects, needs and life projects. In principle, democratic politics should be able to respond to different human needs and not restrict its concerns to the needs of already established citizens. The implications of the politics of difference are profound in suggesting a failure at the heart of the democratic welfare state to apply the universal principle of human rights to the universal needs of humankind.

If the various 'differences' claimed by feminists and other subaltern groups each assumes an ontological status, then the idea of a universal human nature with its common needs defining a set of substantive democratic rights to welfare is even more problematic. For, the politics of difference argues that democracy cannot recognize the needs and identities of different groups, that it has been accountable to only one – male – element of humankind, and that it can acknowledge only one conception of human nature. The real problem for democracy then becomes its inability to address different conceptions of human nature and the presence of different gendered natures. Feminist theory has responded to this problem by developing the politics of difference in four ways. First, liberal and social democratic feminists respond by re-asserting the existence of a fundamental core in human nature that all share, and by proposing that gender differences are either particular ways of expressing this shared core or are peripheral to a shared human nature. For instance, men and women to a large degree share the same health needs, but women may experience common conditions in different ways to men – depressive illness would be an example – that require specific forms of care. However, women also suffer certain conditions that do not affect men, such as gynaecological and obstetric conditions, which require specific forms of intervention and give rise to gender-specific treatments and well-women health programmes. The failure of Social Democratic social policy to extend to women the same equalitarian considerations it gives to men is remedied by a stronger and more extensive application of universal values to different social groups. Secondly, radical feminists respond to the failure to acknowledge the identity of women by asserting the existence of fundamental differences in the gendered natures of men and women, in their biology, physiology, psychology, sexual and genetic make-up, even to the point of advancing men and women as needing different species modes of life (e.g. Firestone 1979).

Thirdly, feminists committed to a politics of deconstruction respond to patriarchal oppression, not by asserting a different gendered nature, but by arguing that human nature as a totality is a social construction without any objective validity, which men impose on women (e.g. Butler 1990). In this vein, feminist politics and policy is about deconstructing oppressive ideology and constructing in its place an alternative view of womankind which is capable of supporting a female power base and opportunities that resist and subvert patriarchy. Finally, some socialist feminists advance a dialectic of recognition which sees the politics of difference as the struggle between subaltern groups of women whose universal needs are not recognized and dominant male groups whose needs are. In the struggle against the 'universality' of social policy and citizenship, a deeper recognition of identity and difference in human nature is sought. Human nature exists in an immanent state of development. Each new stage in the development of the mode of production emerges through the struggle to overcome the obstacles posed by the former productive mode. Human nature passes through different stages of development, each one of which stamps its mark on humankind and establishes a particular set of needs and capabilities. In this sense, the constitution of human nature is defined in terms relative to the particular challenges posed at each stage. However, according to this broadly Marxist account, core qualities of human nature develop at each stage of evolution as new human needs are fulfilled and new potentials realized.

The broadly conceived liberal-social democratic feminist and socialist feminist accounts will be examined specifically – each based on notions of basic needs and human mutuality and praxis respectively. The two accounts are examined in more detail in the context of debates among feminists about the particular nature and needs of womankind and their relation to the notion of universal human nature. The argumentation of each account rests on different suppositions. As in previous chapters, the present one identifies the factual, motivational and normative propositions that frame different feminist conceptions of human nature. These different conceptions, despite sharing a concern with the woman's standpoint, lead to different conclusions about social policy. One of the tasks presently will be to reveal the implications of these different and sometimes conflicting conclusions for policy.

Feminist politics as the extension of universal human nature: liberal and social democratic feminism

In the Liberal tradition of political thought, described for example by Alison Jaggar, humans are essentially rational beings. Each individual is endowed with broadly the same kinds of rational faculties, and so equally empowered to prosecute his or her own interests (1983, 28). This common identity applies to the different social, political and economic projects that individuals engage in. The endowment of human nature with reason (a factual proposition) means that each individual has the capacity to secure his or her own best interests by designing projects that best realize these interests, and to fulfil these projects through rationally motivated action (two motivational propositions).

In addition to the endowment of reason, there are further natural endowments individuals have, namely needs and abilities that motivate the individual's interests. The Liberal tradition of the twentieth centuries conceives these needs as divided into basic needs shared by all and satisfied collectively, and individual needs and abilities which each person seeks to satisfy independently. The different strands of Liberal thought – neo-liberal, Social Democratic and so forth – differ in whether humans share a broad or narrow range of basic needs (a factual difference) and where they assign responsibility for meeting needs between the state and individual (a normative difference). It is these needs and capabilities over which reason is the guiding force in prosecuting human projects of fulfilment. Because the Liberal conception of human nature sees humankind primarily in individualistic terms, all individuals are somewhat self-interested. For neo-liberals, they are primarily self-interested; for Social Democrats, they share a complex of self-interested and altruistic motivations. For the Right the state should defend the individual's freedom to pursue her different interests; whereas Social Democrats see the state as providing a modicum of universal provision for all to enable individuals to realize their different interests independently.

However, there is an important difference between the perspectives of Enlightenment Liberals and feminists. *In principle*, humankind shares a universal nature and each individual is treated as equal in his or her needs and abilities. In a modern democratic culture, such equality translates into a metaphysical conception of persons equally endowed with the faculties of reason and with social, political and economic rights to pursue their own interests within the rule of law and the moral order. However, *in reality*, although individuals start from positions of basic equality, the actual outcome will be one of inequality, resulting in individuals with differing abilities and needs achieving different positions within society. The discrepancy in this account between the original position of equally endowed individuals depicted in essential metaphysical terms and the final outcome that is registered in empirical terms of actual inequalities is not seen as a contradiction. Rather, it is the inevitable outcome of the natural empirical differences in physical and mental capacities that individuals are endowed with, and the environmental circumstances which randomly affect each individual in different ways. For Liberals, these empirical differences do not undermine the underlying metaphysical equality between individuals: the empirical and metaphysical represent the separate realms of the real and the ideal. Nonetheless, for its critics, the Liberal discourse steers a problematic course between the ideal of universality and the reality of differential life chances. A theoretical account of human nature based on metaphysical presuppositions of universality and equality is vulnerable to evidence that social groups are in fact excluded from participating in political and economic institutions, whatever their intrinsic endowments. Although the real and ideal remain forever separate, the purpose of politics should be to seek an acceptable rapprochement between the two so that social institutions and individual life chances are judged according to ideals of equality, however defined.

From the liberal feminist's point of view, women are endowed with the same needs and faculties, including reason, that characterize humankind generally, and share the same rights as men to the essential freedom which, according to Liberal philosophy, all individuals possess in pursuing their own ends. This was the crux of J.S. Mill's argument in supporting the rights of women who should be 'free to employ their faculties, and such favourable chances as offer, to achieve the lot which may appear to them most desirable' (1970, 143). Consequently, the exclusion of women from certain institutions and their subordination within a patriarchal culture represents a serious denial of the rights and humanity of women and infringement of the principle of universal equality.

Consequently from a liberal viewpoint, gender differences that do exist must be justified in ways that conform to a universal characterization of human nature. We will examine the different arguments patriarchal and feminist ideologies use to justify differential treatment of women's needs in a way commensurate with a universalist viewpoint. Patriarchal ideology endeavours to sustain such universalism in the face of the facts of gender inequality in two ways. First, it argues that certain physical or psychological differences in gender *are* compatible with an otherwise universal human nature. For example, the predominately domestic role accorded women in patriarchal society, where their principal tasks are to provide child care, homecraft and homely comforts for men, can be justified on the grounds of the different 'natural' capacities women are endowed with, which because they are peripheral do not undermine the idea of universal human nature. Their peripheral significance is reinforced by the often private context in which women perform household tasks away from the public gaze and the support of government policy. For feminist social policy, it is therefore important that women are entitled to freedom of choice between, for example, child care and housework at home and a career at work and that social policy should remunerate women appropriately in both cases. Secondly, it can be claimed that these differences, whether or not significant, are nonetheless integral to an organic conception of human nature, in which women fulfil important private responsibilities that 'complement' the affairs of men in the public domain of business and work. This argument was voiced by opponents to the ordination of women to the Anglican priesthood: that there is no impediment to women participating in a broadly conceived ministry where men and women with different 'gifts' complement each other, and where women with their unique gifts are able to fulfil different roles complementary to those of an exclusively male priesthood (General Synod 1992). Drawing on the work of Lucy Irigaray, Iris Young points to the violence in this notion of complementarity between male and female:

> The gender system structuring Western culture and philosophy presents the feminine others as *complementing* the masculine subject position, creating for it a wholeness, completeness, and return to origins... But this circular relation displaces and silences the other, as she might speak in a different, incommensurate register.
>
> (1997, 346)

In rejecting these arguments, liberal *feminists* argue that the goal of feminist politics is to extend the formal equality enjoyed by men to all women. This goal is achieved by programmes promoting social reform, education and equal life-chances for women to exercise their talents to the full and to live life in accord with their full human nature – even if there are some significant gender differences in certain capacities (see Jaggar 1983, 37). Essentially the interventions of liberal feminists – as of Liberals generally – are rationally motivated, in the belief that scientific evidence of equal endowments outweighs evidence of different endowments between men and women, and that the real achievements of women are sufficient to persuade men to extend equal rights to women in the interests of all. Fabians referred to this aspect of rational social planning as 'permeation'. By the same token, liberal feminists opposed laws and practices that permitted the unequal treatment of women, denying them, for example, the right to participate in professions after marriage on the grounds that their family obligations detract from their professional vocation. This universalist conception of human needs and capabilities has led liberal and social democratic feminists since the 1930s to adopt the strategy of 'welfare feminism', conducted by women like Vera Brittain and Winifred Holtby around the equalitarian issues of pensions for widows, equal pay for teachers, equal opportunities in the civil service, equal rights of guardianship, and improvement of the laws dealing with child assault and unmarried mothers (Humm 1992, 38–9).

This Social Democratic strand of feminism continues to be influential among the present generation of feminists in academic and professional occupations today, because the feminist welfare goals of the 1930s and 1940s are far from fulfilled. The analysis of British feminists has grown from demonstrating the manifest injustices which continue to limit the opportunities for women to fulfil their needs, to seeking to understand more closely the underlying economic, social and ideological structures that compound gender inequality in societies where there is general acceptance of formal notions of equality. One example of this shift in analysis that has direct implications for public policy is the emerging critique of Social Democratic citizenship theory. Lister, for example, criticizes the public focus of citizenship rights, which accord individuals equal rights to state welfare provisions, but only in those areas that lie within the public domain such as work, health and safety, work-related benefits like contributory national insurance, health care, education and housing (1991). Provision for needs that lie within the private domestic sphere, such as responsibilities for caring for children, the elderly and other dependants, have traditionally received a low priority. Yet these tasks which fall mainly on women are fundamentally important for the welfare of millions, and represent a massive invisible cost in terms of the opportunities for education, careers and leisure that women forgo (see Glendenning 1992). By constructing the concept of citizenship to embrace male areas of public activity and to exclude private dimensions of female caring, the state has been able to maintain one of the mainstays of formal equality without respect for the specific needs and rights of women. Some of the provisions for carers – e.g. income support carer's premium and respite for carers of the elderly and disabled – are provided on a residual, means-tested basis which denies carers a universal right based on need alone to such benefits and confines entitlement to those on low incomes. The universal invalidity carers' allowance was dogged by controversy in its early stages until in 1986 the European Court deemed that it discriminated against married women caring for family members. Entitlement was then extended to working age men and women (Glendenning 1992, 172). Pateman has concluded that

> liberal principles cannot simply be universalized to extend to women in the public sphere without raising an acute problem about the patriarchal structure of private life...the spheres are integrally related and women's full membership in public life is impossible without changes in the domestic sphere.
>
> (1989, 129, quoted in Lister 1991, 70)

The implications of liberal and social democratic feminist theory for understanding human nature can be formulated in weak and strong versions. The strong version argues that there are no significant differences between the sexes and that biological differences are not significant as long as social provisions can rectify the unequal outcomes stemming from them. Modifying the environment can compensate for the lack of opportunities women traditionally receive to produce equally endowed individuals whatever their gender – an argument used earlier in the twentieth century by Social Democrats like the Webbs and Tawney. Provided for in this way, women would demonstrate the same range of achievements as men. Jaggar argues that this view leads to an androgynous conception of human nature whereby 'members of the androgynous society would be physiologically male and female...they would be unlikely to show the same extreme differences in 'masculine' or 'feminine' psychology as those characteristics are currently defined' (1983, 38–9). This androgynous view leads to the strategy of equalitarian feminism of *from difference to equality*.

However, some equalitarian feminists adopt a weaker version, which acknowledges the presence in human nature of differences between men and women that, however minimal, are significant in shaping women's needs. One example is the biologically based needs for which special arrangements should be made. Doyal and Gough (1991, 158) propose that the procreative requirements of women for safe birth control and child bearing represent a need which is specific to women alone. This need should be met by gender-specific provisions if they are to enjoy the same opportunities to participate in society as men. Provision for these needs should therefore be provided by government along with provisions guaranteed for men and women alike. The long-standing demand of government to remove VAT from sanitary towels is but one example. This accords with the Liberal–Social Democratic conception of national-minimum welfare provisions for all citizens, with additional provision for women citizens alone. At base, this weaker version of equalitarian feminism leads to the strategy of *from difference to equal-but-different*.

Some feminist commentators have portrayed the initial pursuit of equalitarian goals, which were then followed later by difference goals based on different conceptions of women's needs, as a way of periodizing feminist politics into first and second waves respectively (e.g. Humm 1992, 11). However, historical studies suggest that the relationship between these two goals is more complex. In social history, the choice of advancing causes that promote either equality or difference has posed a dilemma for equalitarian feminists at different points over the last hundred years. Lewis and Davies describe how social reformers, considering the conditions women experienced at different stages in the twentieth century, were faced with a choice between 'protective legislation' which limited women's participation in certain manufacturing jobs, and equal pay legislation which would outlaw discriminatory practices at work. The choice of strategy 'were firmly embedded in assumptions about sexual difference and the naturalness of sexually segregated work' (1991, 13). Thus 'equalitarians opposed protective legislation as a device that would serve only to undermine women's competitive position in the labour force and reinforce their dependence, whilst those that grounded their views in difference saw such legislation as critical to improving the conditions of a female labour force' (*ibid.*). This suggests that some feminist interpretations of politics have over-simplified matters in suggesting that liberal feminists in principle have been against difference legislation and only committed to egalitarian reforms. The historical evidence shows that reformers conceived the advancement of women as needing measures supporting both equality and difference, though structuring these measures in differing ways at different times. In the context of women's remuneration and conditions of work, difference has been constructed as an equalitarian issue whereby women's *specific* needs are given as much weight as men's. At the same time governments responding to these demands have met them in ways that accord with their own sometimes fundamentally different objectives. By the 1980s, for example, the measures supporting difference enshrined in earlier protective legislation had given way to legislation promoting women's formal equality with men, at a time when the major objective of government policy was to deregulate the labour market. This removed some of the employment regulations protecting women, so posing new issues of difference and equality for women at the end of the twentieth century.

The question for Social Democratic feminists then, as for Social Democrats generally, is how to conceptualize the relationship between common and individually different needs and how to structure provisions for different forms of need-satisfaction. The previous chapter drew on Marxist conceptions of need to argue that basic needs and higher needs were contingent on each other, in that the human mode of life realizes higher needs as part of its satisfaction of basic needs. At the same time, the human mode of achieving autonomy allows different individuals to realize their basic and their higher needs in different ways according to personal desires and cultural differences. This must entail individual choice in determining one's personal projects, and so choice over the means of satisfying need, within the bounds of material feasibility. Individual freedom in this sense is an imperative to securing the basic need for autonomy, for which Liberals, Social Democrats and Marxists argue (though not necessarily sharing the same definition of autonomy). In this case, the human mode of life which men and women share requires equal treatment for basic needs, with different provisions for men and women where circumstances dictate, in order that they can realize their projects for developing higher needs in different ways. For example, basic need provisions for child care and home care enables women to obtain education and work and pursue careers. But such provisions would need to be equally available to men and women, presenting both sexes with more flexible choices over domestic arrangements and between parenting, caring and work. For example, Swedish social policy has sought to address the parenting needs of mothers and fathers in a more even-handed way than elsewhere by granting parental leave and benefits to support fathers as well as mothers when a child is born or is absent from school because of sickness (Johnson 1999, 250).

This discussion suggests that Social Democratic philosophy can respond to feminist claims by organizing the structure of need and provisions into:

(i) provisions for universal basic needs; and
(ii) a range of different options that respond to the differing needs and circumstances affecting men and women. This would require unconstrained choice between these options, compatible with the resources and technologies available.

The two elements would enable basic needs to be met so that individuals can exercise choice over the higher needs which basic needs secure. However, until recently, Social Democratic social policy had given little thought to the different ways in which women access basic needs, and to the serious constraints on their developing personal projects. This structure, though geared to the equal treatment of men and women, is analogous to the traditional Social Democratic structure dividing universal national minimum provisions for basic need from the mixed economy of family, voluntary and market provision for individually different needs. The difference, however, lies in that the state would underwrite the different needs of men and women, and so acknowledge an area of difference that is presently left largely to the mixed economy of for-profit, self-help and informal welfare.

We have argued that need-satisfaction and human fulfilment are secured in part by means of mutual interaction between different individuals. Whilst we have attempted to address the issues surrounding common basic and individually different needs at the levels of basic and higher need-satisfaction, we must now address the issue of recognition and reciprocity entailed in identifying and satisfying different needs. For the differences that determine the satisfaction of basic needs and the unfolding of higher needs are themselves refracted through and shaped by the struggle for recognition between different individuals and between different social groups.

Towards an immanent conception of universal human nature

Several strands of feminism have emerged since the late 1970s, especially among object-relations psychoanalysts, that contribute towards a mutualist conception of human nature. This viewpoint recognizes the significance of gender differences in the biological, social and psychological constitution of men and women. However, these differences are not seen as invariant and unchanging but one grounded in the intersubjective relationships between men and women. Human nature is a dialectically changing nature that unfolds in relations between self and other and especially between women and men. This strand of thought is strongly influenced by Hegel and Marx (though we saw in Chapter 6 that Marxists do not agree on how to characterize evolution of human nature). From Hegel comes the 'dialectic of recognition' portrayed in his account of the master and slave relationship. This account stands as a metaphor for the individual's journey towards absolute knowledge, in which he or she is drawn into the mutual struggle for self-affirmation and mastery over the other (1977, 111–19) – a metaphor for different relationships including those between men and women (Kojeve 1968; Bernstein 1972; Honneth 1995). From Marx comes an account of human labour exploiting the fruits of nature in the struggle for survival and fulfilment. Here individuals are drawn into relations of exploitation and class conflict with each other, which has a decisive effect on the family life of men and women (Engels 1972). Hegelian and Marxist theory recognizes that the human activity to overcome these relations is conscious and purposive (Jaggar 1983, 54), namely *praxis*, which is the core activity determining the fulfilment of human nature. The notion of praxis is implicit in the mutualist model of human nature in the Liberal and Social Democratic tradition that emerges in writings from T.H. Green to Titmuss.

The mutualist perspective of interaction between self and other represents a universal feature of humankind, which we call an *immanent* notion of universal human nature. Here individuals with different social identities are able to recognize in each other a deeper sense of common human nature. This notion differs from the notion of universalism that has dominated twentieth-century politics and social policy, namely a *transcendent* notion. This describes qualities of human nature such as basic needs, and the human rights and social provisions provided for them, in terms of their uniform identity and sameness, which subsumes and negates different human identities such as gender. The distinction between these two notions of universalism is thematized in Habermas' account of the philosophical project of modernity. The Enlightenment saw human consciousness moving towards an understanding that had the power to absorb different viewpoints into a greater unity from which each received its validity (Habermas 1992, 118) – in our terms a *transcendent universalism*. For example, for Hegel absolute consciousness assimilated different forms of consciousness, and for Marx the proletariat became the universal class. By contrast, *immanent universalism* reverses the order of universality and difference that dominated the Enlightenment. Seen from the viewpoint of history, the universal no longer absorbs difference, but rather different viewpoints and experiences become the ground in which universality emerges. This is a development which Habermas refers to as 'the unity of reason in the diversity of its voices' (1992, 115).

We will argue that difference itself can furnish the grounds for unity. In this vein, several feminists – namely Nancy Chodorow, Carol Gilligan, Seyla Benhabib and Jessica Benjamin – present an account of universalism from the standpoint of concrete gender differences rather than from transcendent notions of universality. They move beyond stereotypical conceptions of difference to suggest deeper notions of difference, otherness and recognition, which reveal new horizons of universal understanding. Echoing Habermas' words above, Benjamin argues that universal recognition 'entails being able to perceive commonality through difference' (1990, 171). Each of these writers follows an immanent agenda, which reveals universal human qualities through an encounter with human difference. They appeal to immanent notions of universalism that pose the possibility of more supportive relations between individuals, based on new principles of human conduct and leading to new prescriptions for social policy. The remaining sections of the chapter seek to identify these ethical principles and political prescriptions. The chapter proceeds by outlining the above writers' accounts of the dilemma of difference and commonality and asking what questions this dilemma poses for social policy. Finally the dilemma of difference and commonality is addressed in relation to the recognition of both different needs and shared needs which lies at the heart of this dilemma.

1 Universalism as the reversibility of difference

The implication of Chodorow's work, on the formation of gender identities in children, is that by reversing different gendered roles, men and women can discover new interchangeable abilities and deeper and more fulfilling gender differences and relations. In contrast to the 'absoluteness' of Freud's account of the oedipal resolution (Chodorow 1989, 53), which legitimates the universal patriarchal authority to which sons and daughters submit,

Chodorow provides an account of the social and biological role of the reproduction of mothering in the formation of gender identity. Mothering is the major site on which gender differentiation between boys and girls takes place and different forms of 'relational potential' between men and women are constituted (1978, 166). Chodorow argues that boys must 'break decisively' with their mothers in order to establish their identity. However, the father is not available to the son as an identity model in the same way as the mother to the daughter, because traditionally he spends less time at home. Consequently, boys are forced to adopt a 'positional' rather than an actual identification with the father. They must identify with a fantasized male role rather than a personalized one, and construct this role as a negation of all that is female (1989, 50–1). In Chodorow's view, the son embarks on a course of identity formation that leads to the universal devaluation of women. By contrast, girls' identity formation is less problematic in having the female role continually available in the figure of the mother. Their separation from and identification with the mother and other women is based on a personal not positional identity, and is partial and not decisive. For 'girls come to experience themselves as less differentiated than boys, as more continuous with and related to the external object world and differently oriented to their inner object-world' (Chodorow 1978, 167).

These different patterns of severance from and identity with mother and father lead to different patterns of relationships among men and among women. Men invest less than women do in extended personal relationships and more in structures of power and dominance. Here Chodorow arrives at the core of her thesis on gender identity and relationships among women and among men. For male relations 'tend to be based not on particularistic connections or affective ties, but rather on abstract universalistic role expectations' (1989, 53). With women the continuing proximity between mother and daughter makes for a personality formation that is characterized as 'continuous'; whilst with men the more emotionally distant relationship between father and son is discontinuous (54). With these contrasting personality types come different potentials for relationships that contribute towards different constructions of gendered human nature. Chodorow writes that 'Girls emerge from this period with a basis for "empathy" built into their primary definition of self in a way that boys do not. Girls emerge with a stronger basis for experiencing another's needs or feelings as their own' (1978, 167). We can see how Chodorow introduces two contrasting themes that have shaped the development of the politics of gender difference: first, the male nature of abstract universalism; and, second, the female nature of concrete particularism based on relations of care and empathy. The contention is that women have the capacity to identify with difference in others as if this difference were part of, and not different from, their own selves. In so doing, they exercise an imaginary capacity to put themselves in the place of the other.

Chodorow's work explicitly poses the possibility of overcoming these differences by initiating new ways of seeking universal recognition and founding institutions contributing to greater equality between men and women. She proposes that

> boys need to grow up around men who take a major role in child care, and girls around women who, in addition to their child-care responsibilities, have a valued role and recognized spheres of legitimate control.
>
> (1989, 65)

These exhortations impact on a wide field of social policy that seeks to change social structures embedding mothering and child socialization, such as pre-school child-care provision, schooling, income maintenance and relations between home (conventionally the mother's preserve) and work (the father's preserve).

We can extract two themes from Chodorow's influential thesis that shape the argument of the thesis decisively hereon. First, there is an explicit theme that gender differences are structured around male-abstract and female-affective modes of relating to others – a theme developed in Gilligan's work on the care versus justice characterization of gender differences, to which we next turn. Secondly, there is an equally explicit theme concerning the possibility of role reversibility in overcoming the patriarchal structuring of difference. This theme supports the idea of universality which this chapter explores, and which is developed in the work of Benhabib. However, I want to suggest a different interpretation of Chodorow's notion of role reversibility which I think can be claimed is present in her argument. This is that the extension of a person's capabilities from a traditional to a new role involves him or her in new explorations of common needs and abilities. Reversibility involves a deepening of a person's way of tackling new problems. It implies a deepening of the self's understanding of their needs and abilities, as well as an encounter with the other's needs and abilities.[1] Reversibility implies both universality *and* differentiation. This is a theme central to the work of the psychoanalyst Jessica Benjamin and the political theorist Iris Young.

2   Universalism as a dialogue between justice and care

Gilligan's work on the formation of moral identity develops Chodorow's theory of gender differentiation, based on the polarity of male abstract-universalism and female concrete-particularism. Her study of the cognitive orientations of men and women identifies two different models of male and female moral identity derived from their different experiences as moral subjects and different ways of relating to others. These two models give rise to two contrasting ethics of justice and care – of formal equality and of responsibility for others – which are both unavoidably faced when resolving moral dilemmas (1982). Gilligan argues that women facing a moral crisis will characteristically seek a resolution that sustains the integrity of relations between self and other through personal involvement. The concern with care for others and responsibility for personal relationships is contrasted with the male approach of impersonally weighing up situations and objectively applying rules to arrive at just solutions. Gilligan describes women's moral disposition as universally founded in 'Sensitivity to the needs of others and the assumption of responsibility for taking care', which 'lead women to attend to voices other than their own and to include in their judgement other points of view' (1982, 16). Her work has contributed towards an ethic of care that she contrasts with the male ethic of justice. For 'Morality as care centres around the understanding of responsibility and relationships; just as morality as fairness ties moral development to understanding rights and values' (1982, 19).

Gilligan does not pursue Chodorow's argument that gender differences can be transformed by reversing male and female roles. Instead Gilligan appeals to two gender-specific moral propensities that in the right circumstances can be conjoined in such a way as to transform situations normally characterized by unequal gender roles, relations and opportunities. This transformation is possible because the two propensities appeal to universal ethical principles beyond the contingencies of specific situations, namely the ethic of care based on responsibility for others and the integrity of relationships, and the ethic of fairness based on equal treatment for all. This 'dialogue between fairness and care' (1982, 174) sustains a dialectic of human development based on two different principles that in the end connect. Gilligan appears to suggest that 'convergence' between the two principles is possible because we realize that the failure to link them is ethically unacceptable. For the principles are based on:

> two disparate modes of experience that are in the end connected. While an ethic of justice proceeds from the premise of equality – that everyone should be treated the same – an ethic of care rests on the premise of non-violence – that no one should be hurt. In the representation of maturity, both perspectives converge in the realisation that just as inequality adversely affects both parties in an unequal relationship, so too violence is destructive for everyone involved. (*ibid*.)

What emerges from pitting one ethic against the other is a creative and immanent universalism that challenges the violation of care caused by subjecting different people with different needs to sameness of provision, and the unfairness of caring for some individuals and not others. Social policies governed by a transcendent abstract-universalism in the form of justice, citizenship and the rule of law go to great lengths to apply impartial principles of equity and distributive justice. However, in so doing they lose sight of their responsibility to care for individual recipients. Yet, by the same token, focusing care on those we know rather than those we don't violates impartiality and fairness.

3 Interactive universalism

More explicitly than the other two writers, Benhabib defends universal reasoning. However, in common with these writers, she offers an *immanent* version of universal reasoning which she calls 'interactive universalism'. Benhabib locates the tension between care and justice within a discourse ethics, in which moral conversations take place between real selves, where caring requires taking the standpoint of the other, and where justice requires universal respect for concrete others with different needs (1992). As with Gilligan, the rapprochement between justice and care involves a dialogue between real individuals with their distinct lives. Consequently, universalism in welfare and other practices arises from mutual recognition between concrete individuals who each have their own needs, narratives and histories. In this way, Benhabib argues that 'universal moral respect and reciprocity' have the potential to encompass 'the universal viewpoint of humankind' (1992, 53–4); a two-fold 'regulative ideal'

> that does not deny our embodied and embedded identity, but aims at developing moral attitudes and encouraging political transformations that can yield a point of view *acceptable to all*. Universality is not the ideal consensus of fictitiously defined selves, but the concrete process in politics and morals of the struggle of concrete selves, striving for autonomy.
> (153, stress added)

For Benhabib, the two regulative ideals enjoin members of a moral community to 'reverse perspectives' (1992, 31) and 'appreciate others' points of view' (52). They encourage a moral outlook of openness to others that issues in welfare arrangements promoting individual and group autonomy. Like all propositions that are regulative, these ideals stand as points of reference for ordinary individuals with their own backgrounds to evaluate their conduct and assess how far their projects and aspirations have been realized. Unlike transcendent universalism that treats different others under the rubric of the 'generalized other', interactive universalism, once arrived at, generates contextually-sensitive principles for real-life situations experienced by concrete selves and others, whether engaged in struggle or co-operation, derived from ongoing conversation (53) and 'mutuality of effort' (149). Michael Bach gives an example of the power of interactive universalism between concrete welfare subjects to determine moral and legal outcomes. He describes the competing narratives of a severely disabled litigant pursuing a claim in court to be discharged from an institution into the community, and of his elderly father seeking to deny him this right, both supported by various experts and carers. Bach concludes that in this case 'the standpoint of the concrete other comes to hold sway in contradistinction to the generalized other of the categories of psychiatric discourse and psychometric testing' (1993, 200).

Each of these writers recognizes that universality of needs and abilities arises from different individuals engaging in mutual relationships. For Chodorow, different individuals discover areas of shared nature by reversing or extending roles in new directions. For Gilligan, individuals are embroiled in an inescapable but potentially creative tension between justice and fairness that can issue in a universal understanding of each other's needs and abilities sensitive to their differences. For Benhabib, concretely different individuals can achieve mutual recognition through ongoing dialogue and mutuality of effort, in line with the specific interpretation I have given to Chodorow's care thesis. For each writer, immanent universalism involves both the discovery of commonality shared by different individuals and of differences arising from self-extension and from encountering the situation of others.

Mutual recognition and welfare

The chapter now turns to examine the implications of recent feminist work on the politics of difference for social policy. In particular, this addresses the process of arriving at mutual understandings about the different and common needs of men and women. In addition, this process is relevant in the context of other forms of social difference that are not addressed presently such as race, ethnicity and ability/disability.

First, social policy should facilitate both role reversals to achieve greater mutual understanding about needs between individuals with different backgrounds and experiences *and* new opportunities to develop different needs and capabilities among individuals and groups. At the same time one should repeat the caveat entered in note 1 (see p. 186), that social policy should also respect those limitations of ability associated with difference that it is unreasonable to expect individuals to overcome. Role reversal both extends the range of shared human abilities and deepens the exploration of different needs, identities and abilities. The question for social policy therefore is how to secure a context in which male and female roles – and other differences – are reversed so that different abilities can be extended into new roles without inflicting sameness or loss of difference. Chodorow's approach to universalism addresses the roles and relations that can be achieved in social policies respecting gender differences and potentials. Men and women are endowed with different identities in some areas of their lives, such as reproductive and relational needs. However, by interchanging roles, they are able to enhance their personal capabilities and differences as well as achieving new levels of recognition of shared needs. One consequence is that the gendered worlds of work and home-based parenting would be governed by more universal norms. Policies for equal opportunities should not only equalize life chances among individuals who differ in gender, race, disability, etc., but should also provide opportunities for different groups to explore their own unique perspectives, abilities and otherness and to enrich relations with a diversity of others.

In equal opportunities policy some of these provisions already exist, but much remains to be done, in some cases creating additional costs, in others unleashing new resources of labour. The list includes: new work opportunities for women; legislation to advance equal status and rewards; affordable pre-school and out-of-school child care; subsidized career breaks for men and women, supported by life-long learning banks that adjust education to the needs of individuals throughout their life cycle (Borrie 1994); sickness benefits for parents linked to work breaks when children are sick, as in Sweden; wages for housework, citizens' basic income; and so forth. The list of objectives remains long. However, a major challenge for politics would lie in managing the tension between different roles that converge because they are interchangeable, and the gendered natures of selves that diverge in new directions and relate in new ways that develop their radical otherness. We will return to this problem of difference and commonality later in discussing Benjamin's work.

A second implication for social policy of the politics of difference is how to secure modes of welfare in which the principles of justice and care cohabit together. To see questions of distribution solely in terms of allocating scarce resources in ways that are fair and maximize individual freedom – about which there has been ongoing discussion since Rawls first published *A Theory of Justice* (1972) – without paying sufficient attention to the person's need for care, is to ignore the purpose of welfare. The task of providing welfare becomes a two-pronged one of impartially regarding differences amongst others *and* affording sensitivity to others. This further entails respecting others with detachment and objectivity *and* listening to and regarding others' different needs with a universality that subsumes different needs within a comprehensive framework of need.

For Gilligan and others, the difference between justice and care is an essential fact characterizing all human relations and specifically caring relations. As a fact, it has normative implications for how these relations should be conducted. Yet at the same time, respect for human difference is forever being violated in practical tasks of satisfying human needs. Increasingly in cash-strapped social provision, social workers and other professionals apply a technology of needs assessment which is highly systematic and routinized, and which examines an inventory of needs against a set of quantitative measures and 'tick box' codes. Of course, the violation of difference occurs in all caring relations, personal as well as professional, where resources of time, energy and money are limited (see Fisher and Tronto 1989).

In a universe of cohabiting differences, the principles of fairness and care may not be easily reconciled. First, justice is about principles for allocating goods of differing 'use-values' between individuals with different needs, and between individuals with different levels of the same need rendered in equivalence terms. These principles operate, for example, in determining and applying poverty lines, levels of nutritional adequacy, 'Quality of Life Indicators', and so forth. Secondly, care is given according to the ethic that giving goods or services to others entails personal concern and cannot be rendered impersonally. However, the care of others – perhaps even the regard for the other as preceding all other ethical considerations (see Levinas 1989, 84) – cannot be rendered into just measures of equivalence without threatening the ethic of care. For the moment of care demands that there are no limits on the amount of care one gives to another's needs. Care, or consideration for others, is the means by which one person meets the particular needs of another in a human way. It is a higher basic need that is part of the human mode of life. Yet, at the same time, in the moment of justice we acknowledge that the reality of resource-scarcity poses inescapable limits that must be subject to an ethic of fairness. In welfare relations and practices the principles of justice and care, though irreconcilable, are mutually inextricable and impact on each other, such that one cannot be considered in isolation from the other nor abandoned for the sake of the other. The writers considered presently argue that however fundamentally different and irreconcilable the two principles are, they coexist in relationships between concrete individuals with identifiable but different needs, narratives and resources. This suggests that rapprochement depends on negotiating a working relationship or *modus vivendi* between the two principles in the broader context of democratic action. Moreover, incompatibility is lessened, and scope for rapprochement widened, when resources are adequate to support caring relations between giver and recipient. Considerations of care as well as fairness need to be given when budgeting for welfare.

The third implication of the politics of difference and recognition is that a rapprochement between justice and care requires that the other in need of welfare is seen as both a 'general other' subject to the rule of justice and a 'concrete other' in need of care. Benhabib suggests that politics can secure an outcome where individuals are receptive to each other's concrete needs and abilities, only if there is provision for different parties to engage in moral conversations that help to balance the demands of justice and care. These are provisions that, as argued in the previous chapter, satisfy physical needs as well as human recognition. In moral conversations, including welfare practices, the self relates to the other in two different senses: as the generalized other whose needs are compared with other individuals according to a formula of fairness (comparing individuals on a measure of need alone or on a range of principles such as need, means, desert, merit, etc.); and the concrete other whose specific needs, abilities and life-history come into play in the task of caring (1992, 164). The supposition is that real needs can only be recognized when the perspectives of self and other are reversed in a spirit of mutual respect. Benhabib's two regulative ideals – of universal respect and equal reciprocity – stand as standards for practice and institutional design. Such counterfactual ideals expose the reality of welfare structures that, though conforming to notions of fairness, impede the reversibility of perspective and the satisfaction of real needs. This impediment can be seen in, for example, administrative bureaucracies that serve to routinize 'just' distributions of welfare without reference to an ethic of care; selective procedures of means-testing and needs assessment that exclude and stigmatize; professional dominance and client subordination; and the social and economic disadvantages that can result from insufficiently regulated quasi-markets in the public sector. Despite these unequal welfare relationships, however, Benhabib assumes that intersubjective recognition between two individuals *can* occur despite differences in the positions they occupy within structures of power and material inequality (169–70).[2] Ultimately recognition can transcend the distinction between justice and care.

Benhabib advances an immanent notion of the 'common good' sought in politics and welfare, in preference to transcendent notions of universality and complementarity whose abstraction is in practice detached from everyday needs and problems and open to ideological and selective applications. The work of mutual and self-help welfare associations might be an example of organizations capable of this type of grounded and immanent universalism. The hope is that different individuals will come to realize that their own fulfilment rests as much on the mutual fulfilment of all as on the mutual fulfilment of each individual self and other. Thereby, the universal notion of the 'common good' would be arrived at immanently rather than transcendently. Whilst the notion of the common good has been central to welfare politics since the nineteenth century, modern feminist theory draws on a more immanent and grounded notion derived from Hegelian philosophy and found only on the mutualist tradition of Social Democracy. In particular Nancy Fraser has recently developed such a concept for social policy, which she terms the 'universal care-giver' (1997).

In conclusion, it is important to acknowledge that mutual recognition is not only about welfare relations involving two individuals. For the intersubjective relationship can be generalized to a level that encompasses all of humankind. This generalizable application of mutual recognition is seen most clearly in the work of Titmuss, who showed that the intersubjective recognition of need embraced the general other (e.g. the common good), the impersonal other (the other as stranger) and the personal other (1970).

Different and shared needs

Finally, we address two issues that stem from the politics of recognition, namely, recognition of the other's needs as different from the self's, and recognition of needs as common to all. In reflecting the viewpoints of difference and commonality, these issues are fundamentally at odds with each other. However, the argument throughout is that, however irreconcilable, the two are inseparably implicated in each other when applied to concrete moral problems.

First, how is an immanent universalism that seeks mutual recognition between different parties – emblematically the self and other – to avoid stifling difference under the embrace of a newly emerging shared understanding? How is this understanding to avoid becoming the dominance of one party over the other? This question goes to the heart of the rejection by postmodern thinkers of Hegelian, Marxian and Liberal notions of a transcendent universality that subsumes otherness (see Hewitt 1994). Jessica Benjamin has made an important contribution in understanding the processes of subsuming otherness. In particular, she addresses the genesis of domination in child socialization, human relations, administrative practices and scientific rationality, and present in all forms of mutual recognition (1990). Her response to this problem is to posit an ethic of mutuality and intervention on behalf of the *other* (Benjamin 1994) in order to guard against one-sided structures of domination by the *self*. In Benjamin's preferred model of recognition, structures of domination alternate between self and other, such that commonality can only appear through difference. The ethics of care and justice cannot be rendered into complementary principles but must remain forever in a state of oscillating tension that is the driving force of recognition. Universal recognition rests on giving the other the *paradoxical* recognition by which the self and other mutually recognize each other's commonality, whilst at the same time acknowledging and respecting differences in each other that remain beyond mutual recognition. This limit to mutual recognition exposes the self to his or her own limitations and to the difficulty of reaching new levels of recognition. Recognition is therefore not a state of resolving difference, but an attitude of sustaining paradox (1990, 36). However, such irreducible paradox does not deny that mutual recognition can emerge leading to an immanent universal understanding. For in this universe, the self and other are interchangeable beings: the other is also a self and the self an other to the other's self. Benjamin quotes Drucilla Cornell:

> The strangeness of the other is that the Other is an 'I'. But, as an 'I', the Other is the same as 'me'. Without this moment of universality, the otherness of the Other can be only too easily reduced to mythical projection.
> (244; Cornell 1992, 57)

This paradoxical view of recognition would acknowledge that in welfare relations between self and other – often seen as 'dependency relationships' of subordination – there should be scope for developing the self who gives care as well as the other who receives care. However, ultimately an ethic of intervening on behalf of the other should prevail. It recognizes that the self-recognition and other-recognition flowing from giving and from receiving are mutually contingent on each other. Mutual recognition implies consensually arrived at welfare provision based not only on ascribing universal worth and equality to all parties (a transcendent ascription), but on each party discovering its own worth and conferring equal respect on the other (an immanent ascription). As argued earlier, this notion of immanent universalism reflects the mutual discovery of commonality, the self's discovery of its difference, and the mutual recognition of the other's difference. Thereby welfare practice continually rediscovers and re-affirms the terms of human equality. The renewed interest in mutual welfare organizations lies as much in the space they provide for mutual recognition between individuals and for a greater sensitivity to the needs of others, as in their ability to overcome the oppression of bureaucratic state welfare and the insecurity of market-based welfare. However, as a cautionary note, history shows that mutual organizations like Friendly Societies can be exclusive to members – just as mutual relations of care are exclusive to the parties involved – and are liable to exclude non-members. For this reason in part, basic need provision became a government responsibility.

A second problem concerns the role of basic needs in a theory of recognition, which points to some of the limitations a theory of recognition presents to social policy. Basic needs cannot be fully addressed from a perspective that sees the satisfaction of need as the outcome of mutual recognition alone, as though recognition always comes before need satisfaction. Recognition identifies need but cannot satisfy need – at least not all need. The relationship between recognition and need satisfaction is complex. On the one hand, mutual recognition is itself dependent on satisfying basic needs. Indeed, without basic need satisfaction little else is possible in human life. At its most mundane level, 'life involves before everything else eating, drinking, housing and clothing and various other things' (Marx and Engels 1976, 41–2). On the other hand, identifying most needs and satisfying some is contingent on mutual recognition. Indeed Charles Taylor has pointed to recognition as a 'vital' basic need (1992, 26), but, we would add, only one such need. Recognition and basic needs fulfilment are therefore complementary activities (that are conjoined in human praxis). Mutual intersubjective relations are involved in the recognition of need and in producing for need. The mutual co-operation involved in production must secure the satisfaction of common needs that is a prerequisite for recognition. Undoubtedly the two universal rights that Benhabib stresses, concerning a person's expectation of universal moral respect and recognition of their identity and needs, entail the right not only to be recognized but to have one's basic needs acknowledged as well. We will return to the question of basic needs and recognition as need in the concluding chapter.

The feminist critique of common needs and universalist rights stems from a justifiable concern that these notions reduce human existence and diversity to a common denominator which cancels out claims for social difference. Yet, as we have seen in Chapters 5 and 6, there is a tradition that stems from Marx which stresses the nature of what he calls 'human needs', and that recognizes that human existence entails meeting basic physical needs in a truly 'human' way that gives form to the rich and diverse content of human experience.

The expectation in modern democratic societies that government policies provide for basic needs has been understood in a minimal sense that pays little attention to specific needs that constitute the human mode of existence. This has been partly a matter of financial constraints on government. But it has also been a matter of modes of welfare delivery that have been constrained by government assumptions of recipients as passive and possessing minimum or limited needs (see Borrie 1994, 221). The emergence of new forms of welfare delivery, where government finances mutual assistance and self-help organizations to support their own provisions for need, has helped to promote more active and enriching forms of welfare. This movement both encourages organizations based on a spirit of mutuality and helps to meet basic needs in ways that give form to the satisfaction of the 'many-sided' character of human needs rather than mere physical needs alone.

There is a danger that the renewed interest in the struggle for recognition may ignore the need for basic need-satisfaction at the expense of recognition, and overlook the integral relationship between the two objectives. Honneth and Joas (1988, 23–4) and Honneth (1995, 146–51) provide detailed accounts of why Marx came to abandon the Hegelian perspective on the struggle for recognition in his account of praxis as productive labour. However, Honneth and Joas, in particular, place a severely limiting connotation on Marx's concept of labour, as we saw in the last chapter, which denies it the capacity to generate reflexive mutual understanding (see 1988, 23). This is true of the large corpus that makes up Marx's 'later' work. However, 'labour' is a widely resonant concept that refers to the work expended in the struggle for mutual recognition as well as that performed co-operatively in meeting basic needs.

In the history of social policy, mutual aid and state collective provision for basic needs have gone hand in hand, although the current restructuring of the welfare state involves the abandonment of the universal national minimum and the return to a residual minimum based on selective principles of means-testing and conditional welfare. At the same time, writers on the left and right have rediscovered the importance of mutual aid provisions (e.g. Gray 1993; Holman 1993; Field 1996). These have a potential to develop wider horizons that lead to commonality among different organizations: through government support, inter-organizational subsidies, common contingency funds shared by different associations, and the cross-transferability of standards of practice and quality assurance (see Hirst 1994). This development – perhaps part of a new consensus on welfare – cannot be at the expense of provision for common basic needs, such as a citizen's income (*ibid.*), which forms the foundation on which mutual provision and the struggle for recognition are secured.

8
Conclusion

Introduction

Human nature is a central concern of social policy in providing a set of founding assumptions that lead to empirical, motivational and normative propositions about the needs, abilities and motivations of individuals. It enables us to comprehend the scope and purpose of social policy itself. Julian Le Grand is not alone in arguing that 'assumptions concerning human motivation and behaviour are the key to the design of social policy' (1997, 153). Yet social policy has tended to theorize human nature in simplistic terms, as though the two prevailing welfare ideologies in the twentieth century of Social Democracy and the Radical Right or neo-liberalism have been based solely on altruistic or self-interested accounts of motivation respectively. However, far from relying on simplistic motivational views of human motivation, these ideologies have drawn on a range of different human motivations in constructing social policy. The interesting question therefore concerns the ways in which welfare ideologies have configured different accounts of human nature in their political schemes, institutions and policies, giving rise to complex meta-accounts of human nature. Consequently, recognizing the inadequacies of simplistic accounts, and the uncertainties about which motivations dominate human nature, several writers propose analysing policy and politics in ways that allow for the complexity of motivation. Policy analysis should allow for 'multiple dimensional human subjectivities' (Dryzek 1996, 106); and it should show 'sensitivity to motivational complexity' (Gooden 1996, 41). In a different vein that, like Rawls, seeks to expunge assumptions about human nature from principles of justice and to design policies free of motivational assumptions, Le Grand proposes that we should 'accept our ignorance about what actually motivates people and...try and design what might be termed *robust* strategies: strategies or institutions that are robust to whatever assumption is made about human motivation' (1997, 165). He personifies these motivations as public-spirited *knights*, self-interested *knaves* and compliant *pawns*. This robustness treats assumptions about human nature as ideologies that can dominate and even mislead public policy. Given uncertainties about which core motivations are dominant in human nature, policies should be designed either to accommodate a wide range of *different* motivations or stand independently of such assumptions. Either way, we have what, on epistemic grounds, Hayek called an 'unbounded' view of human nature, one that does not endorse a finite and limited view of human nature and its fulfilment. For some writers the problem of avoiding a bounded view of human nature leads to pragmatism and away from foundational views of human nature. For others it leads in a different direction in which human nature continues to play an important part in guiding social policy. Specifically, I shall argue that in the welfare state of the future, assumptions about common human needs and human mutuality will play an increasingly important part.

Political renewal and human nature

The sea change in the politics of welfare, and in wider social and economic structures, has encouraged an interest in suppositions about human nature in social policy (e.g. Field 1996; Gooden 1996; Page 1996). However, the rejection of Radical Right solutions to the presumed inadequacies of Social Democracy has not yet led to a clearer sense of direction in welfare, despite a Labour government keen to distinguish its policies from the former regime.[1] The response to the political exhaustion characterizing the early 1990s has come from two kinds of discourse. On the one hand, traditional political options of the right and left have collapsed into a pragmatism that seeks immediate, practical and affordable solutions to social problems without recourse to theories of human nature to guide them (see George and Miller 1994, 17). This line of argument proposes policies robustly capable of withstanding different views of motivation (e.g. Le Grand 1997), based on provisional and pragmatically conceived solutions (Mishra 1993), and open to widening diversities of choice (Gray 1992). On the other hand, there is a renewed concern to explore the logic of human nature as reflected in political thought, policy and practice (Plant 1993; Field 1996). The two responses thus develop different approaches to defining the ends of welfare and human fulfilment. The first sees human fulfilment in practical terms of what is possible, limited by what is economically and technically feasible; the second argues that human fulfilment should be defined by what constitutes human nature and ecological nature at large. This response, like the former, addresses the economic limits arising from the existing condition of natural resources. However, unlike the former, it views the human domain as inextricably part of the ecological, and according to some exponents of this view sees the norms that stem from ecological limits as applying to the human world as well as the non-human organic world (including animals).[2]

Consequently, a theory of human nature carries assumptions that also underpin humankind's view of the ecological domain. It raises further issues about whether the way out of the political impasse and towards new social policy is to draw on and revitalize traditional conceptions of human nature; or whether it is to develop new capabilities, such as new forms of mutuality between self and others. We will examine later Anthony Giddens' important contribution to the question of mutuality, or what he terms 'reflexivity'. Uncertainties about which direction the Labour government is following presently arise in part because its leadership appears to be using both discourses at the same time, appealing to both pragmatic and principled strategies founded on notions of human nature.

Despite uncertainties about the direction of welfare, the long-wave transformations of the last twenty-five years have encouraged renewed interest in ideas about mutuality in welfare, which appeal to some version of the mutualist view of human nature (e.g. Green 1993; Holman 1993; Field 1996). Accounts of human mutuality draw on a variety of theoretical sources: Social Democratic notions of fellowship and human giving; New Right notions of buyer and seller interaction in the market; Marx's notion of praxis; and, most recently, feminist accounts of mutuality. Each source addresses the process of the self and other coming to recognize their different needs and identities and co-operating in meeting them. Interaction between self and other is formative of the cultural content of human existence. In this sense it expands our understanding of what Marx meant by the human mode of existence and the satisfaction of truly human needs; namely the desire to meet the many-sided nature of human needs – physical, mutual, cultural and spiritual simultaneously. From this perspective, basic needs and mutual recognition are complementary moments of the human mode of life.

Several critiques of the postwar welfare state are couched in terms of the limitations of its one-sided reasoning about human nature. The gist of these critiques is that welfare policy has emphasized one propensity to the detriment of others, such as altruism rather than self-interest (e.g. Bell *et al.* 1994); that it fails to give a balanced account that reflects the complexity of human motivation, 'where altruism is more equally weighted with self-interest' (Field 1996, iii; Green 1993, 1); that it is not sufficiently independent of motivational assumptions (Le Grand 1997); and that it fails to address the fundamental changes occurring in post-traditional societies responding to the process of globalization and its impact on self-formation (Giddens 1994).

However, we have suggested that the accounts of human nature criticized by the above writers are in fact far from being one-sided. On the contrary, social policy has been configured in ways that belie a simplistic account of human nature. This chapter does three things. First it describes how the four models of human nature introduced in Chapter 2 – atomistic, organic, basic needs and mutual – figure in the complex accounts of welfare that have shaped social policy in the twentieth century. This refers especially to the Social Democratic and neo-liberal accounts described more fully in Chapters 2, 3 and 4. For these four component models have been combined in ways that are far from simple and far from being governed by single axial principles. Alongside the Social Democratic and neo-liberal accounts, a mutualist account of welfare (developing the ideas of the mutualist model of human nature) can be identified which has received scant attention over recent decades. Secondly, the chapter seeks to rectify this lack of attention by describing the assumptions underlying the mutualist account and its relevance for welfare. Finally, it ends by speculating on accounts of human nature that could carry debates beyond traditional Social Democratic and neo-liberal politics and become increasingly important for welfare reform. Specifically, we concentrate on two accounts – 'plastic' human nature and 'full' human nature – that both seek to address the changing nature of the human subject in the context of wider social transformation and globalization.

The *Social Democratic* idea of welfare conjoins three different models of human nature: a model of basic needs which all share and which government national minima underwrite; a model of individual human needs which individuals are free to meet in the market once common needs are met; and a model of mutual needs met by different individuals acting co-operatively to meet their common and different needs. For the Webbs and Beveridge, state welfare was concerned to meet universal basic needs and organized in terms of a range of national minima. Beyond the minimum, an 'extension ladder' of voluntary provision was provided by charity aided by voluntary donations and dispensed by volunteers or paid professionals, by 'voluntary insurance' provided by occupational or private schemes, and by 'mutual aid' based on community self-help organizations and co-operatives. By means of this complex fabric, the national minimum came to represent a 'suture' joining universal, individual and mutual needs constituting the complexity of human nature.[3] Not only different types of need, but also ethical and political responsibilities are patterned in this way, as we saw in the discussion of Beveridge in Chapter 3. Before the emergence of state welfare, mutual aid was an important way of meeting basic needs (see Gladstone 1999). However, after the establishment of the national minimum, mutual forms of welfare concentrated on individual and collective needs above the minimum.

However, the notion of minimum needs as an organizing principle or 'suture' has proved problematic in several ways. First, minimum basic needs are defined in terms of a conventional, and so arbitrary and even inconsistent, understanding of what constitutes basic necessities and how they differ from the particular needs of different individuals. This was a problem that Tawney noted in 1931 in *Equality* (1964, 124). Secondly, it limits the scope of state involvement to providing minimum and often uniform provision alone. In so doing, it places serious limits on the realization of human potential beyond the minimum, including the different potentials of subaltern groups who identify their strength in their difference. Thirdly, minimum needs are defined in narrowly physical terms that ignore a truly human conception of need. Swedish Social Democracy, by contrast, has traditionally pursued an optimal rather than minimum approach to common needs. Similarly, several concepts of deprivation, of which Townsend's is the most well known (1979), are defined by reference to a consensual notion of participation in an enriched common 'life-style', including participation in shared cultural activities, consumption patterns and employment and political rights (Townsend 1987). Finally, until recently the state's role in this respect was sufficiently large for it to be in effect a monopoly provider and sole determinant of what constitutes minimum needs. Before the 1990s, there was limited scope for non-state provision of national minimum welfare.

Recently there has been a renewal in Social Democratic circles of the organic view of human nature as a way of harnessing mutual abilities. This is seen in the idea that individual needs require collective means for their expression and fulfilment; in turn, meeting individual needs contributes to advancing the common good. The common good is achieved by harnessing the collective power of individuals each contributing to the good of all and so enabling each person to better perform their duties and fulfil their rights. This notion of organicism has recently been inscribed in the Labour Party's revised constitution of 1995 (replacing the old Clause IV on the back of membership cards):

> The Labour Party...believes that by the strength of our common endeavour we achieve more than we achieve alone, so as to create for each of us the means to realize our true potential and for all of us a community in which power, wealth and opportunity are in the hands of the many not the few.

Institutions of collective support make possible the realization of the moral qualities in the person – the 'moral personality' of T.H. Green and Rawls – and give rise to an autonomy which ultimately enables individuals to make their own judgements and decisions and to realize their own potential – however much the organic 'we', in the above quotation, appears to supplant the individual 'I'. No one person or group, and no impersonal procedure, can supplant this organically conceived moral autonomy.

Today, New Labour is reviving the rhetoric of the social organic model of human nature in seeking to renew its ethical socialist roots, after nearly two decades during which the language and expectations of the Tories' atomistic model of humankind prevailed. Blair, for example, stresses the 'view that individuals are socially interdependent human beings – that individuals cannot be divorced from the society to which they belong' (1994, 4). Thus the individual's interests are advanced through 'the collective powers of all used for the individual good of each' (7). In this vision of an organic and 'united society', the voice of T.H. Green and the Webbs is unmistakable in Blair's definition of a socialism based on the 'moral assertion that individuals are interdependent, that they owe duties to one another as well as to themselves, that the good society backs up the efforts of the individuals within it, and that common humanity be given a platform on which to stand' (1995, 12).

A revived communitarian spirit within Social Democracy further reinforces this organic view. As the new 'third' or 'middle way', communitarianism supplies the intermediary social bonds between society and individual. For Blair, the community represents 'this different, reconstructed, relationship between individual and society'. Communitarianism also mediates between the overbearing state and the unregulated market in appealing to individual as well as collective responsibilities. It appeals to the individual's sense of duty which 'is at the heart of creating a strong community or society' (1995). At the same time, duty 'draws on a broader and therefore more accurate notion of human nature than one formulated on insular self-interest' (*ibid.*). The idea that fulfilling certain duties should be a condition of receiving welfare, thereby balancing duties and rights, is becoming increasingly prominent in New Labour social policy (Lister 1997; Dwyer 1998). The government's welfare to work strategy requires welfare recipients such as some lone parents, the long-term unemployed and some disabled to actively seek employment with increased support from education, training and childcare.

By comparison with Social Democracy, the *neo-liberal* account of welfare is based on an atomistic notion of human nature in which fulfilment lies in individuals engaging in voluntary transactions to buy and sell their talents and products. Welfare like any other commodity is best sought in the market or in quasi-markets. This market philosophy views the welfare needs of individuals not as common needs but as individually different needs which individuals can meet by access to a variety of markets.

In this model of human nature, the assumption is that individuals have different needs that they are responsible for meeting themselves. Government intervention is to 'enable' individuals to realize their potential as autonomous agents exercising responsibility for themselves and their family. The issue of whether needs are common or different is not a defining one for the radical right; rather it is the principle of individual responsibility for meeting need which is the core issue. Human beings are each responsible for their own circumstances. It is government's role to enable each person to realize this responsibility by means of

(i) maintaining free and unimpeded markets;
(ii) constructing pseudo-markets that in principle enable users to act as consumers and exercise choice, voice and exit as in the normal market, and which expose purchasers and producers to wider market forces;
(iii) providing residual and often deterrent minimum provisions for those who cannot avail themselves of the opportunities provided by (i) and (ii).

In (iii) there is the assumption of a core of common needs which, if individuals fail to meet them themselves, it is for a decent society to provide, as the discussion of Hayek in Chapter 4 showed. The notion of core needs is a residual rather than a national or universal minimum, in the sense of needs being met at a lower level of sufficiency or subsistence than common basic needs. Further, residual needs imply a narrower band of needs than common basic needs. Thus, for the Right, the notion of basic needs represents a residual back up when all else fails. It does not represent the national minimum principle as the first line of welfare support, but rather a residuum on which only the poorest rely when in dire need. In this way the Radical Right reverses the Social Democratic order between basic needs met in the first instance by the national minimum, and individually different needs met in the market or by voluntary charity. For the Right, the first line of welfare is the market and the second the residual minimum.

The idea of the market as the source of the means to satisfy needs assumes that individuals themselves possess both needs and the ability to meet these needs, and that they can harmonize their different needs and abilities through market exchange. This assumption represents a secondary or meta-account. However, it is problematic in conflating two kinds of belief, that individuals like firms can compete for the best advantage *and* at the same time co-operate within the firm. In fact both co-operation and competition stem from the same self-interest. Workers co-operate with co-workers and compete against workers in competitor firms.

The shift from state welfare to an enlarged and diversified mixed economy, providing adequate welfare for those who pay and minimum and not always adequate provision for those who cannot, has removed the clear commitment to national-minimum provision associated with the Beveridge welfare state. The clearly defined line or 'suture' dividing state from market commitment to need has been gradually unpicked and the entire fabric of the welfare state redesigned as a 'patchwork quilt' (Balbo 1987). The assumption underlying the national minimum was that the 'facts' of basic human need were sufficiently indisputable for government to ensure that it not only maintained the minimum, but also increased its value over time to reflect improvements in national prosperity. In theory, government could increase welfare benefits in cash and kind in line with increases in national wealth, wages or prices. However, in 1980 the Conservative government severed the link between long-term benefits and earnings, retaining a link only with prices. The Commission on Social Justice reported in 1994 that the basic state pension had fallen from 20 per cent of male average earnings in 1977/8 to about 15 per cent by the early 1990s (1994, 267).

Labour has clearly departed from the Social Democratic tradition in seeking to find new ways in which markets rather than government can provide basic provisions such as health and education. In this respect, it is retaining elements of market-based allocation and delivery in social provisions of the previous Tory government. It is continuing the Tories' Private Finance Initiatives, establishing Education Action Zones which include private provision, redesigning the Tories' quasi-market arrangements between purchasers and providers into larger consortia of purchasers (e.g. Primary Care Groups), and extending contractual agreements from one to three years (DoH 1997). Labour appears to argue that these arrangements need not signify a newly dominant role for the market with its atomistic approach to human nature, in which the majority would be left to fend for themselves and the poorest to rely on means-tested welfare to meet their needs. What matters most, Labour argues, is that social policy should achieve a stronger organic unity between the individual and society, which redraws the balance between rights and duties and between state dependence and individual independence. The organic unity of society, rather than the market or state basic minimum, becomes the pre-condition for fair distribution. For society is strong if there is

> a thriving civil society, comprising strong families and civic institutions buttressed by intelligent government. When society is weak, power and rewards go to the few and not the many.
>
> (Blair 1998, 3)

It follows that, rather than 'champion indiscriminate and often ineffective public spending', Labour should offer more 'adequate services and not just cash benefits', with 'greater emphasis to partnerships between public and private provision' (1998, 14, 15).

Finally, there has been renewed interest in the *mutualist* account of welfare based on the mutualist model of human nature, with its view of individuals meeting their needs through socially organized acts of co-operation between people with different needs and abilities. In mutual welfare, the stress is on co-operative rather than competitive motivation. In social policy currently, some writers argue that basic needs should be met by public provision, with mutual organizations outside public provision providing additional support at the local level (Holman 1993). Universal public provision is a precondition for mutual acts of individual exchange. Others advocate that the state should confine itself to providing large-scale provision such as a national health service, with other provisions for basic needs provided by independent agencies (Field 1996). Still other writers argue that public provision should be confined to financial support for individuals who are thereby empowered to access voluntary associations (Hirst 1994). The state would be responsible for little direct provision.

We have argued that the notions of basic needs and mutuality should play a central role in formulating social policy. However, both ideas have recently been developed in new directions that disallow simplistic ideas about human nature and needs. In the context of social change, new ideas about social policy are generating new, but not so clearly articulated, meta-accounts of human nature which seek to address the perplexities resulting from sustaining the different motivations driving humankind. Basic needs have been reconstituted within a wider framework of social justice, and mutuality redrawn in terms of a politics of difference open to new demands and needs. In the next two sections we discuss these two reformulated models of human nature and consider their influence on current thinking in social policy.

Social justice and common human needs

Recent Social Democratic thinking about social justice represents a new attempt to revive the basic needs conception of human nature whilst at the same time going beyond the principle of equal provision for equal basic needs. Plant argues that the formulation of new principles of social justice should flow from a 'distributive consensus' in society (1993, 9). A consensus would have to decide on which criteria of justice (e.g. desert, merit, need, etc. or a combination of these), which needs, which mechanisms of delivery, such as universal and selective approaches (with their diverging views of human nature), and what balance between incentives and disincentives should be struck. In each case, we have argued that the choice entails advancing a particular account of human nature. Most of all, a precondition for consensus would require more fluid interaction between different individuals and groups to generate the sense of mutuality and reciprocity that is vital to social solidarity. In this section we discuss new formulations of social justice based on basic minimum provision; and in the next the idea of mutuality.

Chapter 3 discussed how Social Democratic thought has sought to define social justice in ways that balance basic and individually different needs, rather than rely on providing a universal and uniform basic minimum. In this context, Rawls' influence, which held sway in academic circles for two decades until the emergence of communitarian theories of justice in the 1980s, can still be found in mainstream debates on public policy. He proposes that, on condition that individual liberties are maximized, primary goods should be distributed equally to all on the principle of need, but that unequal distribution is permitted if it contributes to the welfare of the least advantaged. In their more policy-oriented discussion of social justice, others such as Raymond Plant (1993), the Commission on Social Justice (CSJ) (Borrie 1994), the Barclay *Inquiry into Income and Wealth* (1995), and Gordon Brown (1999, 44) have all been influenced by Rawls in accepting his case for some degree of inequality. However, they widen the range of principles defining social justice to include desert, a principle which Rawls rejects (1972, 104).

An influential example of the Social Democratic notion of social justice based on the idea of basic needs is found in the CSJ Report. The Commission outlines four ideas about social justice that draw on traditional Social Democratic notions of human nature. The over-riding value of social justice is the 'equal worth of all citizens' achieved by means of civil, political and legal rights. This principle echoes the tradition of Social Democratic thought from Tawney's 'equality of consideration', through Marshall's citizenship (1963), to Benhabib's 'equality of respect'. This idea requires three foundations. First, 'every one is entitled, as a right of citizenship, to be able to meet their basic needs for income, shelter and other necessities'. Secondly, 'opportunities and life-chances' should be provided to enhance self-respect and equal citizenship. Thirdly, in social justice 'unjust inequalities should be reduced and where possible eliminated' (Borrie 1994, 18; cf. Levitas 1998).

The second idea of the CSJ about 'opportunities and life-chances' implies a more active role for the state in helping individuals to realize their aspirations and talents. However, it is unclear whether this refers to the traditional Webbsian idea of freedom to develop individual abilities and needs beyond the state minimum, to Tawney's idea that state provision should enhance the diversity of human talents, or to Rawls' difference principle by which unequal opportunities are allowed if they benefit the least advantaged. The third idea about 'unjust inequalities' has as a rider that 'not all inequalities are unjust' (Borrie 1994, 18), so pointing explicitly to Rawls' difference principle. Similarly, the Barclay Inquiry affirms the Rawlsian principle that 'Economic efficiency need not be damaged if the gainers can both compensate the losers and retain part of their gains' (33).

Returning to the CSJ's founding principle of justice – the equal worth of all citizens – we noted in Chapter 7 on feminist theories of human nature that notions of 'equal worth' cover two principles that are not easily reconciled, namely justice and care. The CSJ does not address this dilemma; however, it lies at the heart of notions of social justice. First, equal worth refers to the formal principle of justice of treating all individuals equally in the welfare state. The rule of law applies to welfare as much as to legal and other public institutions based on law, so that no individual is given preference over others. Justice also refers to the formal principle of distributing resources fairly between individuals. For the CSJ, this means both fairness at the start of one's life (i.e. primary distribution), so that 'structures should be adapted and influenced in ways that can give more people a better chance in the first place' (IPPR 1993, 11), and fairness in *re*-distributing life chances subsequently by maintaining a more even playing field in life chance (secondary distribution). Fair distribution requires that resources are distributed differentially among individuals according to their differing needs and abilities. This represents the equity principle that qualifies equal treatment, by treating different cases differently and like cases alike. This can be seen in the special treatment given to groups such as the sick, children and people with learning difficulties, by treating members of these different groups equally, or equally by degree according to the degree of need in each case.

The second principle implied by equal worth is the informal principle of equality of respect, a principle of mutuality that the CSJ does not address. This principle cannot be legislated for in ways that justice can, because it is realized in the quality of the relationships between people, that is, in the regard that one person has for another. It represents a moral prescription that individuals choose to ascribe to or not. This, for example, applies to the criterion of caring for others and points to Tawney's concern for 'right relationships among free and equal individuals' (Terrill 1994, 217). A non-legislative criterion can only be enforced by social norms that arise from an individual's judgement of another person's conduct, and that cannot be subject to systematic or formal enforcement. To this extent, the two principles of care and justice implied by equal worth are very different and not easily reconciled. However, considerations of mutual regard are subject to the influence of legislation on everyday behaviour, as in the case of legislation outlawing discriminatory and abusive behaviour in race relations. Laws that legislate for social justice in the first sense above can provide a framework that influences social relations between different individuals. In the next section, we examine the organization and norms governing mutual relationships of care.

Given the complex issues surrounding social justice, it is important to note that New Labour's approach to welfare embraces a communitarian philosophy that uses welfare legislation to enforce clearer obligations on the part of individual claimants. Rights to welfare are becoming increasingly conditional. This conditional and communitarian approach to social rights sits uneasily besides a Rawlsian approach with its unconditional view of social rights.

Mutual welfare

Chapters 2 and 3 argued that mutuality was the second important model of human nature, after basic needs, to emerge from the organic model of nineteenth-century Liberal thought, and to influence twentieth-century Social Democratic social policy. It is also, as we have seen, a concept at the core of New Labour's communitarian turn. However, unlike the ideas of basic needs and Rawlsian justice, mutualism remains a less theorized concept and less worked out in policy and practice. We will therefore discuss this conception of human nature in ways that draw on the discussion in the previous chapters.

Mutual welfare exists in the networks of resource-exchange formed between different individuals seeking to maximize the welfare of others as well as themselves. It recognizes that both self-concern and other-concern motivate action. Further, mutual welfare draws on the combined strengths of altruistic and self-interested motivation to achieve a greater overarching good for all. This motivation is different from that of market exchange which is motivated primarily by self-interest, and where concern for the greater good is absent – or represented by non-purposive and non-deliberative concepts such as the 'hidden hand'.

The social organization of mutuality gives rise to three patterns of exchange. First, reciprocal relationships can be formed between two partners in exchange. Secondly, one individual stands at the hub of a circle providing services to different individuals who each enter into a separate partnership of exchange with the central provider. Thirdly, several individuals can be involved in a circle of mutuality where one person gives to another, and the latter to another and so on, until some degree of all-round reciprocity is reached. In the latter, there can be no strict rules of reciprocity or equivalent exchange. Some individuals give to others and yet never receive in return; and some are reciprocated in ways that do not amount to the value of the good or service received initially, other than perhaps as expressions of gratitude. Finally, complex patterns of exchange may combine all three arrangements.

These patterns are clearly open to further conceptual and empirical analysis. However, our present interest lies with the third instance, 'circles' of mutuality. For this is a process of producing economic value that is quite different from other types of exchange. Consequently, there is less scope for instrumental forms of exchange associated with markets governed by strict calculations of equivalence. Likewise, there is less scope for conditional forms of exchange associated with receiving benefits from charities or state bureaucracies, where recipients are obliged to engage in certain activities or conduct, such as workfare, training, segregated residential conditions, or even contraceptive implants (e.g. 'Norplant') as a condition of benefit.

The three patterns of mutuality are found in a variety of mutual aid organizations – self-help groups, co-operative traders, mutual assurance, credit unions, local exchange trading schemes (LETS), neighbourhood care and security groups. Each might be involved in wider forms of exchange with others in the locality, such as credit unions supporting a LETS network or co-operative, and with others further – even globally – afield. Together a network of circles of mutuality would constitute a welfare community, animated by a range of motivations including co-operation and competition.

In mutual forms of exchange, the value of a good or service need not accord with prevailing market rates. Circles of mutuality are distinguished from other types of exchange in several ways. First, the parties will negotiate among themselves the rates of payment in terms of money or equivalent goods. The organization may have an agreed rate of exchange or leave the rate to partners to negotiate informally. There might be, for example, agreed hourly remuneration for baby-sitting or gardening. Whatever way the arrangement is reached, it will be a direct reflection of members' different needs and be based on a full consideration of the value of the goods satisfying these needs. In the language of Marx, goods are exchanged for their use-value rather than their exchange-value. It can be argued that the *raison d'être* of mutual organizations derives from the greater sense of individual and collective control members exercise over the activities of production, exchange and consumption.

A second feature distinguishing mutuality is that processes of social interaction that are rarely acknowledged in other forms of exchange determine the value of goods and services. Their value is determined by the nature of reciprocal giving that enters into acts of mutual support between partners, over and above the intrinsic market value of the goods and services exchanged. Mutuality depends in part on immanently defined notions of exchange. It is based on the intrinsic meanings about needs and resources that the different parties bring to the exchange. The value of the exchange is defined by the parties themselves to a degree not possible under other forms of exchange. Even physical needs, as well as higher needs, require negotiation over their definition. The right to physical needs for food and shelter may be clear cut, but decisions as to what kind of food and shelter have also to be decided, especially with culturally or ethnically different dietary needs. As the discussion in Chapter 5 on Marx's notion of truly human needs argued, physical needs entail aesthetic and cultural definitions which individuals must negotiate with each other.

Thirdly, the value attached to goods and services in circles of mutuality may entail delaying or deferring acts of reciprocation. Titmuss refers to the process of deferred reciprocity in his study of blood donation (Titmuss 1970). In some cases donors explained their giving in terms of their sense of gratitude towards strangers who some time in the past had donated blood which prolonged the life of family members. These donors were thereby referring to an indeterminate but nonetheless obligatory period for redeeming the gift that it would have been impossible to agree in advance. Others, more future oriented, referred to the possibility that at some indefinable time henceforth their life might have need of the gift of blood from others. In these cases, a clear intention of reciprocity existed. However, the norms governing reciprocal giving allow for needs whose satisfaction could not be regulated by other types of institutions based on more calculative or instrumental norms such as prevail in contracts of exchange.

Mutuality then represents an important feature of human nature which social policy has in the past and may increasingly in the future seek to encourage and support. However, the debate over human nature and policy has recently taken a more problematic turn in some quarters, with several writers on post-traditional and postmodern society advancing a plastic conception of human nature that relies on qualities of mutuality that nonetheless deny the existence of shared basic needs. In the next section, we discuss this turn before summarizing what we describe as an alternative account of 'full' human nature that draws on the ideas discussed in Chapters 5, 6 and 7.

The plasticity of human nature

The Social Democratic and Radical Right accounts of human nature arose in response to processes shaping the twentieth century associated with strong nation-states, large-scale organizations for mass production and consumption under welfare-capitalism (Esping-Andersen 1990), mass ideology (Hewitt 1992), and patriarchal modes of work and family life (Williams 1992). In Chapter 1, we noted that each of these features has undergone processes of change during the last thirty years. In particular, the economic dominance of the nation-state has been undermined by processes of globalization accompanying changes in the capitalist world system and affecting labour markets and the modes of production and consumption. Accompanying economic change, welfare states have undergone profound restructuring with governments endeavouring to stem the long-standing growth in welfare expenditure and rise in personal taxation. Further, relations between men and women are experiencing far-reaching changes both at the macro-level of occupational membership and labour market participation, and at the micro-level of domestic relations and the division of household tasks. Finally, Chapter 1 addressed the emergence of late-modern societies characterized by new modes of cultural, political and economic life. The book has argued that each of these four types of change impacted on the nature of the human subject, demanding the development of new abilities and generating new needs among individuals to live and flourish in this new climate. We have argued that mutualism, in complementing the limited perspectives of Social Democracy and the Radical Right, and enhancing state and market provision, is one theory of human nature that appeals to the challenges posed by the late twentieth century. We will examine finally the 'reflexive modernization' and Marxist accounts of human nature; different accounts characterizing human nature respectively by its plasticity or its potential for fullness.

As a leading analyst of late modernity, Giddens suggests that both the Social Democratic and Radical Right projects have relied on a traditional world view that is increasingly less relevant to what he refers to as 'reflexive modernization' (1994). For example, neo-liberal ideology advances, as Hayek argued, the effective dispersion of practical knowledge and custom among networks of individuals comprising markets of producers and consumers. Social Democracy assumes, as did Beveridge, regular and predictable patterns of social and economic life, including the predictability of risks and the contingent nature of needs. Both ideologies saw human nature as flourishing in regular and predictable environments where individuals can plan and co-operate to meet need. In both, individuals are seen as best able to accommodate tradition and custom, where they 'have relatively stable preferences, and where their level of reflexive involvement with wider society and economic processes is relatively low' (67). In the present age of reflexive modernization, marked by the complex processes of social transformation outlined above, individuals develop new abilities for reflexive action, by which they can use the feedback from different situations to regularly reorder and redefine what these situations are about (86). Consequently, these processes of social change impact on the individual in profound ways, including personal aspects of his or her nature, changing the constitution of personal identity so that the conduct of the self becomes a reflexive process. For 'Individuals cannot rest content with an identity that is simply handed down, inherited, or built on a traditional status. A person's identity has in large part to be discovered, constructed, actively sustained' (82).

The notion of social reflexivity chimes in with some of the mutualist values in welfare, in particular the idea that individuals can fashion resources co-operatively to meet their different needs. On the other hand, Giddens presents a view of the self in which needs are far from being basic and are closer to being nebulous and malleable, a socially-constructed view of human nature to which we will return shortly. In short, the reflexive self has mutual but not basic needs – a plastic model of human nature the consequences of which we now examine.

One consequence of the development of these reflexive capacities is that the self acquires new scope for autonomy and a greater capacity to distance itself from different political, inter-personal and social contexts. In politics, individuals are capable of developing a new type of democracy – what Giddens calls 'dialogic democracy' (112) – which impacts on all areas of social life and not just those addressed in representative democracy and government. In inter-personal relationships, friendships, families, marriage and sexual relations, a more autonomous self addresses the other for what he or she is and not according to the role they perform. Thus one has to decide who one is and who the other is as persons. Because of this heightened sense of interpersonal reflexivity, a new level of 'plasticity' and openness enters into relationships and into the construction of the self's identity (118). For Giddens, the reflexive self of late-modern society acquires both the agency to influence events and the capacity to respond to events at the same time. However, whilst reflexivity and autonomy are important qualities of the self, it can be argued that the substance of agency – what constitutes the human subject – takes on a plasticity that escapes definition, whether in empirical or metaphysical terms. In this state of plasticity, self-identity has to be 'routinely created and sustained in the reflexive activities of the individual' (1991, 52). Yet, whilst this conception of self-identity is enigmatic, in the face of the challenge to be more reflexive to others, the individual must perforce understand his or her own identity; in short, 'to open out to the other, one must know oneself' (*ibid*.). Like other recent constructions of the self associated with deconstructionism and postmodernism,[4] the reflexive self presents itself in two contrary ways: as a subject that is socially constructed by external, social and interpersonal processes; and, at a deeper and less explicit level, as a subject who has the capacity to discover and exercise degrees of agency in these processes.

Whilst the concept of reflexivity is central to Giddens' work, its analytical value is problematic.[5] Coming from the theoretical tradition of social interactionism, Giddens stresses throughout the creative and constructionist nature of social action. The human attribute of reflexivity takes on a new significance under conditions of high modernity, which are characterized by a high degree of uncertainty without the security associated with the traditional family, local community and culture. In the new environment of manufactured risk and diversity of life-choices, each person is expected to construct their own self-identity, that is 'routinely created and sustained in the reflexive activities of the individual' (1991, p. 52). She or he must develop a sense of self-hood equipped for the 'run-away world' to which they belong. For the significance of reflexivity is not only because it is 'intrinsic to all human activity' (1991, 20, 35), but also because it now characterizes the central institutions of high modernity and thereby 'extends into the core of the self' and makes 'the self a reflexive project' (1991, 32).

In theory reflexivity grows out of the individual's capacity for intersubjective awareness to respond to the object world, including communications from other individuals, and to initiate action in the object world that is meaningful and purposive. Giddens thus locates reflexivity within the context of language as an intrinsic social practice of communication that provides the basis of social interaction (1991, 51). However, his exposition of reflexivity has the effect of undermining the subjective and objective poles of both language and social interaction without which reflexivity would lose its bearings. Both subject and object are made to be *contingent* on each other. The result, it could be argued, is that neither subject nor object is left with sufficient substance and identity to act reflexively.

What is most at stake here is the Enlightenment view that human nature is made of universal qualities that have sustained the species through time, enabling it to survive each historical period and rise to the challenge of the next. For the challenges of social transformation listed above call for new qualities of human nature that are contingent on specific social, material and cultural processes. If these developments are read in entirely contingent terms, without reference to the idea of an enduring albeit evolving human nature, the result is that humankind is no longer conceived in terms of qualities embedded in human nature itself, but in terms of its responses and adaptations to external forces. Human nature is created by external forces and in itself lacks integral content. Humankind exists merely in response and adaptation, and not in self-determination: a hollowed out presentation of humankind devoid of human nature. Indeed, the hollowed out human subject can be seen as the subjective side of the 'hollowed out state', devoid of collective purpose on behalf of its citizens, that the forces of globalization are shaping (Jessop 1994, 24). Further, the hollowed out subject appears central to the effectiveness of the new techniques of managerialism discussed in Chapter 4 with their open-ended notions of quality and performance. On this reading, the new politics of autonomy and pragmatism, which recent social and political theory proposes in response to social transformation, is not complemented by a substantive account of personhood or human nature that supports the faculty of autonomy. The danger is that, by default rather than by design, the empty or hidden subject is reactive and malleable rather than proactive in its response to changing social conditions. The assertion of autonomy is no more than a testament of faith in human potential. Whilst post-traditional writers like Giddens and Beck (Beck 1994) describe individuals as receptive, reflexive and active in their deliberation of and engagement with a changing world, the nature of this agency is unclear. Without the substantive capabilities associated with deliberation and engagement – in particular the exercise of discernment, freedom and choice – it is not clear wherein lie the moral capacities of agency needed to guide human action in times of rapid change.

This is a central problem for those examples of postmodern and late-modern theory that privilege the notion of contingency over the notion of the endurability of human existence (Hewitt 1994). The familiar answer to these problems is that the new environment of human-made uncertainties is bringing forth new human qualities of self-reflexivity and flexibility. Consequently, humankind can no longer base its existence on 'transcendent' beliefs in, for example, the technological forces of production, scientific progress and the universal appeal of liberal values (e.g. Touraine 1981, 2). Self-reflexivity can be construed as a new quality of human nature induced in individuals forced to confront the new complexes of human-made risk that have been produced in large part unintentionally and unbeknowingly. In coming to terms with the new predicament of risk, humans develop the capacity and sensitivities of self-management, of reflexively adjusting their responses to the environment and designing new modes of existence. For sociologists like Giddens, Beck, Touraine and others, self-reflexivity becomes a particular form of intentionality that is meant to counter the directionless drift of human action towards the abyss of overwhelming risk and contingency, and to reinvest human action with a sense of policy and purpose. However, despite the new burden of responsibility placed on the self in reflexively engaging with manufactured risk, these writers abandon the task of identifying the particular content of human nature needed in the age of risk.

More recently, whilst acknowledging past similarities between his and Giddens' treatments of the human subject, Touraine has posited a contrast between two conceptions of the subject that supports the present analysis, namely what he terms the 'I' and the 'self'. He says: 'Even when he [the human subject] believes he is acting in accordance with his desires, the individual is increasingly an effect of the system and its objectives. Which means that we have to make an even clearer distinction between the I, or the principle that resists the logic of the system so stubbornly, and the Self, which is an individual projection of the demands and norms of the system' (1995, 264). According to this distinction, Giddens is advancing the second conception of the subject or self as a reflexive component of the system. However, if we acknowledge that the notion of reflexivity stands for a process of engagement between a more firmly constituted subject and its object world, which is itself mediated by other subjects, then it is possible to restore to reflexive processes a degree of agency characterizing individuals in the world. Otherwise, the process of reflexivity in the manifold settings Giddens describes is at best a transitional and indeterminate process leading from one contingent moment of existence to another.

The notion of 'reflexivity' is not a specifically post-tradition one, but was developed in Giddens' earlier work on the 'double hermeneutics' (see Lash and Wynne 1992, 8), and has its roots in the much longer traditions of phenomenology and Hegelian and Marxist theory that have addressed problems central to modernity. What is therefore significant in this line of thought is that it derives from a tradition that invests human nature with the inalienable qualities of agency that define the essence of humanity, however profound the experience of alienation has become in modern industrial society. Whilst one can justifiably read some accounts of the contingency of modern existence as questioning and deconstructing the very notion of human nature, it is not necessary that these accounts abandon the notion of human nature altogether in endeavouring to face up squarely to the task of describing the processes of change shaping human existence today. For the notion of human nature remains central to this task, however contingent and implicit it appears. It is reasonable therefore to question the genesis of the new qualities of human nature that postmodern and late-modern societies bring forth. We have argued that the core notions of praxis, derived from Hegel and Marx, and the related notion of human mutuality, describe essential qualities of human nature which provide a bridgehead between the endurability of human agency and the experiences of contingency, neediness and lack characterizing contemporary life. Specifically, the thesis has argued that universal features of human nature are realized, in large part, *immanently* in mutual interaction and praxis.

The fulfilment of human nature

Finally, drawing on the discussion in Chapters 5, 6 and 7, we describe an account of human nature that is different from the idea of the plasticity of needs and abilities in late-modern humans. We will call this *full* or, after Marx, *many-sided* human nature. This account recognizes the need for humans to develop more fully rounded natures that are flexible and diverse in the way they deploy their abilities in engaging with the processes of social change that Giddens and others address. However, this account relies neither on the empty construction of the subject which underpins the assumed plasticity of human nature, nor on a hidden and unspecified agency that the subject, despite its plasticity, is ultimately capable of 'knowing'.

Chapter 6 noted that Marx saw basic needs as consisting of the physical and higher needs necessary for realizing human modes of life. We can use Maslow's account of the hierarchy of needs to describe this. Maslow groups the range of human needs into five sequentially ordered groups: physiological, safety, belongingness and love, esteem, and self-actualization. Given this hierarchy, he states 'the clear emergence of … [the need for self-actualization] usually rests upon some prior satisfaction of the physiological, safety, love and esteem needs' (1970, 47). Each set constitutes a particular stage in the development of human motivation and lays the foundation for satisfying higher basic needs. According to Maslow – and Marx – one cannot be truly human without meeting basic needs for say food and shelter in such a way that higher needs for aesthetic enjoyment, human mutuality and sociability are realized: normally higher need-satisfaction depends on meeting physical needs.

Complementing this insight, Marx argues that the truly human way of satisfying basic physical needs is dependent on achieving higher forms of need-satisfaction that impart aesthetic, cultural and social enjoyment to human life: the human mode of satisfying physical needs depends on reaching full need-satisfaction. Thus, lower and higher need-satisfaction represents a totality of human fulfilment that cannot be sustained by reducing it to lower levels of physical need-satisfaction alone, as much minimum welfare provision does. Modern Marxists have construed this totality in two ways. On the one hand, it is based on a permanent stratum of basic needs that remains constant over time whilst higher needs evolve in relation to the development of productive means. On the other, this totality, consisting of both basic and higher needs, evolves as part of the historically unfolding fulfilment of humankind. Either way, the stratum of basic needs represents a desideratum that is essential to human fulfilment, such that if its satisfaction were undermined human fulfilment in the broad sense would suffer.

The rejection of a full or fuller notion of human nature, implied by the notion of a plastic, 'flexible' or 'constructed' human subject, threatens to undermine the commitment to provide the essential resources that humans need in seeking to achieve new forms of personal and social fulfilment.

It is beyond the scope of this book to speculate, other than on the rudiments, on the precise forms of institutional design for welfare that is required to bring about this vision of human nature and fulfilment. However, movement towards achieving this vision would require government commitment to underwrite, but not necessarily to provide, basic needs provision and a recognition that voluntary and mutual organizations need material support to help them meet the full range of needs. So far this has happened where organizations have been free to interpret social policies creatively. In the example given in Chapter 6 of 'supported living' provisions, housing benefit has been used to cover provisions not only for the physical need for accommodation, but also for the special needs associated with the accommodation of adults with learning and communication difficulties. This might include the provision of counselling, therapy and programmes of assimilation, which meet higher needs for belongingness, self-esteem and self-actualization. Provisions are purchased from the market or from mutual aid organizations, both of which are contracted to provide services in return for payments or contributions. Provision for supported living has become an important issue in recent government policy, leading to the publication of *Supporting People* (DSS 1998c). This new policy sought to re-establish supported living following the High Court decision in 1997, upheld by the Court of Appeal, that any needs covered by housing benefit must be solely physical needs for shelter (*The Guardian*, 25.7.97).

Marx's conception of many-sided human nature as universal to humankind implies that all individuals have rights to share in the human mode of life in all its variety that existing resources permit. Fully human nature represents a view of human abilities and needs that endows humans with the substantive qualities of agency that the plastic conception of human nature lacks. More work, beyond the scope of this book, is needed to show how this model of human nature would apply to social policy in the transformed world of recent decades. Nonetheless, fully human nature represents a positive conception of empowered human subjects able to determine the purpose of their fulfilment and to will the means to this end in a social world characterized by fragmentation, exclusion and deprivation. This type of social policy would be universal. However, unlike the Webbs' and other Social Democratic accounts of universal provision, it would not imply a uniform provision or life-style. We suggested in Chapter 7 that the universalization of practices and resources extends new opportunities to subaltern groups who, being newly empowered to address situations previously denied them, are able to deepen their own individuality and difference within their own human mode of life. The development of different modes of consumption and production among individuals and cultures would contribute towards this diversity. Hence, the concept of full human nature implies sufficient space for the enhanced social differentiation and flexibility that the politics of immanent universalism, described in the last chapter, would generate. However, in addition to integrating basic and higher needs, there would still need to be institutional means to empower different social groups in meeting their different basic needs. This is what Doyal and Gough term the 'dual strategy' of central planning and democratic participation in formulating social policy (1991, 297). The design would have to address social diversity as well as the means to enable individuals to integrate the hierarchy of need-satisfaction contributing to each individual's full human nature. It would have to be sufficiently pluralist in embracing the needs for autonomy of different groups as well as sufficiently universal and unified in addressing the hierarchy of basic and higher needs.

The notion of full human nature, or the 'fully rounded human being', stands as a standard against which actual instances of human nature discourse can be compared, and towards which examples of human practice approach. It represents a standard for comparing different accounts of human action and organization, for identifying those aspects in each account that contribute or inhibit human fulfilment, and for devising programmes of policy and action that reach towards this standard of fulfilment. As a normative standard, it represents a set of criteria for evaluating social practices and policy proposals that democratic societies follow in promoting the collective welfare and personal fulfilment of all its members. Some degree of empirical support for this normative argument is given in Dean and Melrose's recent investigation of popular conceptions and concerns about citizenship and social justice, where they suggest that:

> If people are more inclined than in the recent past to autonomistic social-contractualist conceptions of citizenship, these may be inflected towards more highly focused and instrumentally specific demands upon the state; towards a contract that is quite full and substantive, not rather empty and minimalist.
>
> (1999, 129)

The general argument posed, it is important to acknowledge something that deserves more than an afterword, namely that several writers within Marxist and other traditions have addressed the existence of 'natural limits' to human fulfilment in addition to the limits posed by the dominant mode of production. These may reside in the human psyche and biology and in the ecological system (e.g. Soper 1981; Benton 1989; Dickens 1992).

Conclusion

The last two decades have seen fundamental changes in social policy associated with a sea change in thinking about human nature, needs and fulfilment. The concept of human nature itself has become increasingly central to debates about policy and politics. The postwar decades saw welfare playing a central role in protecting individuals from destitution, limiting the extremes of inequality that unfettered capitalism produced, and extending universal rights to most citizens. The national minimum was the principal apparatus for achieving these three aims. At the same time, the welfare state was supposed to buttress solidarity partly by securing basic minima for all, and partly by engendering new types of relationships between citizens based on mutual support and reciprocity. In these ways the welfare state appealed to ideas about human needs and fulfilment that drew on the universalist spirit of the Enlightenment represented in Liberal and Social Democratic thought, and, to a lesser extent, on communitarian sentiments that emerged in more immanent ways in practical social relationships of care, responsibility and obligation. The last twenty-five years, however, saw the emergence of New Right values that replaced ideas of social justice and mutuality with concerns for greater productivity and enterprise in the economy and managerial efficiency in welfare delivery, targeting resources on the residual poor rather than on the population at large.

However, despite these developments, and the Labour government's acceptance of parts of the previous Tory government's legacy, the book has suggested that there is still space within the transformed structures of welfare for evolving the Social Democratic tradition. This is seen in the continuation of certain ideas about human nature in New Labour's project, namely basic needs and mutuality. The challenge for Labour is to re-affirm its commitment to meeting basic needs, either directly or indirectly by means of non-state agencies such as mutual providers. Provisions for basic and mutual needs would in this way support each other. Beveridge's way would appear to be closer to Labour's Third Way than is often perceived (e.g. DSS 1998a, iv; see Hewitt and Powell 1998). This is not a plea to regress back to the classic welfare state, but to draw on the political and intellectual movements that are rediscovering and re-inventing ideas and practices around mutualism and recognition.

This chapter has suggested in a spirit of optimism that the future of welfare could involve revitalizing concerns for social justice that are currently being conceptualized in new ways. The hope is that in the new welfare state concern for human fulfilment will be more prominent than previously, and will involve an understanding of social justice based on integrating new notions of common basic needs and mutually satisfied needs, needs that are both universal and sensitive to difference. In this way new thinking about human nature seeks to extend the discourse on human nature to embrace a wider range of motivations rather than single or narrowly conceived motivations.

Notes

1 Introduction

1. For an alternative view of the nation-state exercising some autonomy over global influences, see Hirst and Thompson (1996) and Weiss (1997).

Part I
Mainstream Traditions in Social Policy

1. Studies of nineteenth-century Liberalism disagree over the influence of Green and the Idealists. For example, Freeden lists British Idealism as one among other influences such as biologism and evolutionism (1978, 16); whereas Vincent and Plant stress its prime importance (1984, 2). The latter (2–3) also refer to Lichtheim (1967), Pugh (1982), Dyson (1980), and others in support. We argue below that early twentieth-century Social Democratic thinkers came to reflect some of Green's central ideas.

2 Social Democracy and Human Nature

1. See, e.g. Freeden (1978); Clarke (1978); Vincent and Plant (1984); Collini (1991).
2. See Veit-Wilson (1986) for a detailed analysis of Rowntree's methods and his culturally constructed view of needs.
3. See Vincent and Plant (1984, 96–7) for an assessment of this view.
4. See Lister (1995) discussion of the 'Republican' approach to citizenship as a holistic alternative to Marshall's approach.

4 Human Nature and the Right

1. For example, see Elliott and Hutton's interview with Kenneth Clarke, the former Chancellor of the Exchequer (1995).
2. For his comparison of the two traditions, see Hayek (1960, ch. 4).
3. However, some suggestions of Nozick (1974) and Murray (1984, ch. 16) imply that the state should not exercise a role in welfare provision.
4. Von Mises developed a theory of 'praxeology' to explain this process (see Barry 1979).
5. The Labour government has reformed some, but not all, aspects of the internal market by replacing GP fundholders with Primary Care Groups or trusts which represent all the GP practices within each area. These new bodies will still purchase services from providers such as NHS hospital trusts.
6. In (1992, 69) Gray voices one of the strongest endorsements for universal welfare heard on the Right.

Part II
5 Marx, Marxism and Human Nature

1 The italicized rendering of the quotations taken from Marx is from the original, unless otherwise stated.
2 By contrast, knowledge abstracted in the form of a disembodied consciousness of the world is not real knowledge – a problem that Marx criticizes Hegel for (1975a, 382), just as recent feminists have modern liberal theorists of distributive justice such as Rawls (e.g. Benhabib 1992).

6 Marxism, Human Nature and Need

1 For one of the fullest accounts of need content, see Doyal and Gough 1991.

7 Feminism, the Politics of Recognition and Social Policy

1 Reversibility can also involve confronting fundamental limitations in one's capacities to take on new tasks and acquire new skills and insights. In this case one also learns about the significance of difference. The lack of space for a discussion of psychoanalytic theories of human nature does not deny the importance of the intrinsic limits circumscribing personal resources that can limit human achievements.
2 Iris Young has suggested that such spatial, as well as ontological, differences may make it difficult to put one's self in another's place and that trying to do so may lead to misunderstanding. She suggests nonetheless that understanding across difference is both possible and necessary. However, this takes place on the basis of a different account from Benhabib's view of 'symmetrical' reciprocity in that understanding occurs between asymmetrically different selves (1997, 353–4).

8 Conclusion

1 Recent discussions of the provenance of the social policy of the New Labour government include Oppenheim 1997; Lister 1997; Hewitt and Powell 1998; Powell 1999.
2 See Benton (1993) for an examination of debates around the issue of 'human/animal continuism'.
3 The concept of 'suture' is taken from Laclau and Mouffe (1985) who provide an account of its role in hegemonic discourse.
4 Giddens in fact has distanced himself from postmodernism as an intellectual movement on several occasions.
5 See O'Brien (1999) for an extended critical exposition of Giddens' notion of reflexivity.

Bibliography

Ackerman, B. (1980) *Social Justice in the Liberal State*, New Haven (USA): Yale University.
Althusser, L. (1969) 'On the Materialist Dialectic', ch. 6 in L. Althusser, *For Marx*, Harmondsworth: Penguin.
Anderson, D. (ed.) (1993) *The Loss of Virtue: Moral Confusion in Britain and America*, London: Social Affairs Unit.
Armitage, B. and Scott, M. (1998) 'British labour force projections: 1998–2011', in *Labour Market Trends* (DfEE), Vol. 106, No. 6, June, 281–97.
Bach, M. (1993) 'Welfare work: discursive conflicts and narrative possibilities', ch. 12 in G. Drover and P. Kerans (eds) *New Approaches to Welfare Theory*, Aldershot: Elgar.
Balbo, L. (1987) 'Crazy quilts: rethinking the welfare state debate from a woman's point of view', ch. 1 in A.S. Sassoon (ed.) *Women and the State*, London: Hutchinson.
Barclay, P. (chair) (1995) *Inquiry into Income and Wealth*, York: Joseph Rowntree Foundation.
Barry, N.P. (1979) *Hayek's Social and Economic Philosophy*, London: Macmillan.
Barry, N.P. (1987) 'Understanding the market', ch. 11 in M. Loney (ed.) *The State or the Market*, London: Sage Publications, 161–71.
Beck, U. (1992) *The Risk Society: towards a New Modernity*, London: Sage.
Bell, D. (1993) *Communitarianism and its Critics*, Oxford: Oxford University.
Bell, I., Butler, E., Marsland, D. and Pirrie, M. (1994) *The End of the Welfare State*, London: Adam Smith Institute.
Benhabib, S. (1992) *Situating the Self: Gender, Community and Postmodernism in Contemporary Ethics*, Cambridge: Polity.
Benjamin, J. (1990) *The Bonds of Love: Psychoanalysis, Feminism and the Problem of Domination*, London: Virago.
Benjamin, J. (1994) 'The shadow of the other (subject): intersubjectivity and feminist theory', *Constellations*, Vol. 1, No. 2, 231–55.
Benton, T. (1988) 'Humanism = speciesism: Marx on humans and animals', *Radical Philosophy*, 50, 4–18.
Benton, T. (1989) 'Marxism and natural limits: an ecological critique and reconstruction', *New Left Review*, No. 178, 51–86.
Bergman, B. and Klefsjo, B. (1994) *Quality: from Customer Needs to Customer Satisfaction*, London: McGraw-Hill.
Bernstein, R.J. (1972) *Praxis and Action*, London: Duckworth.
Berry, C.J. (1986) *Human Nature*, Basingstoke: Macmillan.
Beveridge, W.H. (1942) *Social Insurance and Allied Services* (Cmd. 6404), London: HMSO.
Beveridge, W.H. (1948) *Voluntary Action*, London: George Allen and Unwin.
Blair, T. (1994) *Socialism* (Fabian Pamphlet 565), London: Fabian Society.
Blair, T. (1995) 'End the give and take away society', *The Guardian* 23.3.95, 24.
Blair, T. (1998) *The Third Way* (Fabian Pamphlet), London Fabian Society.
Borrie, G. (chair) (1994) *Social Justice: Strategies for National Renewal* (The Report of the Commission on Social Justice), London: Vintage.

Boulding, K.E. (1967) 'The boundaries of social policy', *Social Work*, Vol. 12, No. 1, 3–11.
Briggs, A. (1961) 'The welfare state in historical perspective', *European Journal of Sociology*, Vol. 2, 221–58.
Brown, G. (1999) 'Equality – then and now', ch. 4 in D. Leonard (ed.) *Crosland and New Labour*, Basingstoke: Macmillan.
Butler, J. (1990) *Gender Trouble: Feminism and the Subversion of Identity*, London: Routledge.
Butler, J.R. (1993) 'A case study in the National Health Service: *Working for Patients*', ch. 4 in P. Taylor-Gooby and R. Lawson (eds) *Markets and Managers: New Issues in the Delivery of Welfare*, Buckingham: Open University.
Callender, C. (1996) 'Women and employment', ch. 3 in C. Hallett (ed.) *Women and Social Policy*, Hemel Hempstead: Harvester Wheatsheaf.
Chamberlayne, P. (1991/2) 'New directions in welfare?' *Critical Social Policy*, No. 33, 5–21.
Checkland, S.G. and E.O.A. (eds) (1974) *The Poor Law Report of 1834* (The Poor Law Commission), Harmondsworth: Penguin.
Chodorow, N. (1978) *The Reproduction of Mothering: Psychoanalysis and the Sociology of Gender*, California: University of California.
Chodorow, N. (1989) 'Family structure and feminine personality', ch. 2 in N. Chodorow, *Feminism and Psychoanalytic Theory*, Cambridge: Polity.
Clarke, J. and Newman, J. (1997) *The Managerial State: Power, Politics and Ideology in the Remaking of Social Welfare*, London: Sage.
Clarke, P. (1978) *Liberals and Social Democrats*, Cambridge: Cambridge University .
Collini, S. (1991) *Public Moralists: Political Thought and Intellectual Life in Britain*, Oxford: Clarendon.
Cornell, D. (1992) *Philosophy of the Limit*, London: Routledge.
Cowen, H. (1994) *The Human Nature Debate: Social Theory, Social Policy and the Caring Professions*, Pluto.
Crosland, C.A.R. (1963) *The Future of Socialism*, London: Cape.
Cutler, T. and Waine, B. (1994) *Managing the Welfare State: the Politics of Public Sector Management*, Oxford: Berg.
Cutler, T., Williams, K. and Williams, J. (1986) *Keynes, Beveridge and Beyond*, London: Routledge and Kegan Paul.
Dahrendorf, Lord R. (chair) (1995) *The Report on Wealth Creation and Social Cohesion in a Free Society*, London: Commission on Wealth Creation and Social Cohesion.
Dean, H. and Melrose, M. (1999) *Poverty, Riches and Social Citizenship*, Basingstoke: Macmillan.
DHSS (Department of Health and Social Security) (1989) *Working for Patients* (Cm 555), London HMSO.
Dickens, P. (1992) *Society and Nature: towards a Green Social Theory*, Hemel Hempstead, Harvester Wheatsheaf.
Digby, A. (1989) *British Welfare Policy*, London: Faber.
DoH (Department of Health) (1997) *The New NHS: Modern, Dependable* (Cm 3807), London: The Stationary Office.
Doyal, L. and Gough, I. (1991) *A Theory of Social Need*, Basingstoke: Macmillan.
Doyal, L. and Harris, R. (1983) 'The practical foundations of human understanding', *New Left Review*, No. 139, 59–78.
Dryzek, J.S. (1996) 'The informal logic of institutional design', ch. 4 in R.E. Gooden (ed.) *The Theory of Institutional Design*, Cambridge: Cambridge University.

DSS (Department of Social Security) (1998a) *A New Contract for Welfare: new ambitions for our country* (Cm 3805), London: The Stationery Office.
DSS (1998b) *A New Contract for Welfare: Partnership in Pensions* (Cm 4179), London: The Stationery Office.
DSS (1998c) *Supporting People: a New Policy and Funding Framework for Support Services* (DSS consultation paper), London: Department of Social Security.
Dunleavy, P. (1991) *Democracy, Bureaucracy and Public Choice: Economic Explanations in Political Science*, Hemel Hempstead: Harvester Wheatsheaf.
Dwyer, P. (1998) 'Conditional citizens? Welfare rights and responsibilities in the late 1990s', *Critical Social Policy*, Vol. 18, 493–517.
Dyson, K.H.F. (1980) *The State Tradition in Modern Europe: a Study of an Idea and an Institution*, Oxford: Martin Robinson.
Elliott, L. and Hutton, W. (1995) 'Building in the centre' (an interview with Kenneth Clarke), *The Guardian*, 20.7.95, 15.
Engels, F. (1972) *The Origin of the Family, Private Property and the State*, New York: Pathfinder.
Esping-Anderson, G. (ed.) (1996) *Welfare States in Transition: National Adaptations in Global Economies*, London: Sage.
Etzioni, A. (1995) *The Spirit of Community: Rights, Responsibilities and the Communitarian Agenda*, London: Fontana.
Falkingham, J. and Hills, J. (eds) (1995) *The Dynamic of Welfare: the Welfare State and the Life Cycle*, Hemel Hempstead: Prentice Hall.
Field, F. (1989) *Losing Out: the Emergence of Britain's Underclass*, Oxford: Blackwell.
Field, F. (1996) *How to Pay for the Future: Building a Stakeholders' Welfare*, London: Institute of Community Studies.
Field, F. (1997) 'Frank Field's response to Alan Deacon', 141–53 in A.R. Morton (ed.) *The Future of Welfare*, Edinburgh: Centre for Theology and Public Issues, University of Edinburgh.
Finch, J. and Groves, D. (1980) 'Community care and the family: a case for equal opportunities', *Journal of Social Policy*, Vol. 9, pt. 4, 487–511.
Firestone, S. (1970) *The Dialectic of Sex: the Case for Feminist Revolution*, London: The Women's Press.
Fisher, B. and Tronto, J.C. (1989) 'Towards a feminist theory of caring', ch. 2 in E. Abel and M. Nelson (eds) *Circles of Caring*, Albany, New York (US): SUNY.
Foucault, M. (1979) *The History of Sexuality: Volume I, An Introduction*, trans. R. Hurley, London: Allen Lane.
Fraser, N. (1997) *Justice Interruptus: Critical Reflections on the 'Postsocialist' Condition*, London: Routledge.
Freeden, M. (1978) *The New Liberalism*, Oxford: Clarendon.
Friedman, M. and R. (1980) *Free to Choose*, Harmondsworth: Penguin.
Galbraith, J.K. (1992) *The Culture of Contentment*, London: Sinclair-Stevenson.
Gamble, A. (1979) 'The free market and the strong state: the rise of the social market economy', in R. Miliband and J. Saville (eds) *The Socialist Register, 1979*.
Gamble, A. (1988) *The Free and the Strong State: the Politics of Thatcherism*, London: Macmillan.
Gamble, A. (1996) *Hayek: the Iron Cage of Liberty*, Cambridge: Polity.
General Synod (1992) *The Ordination of Women to the Priesthood: the Synod Debate, 11 November 1992, the Verbatim Record*, London: Church House.
George, V. and Miller, S. (eds) (1994) *Social Policy Towards 2000: Squaring the Welfare Circle*, London: Routledge.

Geras, N. (1983) *Marx and Human Nature: Refutation of a Legend*, London: Verso.
Giddens, A. (1991) *Modernity and Self-identity: Self and Society in the Late Modern Age*, Cambridge: Polity.
Giddens, A. (1994) *Beyond Left and Right: the Future of Radical Politics*, Cambridge: Polity.
Gilligan, C. (1982) *In a Different Voice: Psychological Theory and Women's Development*, Cambridge, Mass: Harvard University.
Gladstone, D. (ed.) (1999) *Before Beveridge: Welfare Before the Welfare State*, London: Institute of Economic Affairs.
Glendenning, C. (1992) '"Community care": the financial consequences for women', ch. 7 in C. Glendenning and J. Millar, *Women and Poverty in Britain*, Hemel Hempstead: Harvester Wheatsheaf.
Glennerster, H. (1991) 'The radical right and the future of the welfare state', ch. 9 in H. Glennerster and J. Midgley (eds) *The Radical Right and the Welfare State: an International Assessment*, Hemel Hempstead: Harvester Wheatsheaf.
Glennerster, H. (1995) *British Social Policy Since 1945*, Oxford: Blackwell.
Glennerster, H. (1998) 'Welfare with the lid on', ch. 8 in H. Glennerster and J. Hills (eds), *The State of Welfare: the Economics of Social Spending*, Oxford: Oxford University.
Gooden, R.E. (ed.) (1996) *The Theory of Institutional Design*, Cambridge: Cambridge University.
Gough, I. (1979) *The Political Economy of the Welfare State*, London: Macmillan.
Gray, J. (1986, 2nd ed.) *Hayek on Liberty*, Oxford: Blackwell.
Gray, J. (1992) *The Moral Foundations of Market Institutions*, London: Institute of Economic Affairs.
Gray, J. (1996) *Endgames: Questions in Late Modern Political Thought*, Cambridge: Polity.
Gray, J. (1997) 'After Social Democracy', ch. 22 in G. Mulgan (ed.) *Life After Politics*, London: Fontana.
Gray, J. (1998) *False Dawn: the Delusions of Global Capitalism*, London: Granta.
Green, A.E. (1996) 'Aspects of the changing geography of poverty and wealth', ch. 11 in J. Hills (ed.) *New Inequalities: the Changing Distribution of Income and Wealth in the U.K.*, Cambridge: Cambridge University Press.
Green, D.G. (1987) *The New Right: the Counter Revolution in Political, Economic and Social Thought*, Brighton: Wheatsheaf.
Green, D.G. (1988) *Everyone a Private Patient*, London: Institute of Economic Affairs.
Green, D.G. (1993) *Reinventing Civil Society: the Rediscovery of Welfare without Politics*, London: Institute of Economic Affairs.
Green, T.H. (1986) *Lectures on the Principles of Political Obligation and Other Writings*, edited by P. Harris and J. Morrow, Cambridge: Cambridge University.
Habermas, J. (1979) 'What is universal pragmatics?' ch. 1 in *Communication and the Evolution of Society*, trans. T. McCarthy, London: Heinemann.
Habermas, J. (1987) *The Theory of Communicative Action, Volume II: Lifeworld and System*, trans. T. McCarthy, Cambridge: Polity.
Habermas, J. (1992) *Postmetaphysical Thinking: Philosophical Essays*, trans. W.H. Hohengarten, Cambridge: Polity.
Hadley, R. and Hatch, S. (1981) *Social Welfare and the Failure of the State*, London: Allen and Unwin.
Hakim, C. (1978) 'Sexual divisions within the labour force', *Department of Employment Gazette*, Vol. 86, No. 11, November, 1264–68.

Hall, S. (1983) 'The Great Moving Right Show', ch. 1 in S. Hall and M. Jacques (eds) *The Politics of Thatcherism*, London: Lawrence and Wishart.
Halsey, A.H. (ed.) (1972), *Educational Priority: EPA Problems and Priorities, Volume I* (Department of Education and Science), London: HMSO.
Harris, D. (1983) 'Returning the social to democracy', ch. 14 in G. Duncan (ed.) *Democratic Theory and Practice*, Cambridge: University.
Hayek, F.A. (1943) *The Road to Serfdom*, London: Routledge.
Hayek, F.A. (1960) *The Constitution of Liberty*, London: Routledge and Kegan Paul.
Hayek, F.A. (1973) *Law, Legislation and Liberty, Volume I: Rules and Order*, London: Routledge and Kegan Paul.
Hayek, F.A. (1975) *Law, Legislation and Liberty, Volume II: The Mirage of Social Justice*, London: Routledge and Kegan Paul.
Heelas, P. and Morris P. (eds) (1992) *The Values of the Enterprise Culture: the Moral Debate*, London: Routledge.
Hegel, G.W.F. (1977) *Phenomenology of Spirit*, trans. A.V. Miller, Oxford: Oxford University.
Heller, A. (1976) *The Theory of Need in Marx*, London: Allison & Busby.
Hewitt, M. (1992) *Welfare, Ideology and Need: Developing Perspectives on the welfare state*, Hemel Hempstead: Harvester Wheatsheaf.
Hewitt, M. (1994) 'Social policy and the question of postmodernism', in R. Page and J. Baldock (eds) *Social Policy Review 6*, Canterbury: Social Policy Association.
Hewitt, M. (1996) 'Social movements and social need: problems with postmodern political theory', ch. 11 in D. Taylor (ed.) *Critical Social Policy: a reader*, London: Sage.
Hewitt, M. and Powell, M. (1998) 'A different "back to Beveridge"', ch. 5 in E. Bransden, H. Dean and R. Woods (eds) *Social Policy Review 10*, London: Social Policy Association.
Hirst, P. (1994) *Associative Democracy: New Forms of Economic and Social Governance*, Cambridge: Polity.
Hirst, P. and Thompson, G. (1996) *Globalization in Question*, Cambridge: Polity.
HMSO (1909) *Report of the Royal Commission on the Poor Laws and the Relief of Distress; Minority Report* (cd. 4499), London: HMSO.
Hollis, M. (1977) *Models of Man: Philosophical Thoughts on Social Action*, Cambridge: Cambridge University,
Holman, B. (1993) *A New Deal for Social Welfare*, Oxford: Lion.
Honderich, T. (1990) *Conservatism*, London: Hamish Hamilton.
Honneth, A. (1995) *The Struggle for Recognition: the Moral Grammar of Social Conflicts*, trans. J. Anderson, Cambridge: Polity.
Honneth, A. and Joas, H. (1988) *Social Action and Human Nature*, trans. R. Meyer, Cambridge: Cambridge University.
Humm, M. (ed.) (1992) *Feminisms: a Reader*, Hemel Hempstead: Harvester Wheatsheaf.
Hutton, W. (1996a) *The State We're In*, London: Vintage.
Hutton, W. (1996b) 'The Stakeholder Society', ch. 12 in D. Marquand and A. Seldon (eds) *The Ideas That Shaped Post-War Britain*, London: Fontana.
IPPR (Institute for Public Policy Research) (1993) *The Justice Gap*, London: Institute for Public Policy Research.
Jaggar, A.M. (1983) *Feminist Politics and Human Nature*, Totowa, New Jersey: Rowman & Littlefield.

Jessop, B. (1994) 'The transition to post-Fordism and the Schumpeterian workfare state', ch. 2 in R. Burrows and B. Loader, *Towards a Post-Fordist Welfare State*, London: Routledge.
Johnson, N. (1999) *Mixed Economies of Welfare: a Comparative Perspective*, Hemel Hempstead: Prentice Hall Europe.
Jordan, B. (1998) *The New Politics of Welfare: Social Justice in a Global Context*, London: Sage.
Joseph, K. (1976) *Stranded in the Middle Ground: Reflections on Circumstances and Politics*, London: Centre for Policy Studies.
Joseph, K. and Sumption, J. (1979) *Equality*, London: Murray.
Kant, I. (1982) *Kant's Critique of Practical Reason and Other Works on the Theory of Ethics*, trans. T.K. Abbott, London: Longman.
Keat, R. and Abercrombie, N. (1991) *Enterprise Culture*, London: Routledge.
King, D. (1987) *The New Right: Politics, Markets and Citizenship*, London: Tavistock.
Klein, R. (1996) 'Self-inventing institutions: institutional design and the UK welfare state', ch. 9 in R.E. Gooden (ed.) *The Theory of Institutional Design*, Cambridge: Cambridge University.
Kojev, A. (1970) *An Introduction to the Reading of Hegel*, London: Cornell University.
Laclau, E. and Mouffe, C. (1985) *Hegemony and Socialist Strategy: Towards a Radical Democratic Politics*, London: Verso.
Lash, S. and Wynne, B. (1992) 'Introduction' in U. Beck, *The Risk Society: towards a New Modernity*, London: Sage.
Le Grand, J. (1990) 'The state of welfare', in J. Hills (ed.) *The State of Welfare*, Oxford: Clarendon.
Le Grand, J. (1997) 'Knights, knaves and pawns: human behaviour and social policy', *Journal of Social Policy*, Vol. 26, pt. 2, 149–69.
Le Grand, J. and Bartlett, W. (1993) *Quasi-Markets and Social Policy*, Basingstoke: Macmillan.
Leonard, D. (ed.) (1999) *Crosland and New Labour*, Basingstoke: Macmillan.
Levinas, E. (1989) 'Ethics as first philosophy', ch. 5 in E. Levinas, *The Levinas Reader*, ed. S. Hand, Oxford: Blackwell.
Levitas, R. (1986) 'Competition and compliance: the utopias of the New Right', ch. 3 in R. Levitas (ed.) *The Ideology of the New Right*, Cambridge: Polity.
Levitas, R. (1998) *The Inclusive Society? Social Exclusion and New Labour*, Basingstoke: Macmillan.
Lewis, J. and Davies, C. (1991) 'Protective Legislation in Britain, 1870–1990: equality, difference and their implications for women', *Policy and Politics*, Vol. 19, No. 1, 13–25.
Lichtheim, G. (1961) *Marxism*, London: Routledge and Kegan Paul.
Lilley, P. (1995) *Winning the Welfare Debate*, London: Social Market Foundation.
Lister, R. (1990) *The Exclusive Society*, London: Child Poverty Action Group.
Lister, R. (1991) 'Citizenship Engendered', *Critical Social Policy*, No. 32, 65–71.
Lister, R. (1995) 'Dilemmas in Engendering Citizenship', *Economy and Society*, Vol. 24, No. 1, 1–40.
Lister, R. (1997) *Citizenship: Feminist Perspectives*, Basingstoke: Macmillan.
Lister, R. (1997) 'From fractured Britain to one nation: the policy options for welfare reform', *Renewal*, Vol. 5, No. 3/4, 11–23.
Lonsdale, S. (1992) 'Patterns of paid work', ch. 7 in J. Millar and C. Glendenning (eds) *Women and Poverty: Britain in the 1990s*, Hemel Hempstead: Harvester Wheatsheaf.

Lowe, R. (1993) *The Welfare State in Britain since 1945*, Basingstoke: Macmillan.
Lowndes, B. (1994) 'Supported living for people with Asperger syndrome', *Communication* (The Journal of the Autistic Society), London: National Autistic Society, 13.
Mack, J. and Lansley, S. (1985) *Poor Britain*, London: Allen & Unwin.
Macpherson, C.B. (1973) 'The maximisation of democracy', ch. 1 in *Democratic Theory: Essays in Retrieval*, Oxford: Oxford University.
Markus, G. (1978) *Marxism and Anthropology: the Concept of Human Essence in the Philosophy of Marx*, Assen (The Netherlands): Van Gorcum.
Marshall, T.H. (1963) 'Citizenship and social class', ch. 4 in T.H. Marshall, *Sociology at the Crossroads and Other Essays*, London: Heinemann.
Marsland, D. (1996) *Welfare or Welfare State?*, Basingstoke: Macmillan.
Marx, K. (1967) *Capital: a Critique of Political Economy: Volume I*, New York: International Publishers.
Marx, K. (1973) *Grundrisse: Foundation of the Critique of Political Economy*, trans. and ed. M. Nicolaus, Harmondsworth, Penguin.
Marx, K. (1975a) 'Critique of Hegel's Dialectic of the State', trans. G. Benton, in K. Marx, *Early Writings*, introduced by L. Colletti, Harmondsworth: Penguin.
Marx, K. (1975b) 'Economic and Philosophical Manuscripts (1844)', in K. Marx, *Early Writings*, introduced by L. Colletti, Harmondsworth: Penguin Books.
Marx, K. (1975c) 'Excerpts from James Mill's 'Elements of Political Economy', trans. R. Livingstone, in K. Marx, *Early Writings*, introduced by L. Colletti, Harmondsworth: Penguin Books.
Marx, K. (1976) 'The theses on Feuerbach', in K. Marx and F. Engels, *Collected Works, Volume 5*, trans. G. Benton, London: Lawrence and Wishart.
Marx, K. and Engels, F. (1976) *The German Ideology*, trans. G. Benton, in K. Marx and F. Engels, *The Collected Works, Volume 5*, London: Lawrence & Wishart.
Maslow, M. (1970) *Motivation and Personality*, 2nd edn, New York: Harper & Row.
Miliband, D. (ed.) (1994) *Reinventing the Left*, Cambridge: Polity.
Mill, J.S. (1970) 'The subjection of women', ch. 4 in J.S. Mill and H.T. Mill, *Essays on Sex Equality*, (edited by A.S. Rossi), Chicago: Chicago University.
Millar, J. and Glendenning, C. (1989) 'Gender and poverty', *Journal of Social Policy*, Vol. 18, No. 3, 363–81.
Ministry of Health (1944) *A National Health Service* (Cmd 6502), London HMSO.
Mishra, R. (1993) 'Social policy in the postmodern world', ch. 2 in C. Jones (ed.) *New Perspectives on the Welfare State in Europe*, London: Routledge.
Mulhall, S. and Swift, A. (1996, 2nd edn) *Liberals and Communitarians*, Oxford: Blackwell.
Murray, C. (1984) *Losing Ground: American Social Policy 1950–1980*, New York: Basic Books.
Murray, C. (1990) *The Emergence of the British Underclass*, London: Institute of Economic Affairs.
Noble, M. and Smith, G. (1996) 'Two nations? Changing patterns of income and wealth in two contrasting areas', ch. 12 in J. Hills (ed.) *New Inequalities: the Changing Distribution of Income and Wealth in the U.K.*, Cambridge: Cambridge University Press.
Nolan, P. and Walsh, J. (1995) 'The structure of the economy and the labour market', ch. 3 in P.K. Edwards (ed.) *Industrial Relations: Theory and Practice in Britain*, Oxford: Blackwell.
Novak, M. (1991) *The Spirit of Democratic Capitalism*, New York: Madison Books.

Novak, M. and Preston, R. (1994) *Christian Capitalism or Christian Socialism*, London: Institute of Economic Affairs.
Nozick, R. (1974) *Anarchy, State and Utopia*, Oxford: Blackwell.
O'Brien, M. (1999) 'Theorizing modernity: reflexivity, identity and environment in Giddens' social theory', ch. 1 in M. O'Brien, S. Penna and C. Hay, *Theorizing Modernity*, Harlow: Addison Wesley Longman.
Oppenheim, C. and Harker, L. (1996, 3rd edition) *Poverty: the Facts*, London: Child Poverty Action Group.
Page, R. (1996) *Altruism and the British Welfare State*, Aldershot: Avebury.
Pateman, C. (1989) *The Disorder of Women: Democracy, Feminism and Political Theory*, Cambridge: Polity.
Plant, R. (1991) *Modern Political Thought*, Oxford: Blackwell.
Plant, R. (1993) *Social Justice, Labour and the New Right* (Fabian Pamphlet 556), London: Fabian Society.
Plant, R. (1996) 'Social Democracy', in D. Marquand and A. Seldon (eds) *The Ideas That Shaped Post-War Britain*, London: Fontana.
Powell, M. (ed.) (1999) *New Labour, New Welfare State? the Third Way in British Social Policy*, Bristol: Policy.
Pruger, R. (1973) 'Social policy: unilateral transfer or reciprocal exchange', *Journal of Social Policy*, Vol. 2, No. 4, 289–302.
Pugh, M.(1982) *The Making of Modern British Politics: 1867–1939*, Oxford: Blackwell.
Rawls, J. (1972) *A Theory of Justice*, Oxford: Clarendon.
Rawls, J. (1993) *Political Liberalism*, New York: Columbia University.
Raz, J. (1986) The Morality of Freedom, Oxford: Clarendon.
Robson, W.A. (1976) *Welfare State and Welfare Society: Illusion or Reality*, London: Allen and Unwin.
Rose, N. (1979) 'The psychological complex: mental measurement and social administration', *Ideology and Consciousness*, No. 5, 5–68.
Rowntree, B.S. (n.d.) *Poverty: a Study of Town Life*, London: Nebon.
Runciman, W.G. (1966) *Relative Deprivation and Social Justice: a Study of Attitudes to Social Inequality in Twentieth-century England*, London: Routledge & Kegan Paul.
Sandel, M.J. (1982), *Liberalism and the Limits of Justice*, Cambridge: Cambridge University Press.
Scott, J., Braun, M. and Alwin, D. (1998) 'Partner, parent, worker: family and gender roles', ch. 2 in Jowell, R., Curtice, J., Park, A., Brook, L., Thomson, K. and Bryson, C. (eds) *British and European Social Attitudes: The 15th Report*, Aldershot: Ashgate.
Smith, C. (Member of Parliament) (1996) *Social Justice in a Modern World*, (Lecture at the Institute for Public Policy Research on 7.5.96).
Soper, K. (1981) *On Human Needs*, Brighton: Harvester.
Springborg, P. (1981) *The Problem of Human Needs and the Critique of Civilisation*, London: George Allen & Unwin.
Stewart, J., Kendal, E. and Coote, A. (1994) *Citizens' Juries*, London: Institute for Public Policy Research.
Tawney, R.H. (1964) *Equality*, London: Allen & Unwin.
Taylor, C. (1992) *Multiculturalism and 'the Politics of Recognition': an essay by Charles Taylor; with commentary by Amy Gutmann (ed.) et al.*, Princeton, New Jersey: Princeton University.
Taylor-Gooby, P. and Lawson, R. (1993) *Markets and Managers: New Issues in the Delivery of Welfare*, Milton Keynes: Open University.
Terrill, R. (1974) *R.H. Tawney and his Times: Socialism as Fellowship*, London: Deutsch.

Thair, T. and Risdon, A. (1999) 'Women in the labour market: results from the spring 1998 LFS', *Labour Market Trends*, Vol. 107, No. 3, March, 103–14.
Thorne, M.J. (1990) *American Conservative Thought since World War II: the Core Ideas*, Connecticut (USA): Greenwood.
Timmins, N. (1996) *The Five Giants: a Biography of the Welfare State*, London: Fontana.
Titmuss, R.M. (1950) *The Problems of Social Policy*, London: HMSO.
Titmuss, R.M. (1968) *Commitment to Welfare*, London: Allen & Unwin.
Titmuss, R.M. (1970) *The Gift Relationship*, London: Allen & Unwin.
Touraine, A. (1981) *The Voice and the Eye: an Analysis of Social Movements*, trans. D. Macey, Cambridge: Cambridge University.
Touraine, A. (1995) *Critique of Modernity*, trans. D. Macey, Oxford: Blackwell.
Townsend, P. (1979) *Poverty in the United Kingdom: a Survey of Household Resources and Standards of Living*, Harmondsworth: Penguin Books.
Townsend, P. (1987) 'Deprivation', *Journal of Social Policy*, Vol. 16, pt. 2, 125–46.
Townsend, P. (1995) 'Persuasion and conformity: an assessment of the Borrie Report on social justice', *New Left Review*, No. 213, 137–50.
Veit-Wilson, J.H. (1986) 'Paradigms of poverty: a rehabilitation of B.S. Rowntree', *Journal of Social Policy*, Vol. 15, pt. 1, 69–99.
Vincent, A. and Plant, R. (1984) *Philosophy, Politics and Citizenship: the Life and Thought of the British Idealists*, Oxford: Blackwell.
Wainwright, H. (1994) *Arguments for a New Left; Answering the Free Market Right*, Oxford: Blackwell.
Walker, R. (1987) 'Consensual approaches to the definition of poverty: towards an alternative definition of poverty', *Journal of Social Policy*, Vol. 16, No. 2, 213–26.
Wallerstein, I. (1974) *The Modern World System*, New York: Academic.
Wallerstein, I. (1995) *After Liberalism*, New York: The New Press.
Waters, M. (1995, 1st ed) *Globalisation*, London: Routledge.
Weale, A. (1983) *Political Theory and Social Policy*, London: Macmillan.
Webb, S. (1911) *The Necessary Basis of Society*, London: Fabian Society.
Webb, S. and B. (1910) *English Law Policy*, London: Longman Green (reprinted by Cass and Co., 1963).
Webb, S. and B. (1911) *The Prevention of Destitution*, London: Longman Green.
Webb, S. (1994) 'Social Insurance and Poverty Alleviation: an empirical analysis', ch. 1 in S. Baldwin and J. Falkingham (eds) *Social Security and Social Change: New Challenges to the Beveridge Model*, Hemel Hempstead: Harvester Wheatsheaf.
Weiss, L. (1997) 'Globalisation and the myth of the powerless state', *New Left Review*, No. 225, 3–27.
Wilding, P. (1992) 'The British welfare state: Thatcher's enduring legacy', *Policy and Politics*, Vol. 20, No. 3, 201–12.
Willetts, D. (1992) *Modern Conservatism*, Harmondsworth: Penguin.
Williams, F. (1989) *Social Policy: a Critical Introduction*, Cambridge: Polity.
Williams, F. (1992) 'Somewhere over the rainbow: universality and diversity in social policy', ch. 11 in N. Manning and R. Page (eds) *Social Policy Review 4*, Canterbury: Social Policy Association.
Wilson, W.J. (1987) *The Truly Disadvantaged*, Chicago: University of Chicago.
Young, I.M. (1997) Asymmetrical reciprocity: on moral respect, wonder, and enlarged thought', *Constellations*, Vol. 3, No. 3, 340–63.

Index

abstract universalism (Chodorow), 151
  see concrete particularism
Ackerman, B., 140
active welfare state, 44
aesthetic fulfilment, 56, 127
agency, 76, 92, 94, 177–80, 182
aims of social policy, 3, 8, 61, **135–8**
alienation, 106, **110–12**, 114–5, 118, 120, 136, 180
Althusser, L. 119
altruism, 12–13, 15–16, 23, 53, **62–3**, 69, 75, 80–1, 83, 87, 93, 142, 163, 165, 174
anarchy in human nature, 75, 76, 77, 78
Anderson, D., 97
antinomies of need (Heller), 131
area deprivation, 57–9
Aristotle, 25
Armitage, B. and Scott, M., 8
Asperger's Syndrome, 128
associationalism (Hirst), 2, 162
atomistic model of human nature, 12, 17–18, 20, **21**, 22, 24, 29, 39, 69, 71–2, 88, 90–2, 97, 102, 165, 168, 170
autism, 128
autonomous, 11, 59, 100, 168
autonomy, 54, 66, **98**, 129, 131, 133, 147–8, 154, 177, 183

Bach, M., 154–5
Balbo, L., 169
Barclay, P., 6–7, 65, 172
Barry, N., 76, 79, 82, 84, 185
basic needs model of human nature, **22**, 28, 39, 42, 49, 62, 66–7, 70–1, 107, 116, 142, 165
Beck, U., 10, 61, 179
Bell, D., 70
Bell, I. *et al.*, 98, 165
benefits, 7, 31–3, 40, 47–8, 50–1, 53, 64, 81, 87, 98–9, 116, 128–9, 145, 148, 156, 170, 174, 182

disability living allowance, 128
earnings-related, 48
flat-rate, 48, 51
housing, 81, 128, 129, 182
invalidity carers allowance, 145
in-work, 50
job seekers allowance, 87
mobility, 128
national assistance, 32, 47, 50
occupational pensions, 7
pensions, 47, 98, 101, 170
Benhabib, S., 140, 150, 152, 154–5, 157–8, 160, 172, 186
Benjamin, J., 150, 152, 156, **159**
Bentham, J., 35
Benton, T., 119, **122–4**, 125–7, 129, 132–3, 136, 146, 183, 186
Bergman, B. and Klefsjo, B., 95
Bernstein, R.J., 149
Berry, C.J., 11, 13
Beveridge, W.H., 7–9, 18, 22–3, 27, 31–2, 34–6, 38, 44, 47–8, **49–54**, 60–2, 71, 99, 114, 139, 166, 169, 177, 184
  Social Insurance and Allied Services, 32, 38, 47–9, 128
  Voluntary Action, 48, 53
biologism, 185
bio-politics (Foucault), 52
birth control, 146
Blair, T. (Right Hon.), 2, 23, 27, 48, 168, 170
blood donation, 61–3, 175
Booth, C., 31–2, 114
Borrie, G., 44, 65, 70, 156, 161
Bosanquets, B. and H., 36
Boulding, K., 61
Briggs, A., 29
British empiricism, 35
British Idealists, 22, 23–5, 27, 30, 34, 36, 39–40, 71–2, 86, 185
British Social Attitudes survey, 9
Brittain, V., 145
Brown, G. (Right Hon.), 65, 172

Budapest School, 119
Butler, Judith, 141
Butler, J.R., 94,

Callender, C., 9
Capital (Marx), 105, 125
capitalism, 6, 16, 23–4, 29, 54–5, 65, 77, 79, 91, 97, 106, 110–2, 120–2, 129, 131–5, 176, 184
capitalist consumption, 132
capitalist production, 114, 116, 132
capitalist relations of production, 106, 116, 121
capitalist social relations, 115
carers, 145, 155
carers allowances, 128
Cartesian rationalism, 85
  anti-Cartesianism, 91
Chamberlayne, P., 7
charities, 71, 82, 85, 116
Charity Organization Society, 22, 36, 37, 41, 44
Checkland S.G. and E.O.A, 50
child care, 34, 35, 140, 144, 148, 152, 156, 168
child neglect, 38
Chodorow, N., 150, 151, 152, 153, 155
  on child socialization, 159
Christian Democracy, 9
citizens' basic income, 156, 162
citizens' charters, 93, 94, 95
citizenship, 7, 9, 10, 27, 35, 45, 64, 70, 139, 140, 141, 145, 146, 153, 172, 183, 185
  active citizenship, 3
Citizenship and Social Class (Marshall), 45
civil service, 145
civil society, 26, 46, 97, 170
Clarke, P., 54, 185
Clarke, J. and Newman, J., 94
class conflict, 6, 149
classic welfare state, 7, 9–10, 47–8, 64, 74, 184
classical political economists, 114
Clause IV (Labour Party), 167
collective action, 34, 42, 81, 89, 92
collective provision, 28, 32, 33, 36, 38, 64
collective welfare, 20, 22, 32, 183

collectivism, 49, 52, 53, 56
Collini, S., 185
colonization of the life world (Habermas), 91
Commission on Social Justice, 44, 70, 170, 172
commissioning and providing, 93, 128
commodities, 21, 92
commodity form, 65
common and different needs, 156
common good, 13, 21–2, 25–8, 30, 33, 35–8, 39, 42, 45–6, 53, 64, 67, 69, 71, 79, 86, 90, 101, 158, 167
common human needs, 18, 22, 24, 26, 28, 32–3, 39–40, 42, 48, 56–7, 63, 67, 69, 73, 87, 89, 92, 104, 123, 125, 139, 160, 166–9
communication, 178
communicative action (Habermas), 91–2
communism, 83, 97, 113, 115
communitarianism, 22, 48, 65, 70, 77, 97, 102, 105, 168, 171, 173, 184
communitarian liberalism (Gray), 97, 101
community, 21, 26–7, 29, 34, 35, 37–9, 42, 44–5, 51, 53, 58–9, 61–4, 68, 70–1
community care, 124, 128
community development, 58
compensation, 43, 60–1, 65, 140
competition, 13, 15–16, 74, 77–81, 83, 89, 92–3, 97, 169, 174
competitive individualism, 82, 83, 90, 93, 98
compulsory competitive tendering, 93
compulsory insurance, 35, 51
concrete other
  see generalized other
concrete particularism (Chodorow), 151
  see abstract universalism
conditional welfare, 161, 174
consensual notion of participation, 167
consensus formation, 68, 79, 100
Conservatism, 1, 6, 8, 17, 20–1, 75–6, 78, 82, 170
Conservative government, 98, 170
Conservative Party, 1, 6, 74, 80
Conservative social policy, 8, 20, 92–7
constitutional ignorance (Barry), 76, 84
constructivist rationalism (Hayek), 85
consumerism, 5, 56 74, 93

consumption, 167, 175, 176, 182
contraceptive implants, 174
contracts in welfare, 94, 170
contradictions
　in Marx's notion of human nature, 119
　in Right's notion of human nature, 94
co-operation, 5, 14–15, 18, 22, 25–7, 30–1, 40, 42, 71, 83, 91, 106, 133, 136–7, 139, 160, 169–70, 174
Co-operative Commonwealth (the Webbs), 33
co-operatives, 20, 53, 71, 166
Cornell, D., 159
costs and benefits, 86–7
council houses, sale of, 93
counterfactual reasoning, 131, 158
Court of Appeal, 182
criminality, 59, 81
Crosland, C.A.R., 18, 34, 41, 48–9, **54–7**, 72, 127
Cowen, H., 17
Culture of Contentment (Galbraith), 55
Cutler, T. and Waine, B., 94, 96
Cutler, T. *et al.*, 23, 29, 49

Dahrendorf, R. 21
day care, 128
Dean, H. and Melrose, M., 183
death grants, 49
deconstruction, 139, 141 178, 180
democracy, 29, 32, 65, 96, 100, 140, 143, 157, 161, 177, 183
demography, 52
demographic time bomb, 9
dependency, 7, 27, 160
dependency culture, 3, 59, 81
depressive illness, 141
deprivation, 56–9
deprived areas, 57–8
deregulation, 6, 74, 93
deserving and undeserving poor, 37–8
destitution, 37–8
detention colonies, 38
dialectic of human development (Marxism), 125–6
dialectic of recognition (Hegel), 141, 149
dialectical development of human nature, 149

dialogic democracy (Giddens), 177
Dickens, P., 183
difference, social, 49, 52, 56–7, 66–9, 184
difference principle (Rawls), 66–8, 70, 172
different and common needs, 69, 159
Digby, A., 47
disability, 47, 58, 119, 128, 168
disadvantaged, 57–60, 65, 67–8
discourse ethics, 68, 154
discourse, reading, 11–14
discrimination, 57, 59, 63
distribution, welfare, 66, 72, 76, 158
distributive consensus (Plant), 171
distributive justice, 44, 99, 112, 114, 140, 153, 186
diswelfares (Titmuss), 61, 65
diverse human nature, 15–17, 27, 40, 76, 79, 81, 98, 183
diverse needs, 29, 34, 42, 56, 72, 75
diversity of life-choices, 178
diversity, concept of, 56
divine order, 76, 78
division of labour, 8–9, 83
domestic division of labour, 8
domestic relations, 7, 176
domiciliary provisions, 128
double hermeneutics (Giddens), 180
Doyal, L. and Gough, I., 2, 65, 70, 72, 84, 100, 123–4, 146, 172, 183, 186
　dual strategy, 183
Doyal, L. and Harris, R., 109
Dryzek, J.S., 13, 163
dual labour market, 6
dualist account of human nature, 121, 122, 124
dualistic interpretations, 119
Dunleavy, P., 95
duties, 26–7, 34, 40, 42, 62–4, 168, 173
duties and rights, 168
Dwyer, P., 10, 168
Dyson, K.H.E., 185

ecology, 164, 165, 183
ecological limits, 164
Economic and Philosophical Manuscripts (Marx), 105, 110, 122, 125, 126

economic cycles, 48, 52
  exchange, 60, 64–5, 115–6
  freedom, 76, 83, 89
  prosperity, 54
  rationality, 64
  recession, 61
  reductionism, 88–9
  risks, 52
economy, 23, 29, 43–4, 46, 140
education, 1, 3, 6–7, 24, 33–5, 38, 44, 47, 54, 58, 69, 74, 94, 96, 106, 128, 140, 144–5, 148, 156, 168, 170
Education Action Zones, 170
egalitarianism, 70, 72
elderly, 145
Elliott, L. and Hutton, W., 185
empirical differences, 42
  generalizations, 16
  needs, 39
employment, 3–9, 51–2, 54, 147, 167–8
employment exchanges, 38
employment protection for women, 147
empowerment, 43, 95, 182
enabling government, 168–9
enabling welfare state, 99
Engels, F., 149
Enlightenment, 4, 10, 98, 102, 139, 143, 150, 178, 184
  anti–Enlightenment, 101
enterprise, 3, 53, 74, 93, 96, 184
environment, 39–41, 43–4, 58, 61, 124, 143
epistemic individualism, 14–15, 76, 83–4, 88, 90, 92
epistemic object, 76
epistemological break in Marx (Althusser), 119
epistemology, 12, 14–15, 84
equal distribution of liberties, 65
equal opportunities, 145, 156
equal pay, 8, 145, 147
equalitarian feminism, 146
equalitarianism, 26, 42–3, 49, 51, 56, 59, 65, 67, 72, 145, 172
Equality (Tawney), 166
  of achievement, 57
  of consideration, 40, 41, 42, 172
  of endowments, 57
  of opportunity, 43, 57, 58, 66
  of outcome, 58–9
  of respect, 41, 172
equality, 23, 25–7, 39–42, 44–6, 49, 52, 54–5, 57–9, 65–6, 139–40, 143–4, 146–7, 152–3, 160, 173
equity, 51, 57, 153, 173
Esping-Andersen, G., 9, 176
ethical code, 84
ethical naturalism (Berry), 13
Ethical or Christian Socialism, 23, 30, 39, 41, 45, 60
ethics of care, 153
  of justice, 152–3, 157
  of mutuality, 64, 159
  of altruism, 63
  of justice and care as dialogue, 153–7, 159
ethnic minorities, 58–9
Etzioni, A., 22, 48
European Court, 145
evolutionism, 18, 185
Excerpts from James Mill's 'Elements of Political Economy' (Marx), 105, 115
exchange (Titmuss),
  bilateral, 60, 116
  unilateral, 61, 63, 116
expert knowledge, 91
exploitation, 106, 111–12, 114, 118, 120, 149
exploitation of nature, 122
extension ladder (the Webbs), 34, 71, 90, 166
externalities, 60
extra-proportionality, 43–4

Fabians, 23, 30, 34–5, 40–1, 57, 145
factual generalizations, 13, 76, 79
factual propositions, 75, 142
Falkingham, J. and Hills, J., 52
fallacy of conceptual realism (Gray), 85
fallibility, 77–9, 83–4
familialist assumptions, 8
families, 21, 29, 37, 38, 170, 175
family allowances, 47
family life, 3, 8, 29, 37, 56, 99, 122, 149, 176
Far East, 6
fellowship, 23, 25, 30, 39–40, 60, 165

feminism, 5, 18, 48, 65, 72, 104, 119, 139, 140, 145, 146, 149, 186
  first and second waves in, 147
  feminist critique of universal welfare, 161
  feminist critiques 7–9, 141, 145, 158
    of ideology, 7
    of politics, 141, 144, 147
    of social policy, 144, 152
    of theories of human nature, 139, 172
    of thought, 2
Field, F., 3, 21, 23, 39, 161, 164–5, 171
Finch, J. and Groves, D., 8
Firestone, S., 141
Fisher, B. and Tronto, J.C., 157
flexible labour, 6, 8, 9
forces of production, 106, 111, 120–1, 179
formation of moral identity, 152
formula-funding for schools, 7
Foucault, M., 52
founders of the US Constitution, 79
Fraser, N., 158
free labour time, 132
Freeden, M., 21, 31, 185
freedom, 4, 23, 36, 44, 50, 53–6, 66, 76–9, 84, 87, 90, 96, 98, 120, 132–3, 142–4, 148, 156, 172, 179
free-market, 10, 23, 27, 60, 83, 87, 89–90, 94, 101
Freud, S., 121, 150
Friedman, M., 14, 15, 75, 92
Friedman, M. and R., 15, 75, 80, 86, 96
Friendly Societies, 20, 30, 50, 53, 160
full human nature, 166, 183
  see many-sided human nature
fundamentalist notion of gender, 139, 141

Galbraith, J.K., 55
Gamble, A., 17, 82, 86, 89, 92
gender, 7–9, 16, 18, 52, 57–8, 119, 141, 143–6, 150–2, 155–6
  and ethnic identities, 16
  differences, 146, 147, 149–50, 152–3
  identity, 140–2, **150–2**
  identity in children, 150
  in human nature, 141, 151, 156
general practitioners, 24
  fundholders, 94, 96, 185

General Synod, 144
generalized other, 154, 157
George, V. and Miller, S., 164
Geras, N., 110–11, 119, 121, 125–9, 131–4, 136, 138
gestalt, 12
Giddens, A., 10–11, 61, 165, **176–81**, 186
gift and gift relationship (Titmuss), 60–4, 114, 116, 175
Gilligan, C., 150, **152–6**
Gladstone, D., 166
Glendenning, C., 145–6
Glennerster, H., 7, 10, 47, 49
globalization, **6–7**, 48, 130, 165, 166, 176, 179
Gooden, R.E., 163–4
Gough, I., 122
government, 23, 31, 53–5, 67, 73, 76–7, 87, 90, 93–4, 96–7, 98, 101–2, 160, 182
Gray, J., 2, 4, 6, 71, 77, 82–3, 85–6, 91, 95, **97–102**, 161, 164, 185
green theory, 18
Green, A.E., 7
Green, D.G., 2, 77, 80, 82, 86, 97, 165
Green, T.H., **24–8**, 30, 34–5, 40, 53, 60, 71, 149, 167, 168, 185
Grundrisse (Marx), 105, 110, 121

Habermas, J., 91, 140, 150
Hadley, R. and Hatch, S., 48
Hakim, C., 8
Hall, S., 80, 82
Halsey, A.H., 48, 58–9
Harris, D., 54
Hayek, F.A., 14–7, 21, 44, 60, 74–9, 81, 82–92, 95–9, 101–2, 164, 169, 176, 185
  theory of knowledge, 12, **14–15**, 76, **85–6**
health, 1, 3, 6–7, 32–5, 38, 47, 57, 62, 69, 74, 86, 89, 90, 93–4, 96, 101, 114, 124, 126, 140, 145, 170, 171
health and safety, 145
health authorities, 36, 93
health needs of men and women, 141
Heelas, P. and Morris, P., 3
Hegel, G.W.F., 11, 18, 22, 115, 136, 149–50, 159, 161, 180, 186

Hegelianism, 149, 158, 180
  master and slave relationship, 149
  see dialectic of recognition
  hegemonic discourse, 186
Heller, A., 119, 126, 129–2, **133–4**
Hewitt, M., 119, 159, 176, 179
Hewitt, M. and Powell, M., 184
hidden hand of the market (Adam Smith), 69, 79, 174
High Court, 182
Hirst, P., 23, 162, 171
Hirst, P. and Thompson, G., 185
historical materialism (Marx), 105–6, 118–9, 129, 135
history, 105–6, 108–10, 116, 119, 122, 125–7, 130–1, 133–4
holistic conception of human nature, 85, 119, 131
Hollis, M., 2
hollowed out human subject, 179
hollowed out notions of need, 96
Holman, B., 23, 64, 161, 165, 170
Holtby, W., 145
Honderich, T., 82
Honneth, A., 137, 138, 149, 161
Honneth, A. and Joas, H., 129, **137–8**, 161
housing, 3, 10, 31, 57, 96, 109, 124, 128, 145, 182
housing benefit, 81, 128, 129, 182
human abilities and attributes, 11, 31, 57, 59, 67–9
human character, 2, 27, 32, 34, 38, 41, 57, 62, 67, 71, 115, 125,
human diversity, 40, 82, 87, 108, 122, 125–6, 133, 156
human fallibility, 77–9, 83
human mode of existence, 165
human motivation, 4, 12–3, 32, 55, 163, 165, 181
human nature, accounts of, 7, 9–10, **11–17**, 21, 93, 105–7, 115–25, 136–8, 139, 143, 149, 163, 165–6, 171, 176, 181
  bounded or limited, 17, 31, 75, 78, 84, 164, 167, 186
  darker side of, 39
  diverse, 101
  first-order propositions about, 16
  holistic, 85, 119, 131

Index 201

  ideologies of, 119
  social policy and, 4–5, 48, 72, 139, 164
  unbounded, 15–16, 75, 79, 81–4, 87, 92–3, 96, 108, 164, 169
human resources management, 93–5
human species, 107, 109, 115, 123, 134–5, 137
human subject, 3, 10, 12, 53, 93, 109, 166, 176, 178, 180, 182
  biological and psychological, 76
human/animal continuism, 186
humanized capitalism (Crosland), 54, 127
humanizing nature (Marx), 119, **122–4**
Hume, D., 35
Humm, M., 145, 147
Hutton, W., 23, 58
  '30:30:40 society', 58

ideal types, 46
identity, 21, 61–2, 117, 152, 154, 161, 177–8
  see gender identity
ideologies, 1, 8, 9, 12, 16, 24, 47, 82, 87, 101–2, 106, 136, 143–5, 163–4, 176
  of social policy, 18, 29
  see feminist critiques of
immanent notions of human nature, 104, 106–7, 121, 141, 158, 175, 181
immanent notion of universalism, 11, 104, 106–7, 118, 121, **149–55**, 158, 159–60, 181, 183
  see transcendent notion
income support, 87, 128
  carers' allowance, 145
individualism, 51, 53, 59–60, 74, 76, 81–2, 88, 90–1
industrial assurance (Beveridge), 49–50
industrialization, 10, 22, 39, 61, 180
inequalities, 6–8, 27, 39–41, 48, 55, 57–60, 66–7, 70, 97, 143, 158, 172, 184
Inquiry into Income and Wealth (Barclay) 172
Institute of Economic Affairs, 60
institutional design for welfare, 182
instrumental mode of rationality, 60–1, 91, 175
interactive universalism (Benhabib), 154–5

intermediate needs (Doyal and Gough), 123–4
internal markets, 7, 90, 93, 96
  see quasi-markets
International Standard Quality Vocabulary, 95
intersubjectivity, 68, 72, 149, 158
investment, 43–5, 52
investor's strategy (Borrie), 44
Irigaray, L., 144

Jaggar, A., 142, 144, 146, 149
Jessop, B., 179
Jordan, B., 6
Joseph, K., 78, 80
Joseph, K. and Sumption, J., 44
justice, 171
justice as fairness (Rawls), 65–7, 70

Kant, I., 85–6
Keat, R. and Abercrombie, N., 3
Keynes, J.M., 23
Keynesian demand management, 48, 52
King, D., 82
Klein, R., 93
Kojeve, A., 149

labour, 6–9, 11, 18, 21–2, 28, 43, 53, 83, 106, 108–10, 112, 114–6, 120, 127, 129, 130–2, 136–8, 147, 149, 156, 161
labour market, 6–9, 21, 48, 50, 97, 147, 176
labour process, 131, 132
labour relations, 6
Labour governments, 9, 10, 47, 50, 54, 65, 87
Labour Party, 1–2, 8–10, 23–4, 30, 49, 136, 164–5, 167, 170, 184
Laclau, E. and Mouffe, C., 186
language, 178
Lash, S. and Wynne, B., 180
late-modernity, 10, 64, **176–81**
  see postmodernity
Lawson, R. and Taylor-Gooby, P., 95
Le Grand, J., 2, 10, 163–5
Le Grand, J. and Bartlett, W., 93
leagues tables, 94
Lectures on the Principles of Political Obligation (T.H. Green), 25

Left, 2–3, 10, 44, 59, 82, 86, 90, 98
Leonard, D., 56
less eligibility, 50
leveller's strategy (Borrie), 44
Levinas, E., 157
Levitas, R., 23, 82, 172
Lewis, J., and Davies, C., 147
Liberal government 1906–14, 31
liberal collectivism (Cutler *et al.*), 23–4, 30–1, 39, 49
liberal communitarianism, **97**, 105
liberal feminism, 141–7
liberal individualism, 66, 96
liberal principles, 49, 82, 179
liberal theorists, 140, 179, 186
liberalism, 23–4, 86, 98, 146, 163
Liberals, 6, 20–3, 35, 60, 86, 89, 143–4, 148
  market liberals, 86, 92, 97
Lichtheim, G., 185
life cycle, 52, 156
life-long learning, 156
Lilley, P., 83
limitations of human nature, 17, 31, 75, 78, 84, 164, 167, 186
Lister, R., 139, 145–6, 168, 185–6
local authorities, 7, 93, 94
logic of social action, 11–2
lone mothers, 9, 58, 81, 98, 145
lone parents, 57–9, 168
lone-parent families, 48
Lonsdale, S., 8
Losing Ground (Murray), 98
low pay, 8, 50
Lowe, R., 29
Lowndes, B., 128

Mack, J. and Lansley, S., 138
Macpherson, C.B., 35
mainstream social policy, 20, 72, 105
Majority Report, *Royal Commission on the Poor Laws* (1909), 36
managerial state (Clarke and Newman), 94
managerialism, 6, 94, 96, 179, 184
manufactured risks, 10–11, 178, 180;
  see risks
  uncertainties, 10
many-sided human nature (Marx), 113, 126, 132, 134, 161, 181–2

markets, 1, 13–15, 17, 51, 61, 77, 87, 96, 102
market exchange, 39, 74, 91, 169, 174, 177
  freedoms, 10, 97, 101
  liberalism, 86, 92, 97
  order, 79, 88
  provision
  see mixed economy of welfare
Markus, G., 111, 119, 129–31, 133, 137–8
Marshall, T.H., 27, 34, 35, 41, 48, 72, 172, 185
  theory of citizenship, 45
Marsland, D., 77, 98
Marx, K., 11, 18, **Ch. 5**, 118–23, 125–9, 131–8, 149–50, 161, 165, 175, 180–2, 185, 186
  cognitive and normative discourses (Soper), 119–20, 131
  early works, 18, 92, 105, 108, 119
  notion of human needs, 119
  theory of human nature, 100, 105, 107, 120–1, 125, 129, 134–5, 176
Marx, K. and Engels, F., 108, 123, 126–7, 160
Marxism, 2, 5, 18, 24, 48, 65, 72, 104, 107, 111, 114, **Ch. 7**, 139, 141, 147–9, 159, 180–1, 183
Marxist ethics, 125
Marxist theory of human nature, Ch. 7
Maslow, A., 84, 124, 181
  conception of need, 127
  hierarchy of need, 124, 181, 183
materialist naturalism (Markus), 129
means of production, 106, 110–11, 114–15, 118, 127
  production, 175, 176
means-testing, 7, 21, 24, 32, 47, 50, 59, 72, 86, 87, 89, 98, 102, 114, 128, 145, 158, 161, 170
medical technologies, 48
meta-accounts of human nature (also theories), 17, 42, 54, 68, 71, 72, 74, 83, 90, 93, 113, 114, 134, 169
  see secondary accounts of human nature
metaphors of need in Marx, 113
metaphysical accounts of human nature, 12, 14–15, 29, 31, 143

meta-theoretical discourse, 29
Miliband, D., 30
Mill, J.S., 143
Millar, J. and Glendenning, C., 139
minima
minimum, 20–2, 24–5, 27–33, 44, 47, 50–1, 56–7, 67, 72, 89
minimum needs, 20, 21, 34, 45, 49, 59, 87, 166, 167
minimum needs model, 20
minimum welfare, 181
Minority Report, *Royal Commission on the Poor Laws* (1909), 32
Mishra, R., 5, 164
mixed economy of welfare (voluntary, private and informal sectors), 8–9, 34, 48, 55, 90, 148, 169
mode of life, 106–9, 123–5, 127–30, 132–4, 136, 138, 141, 157, 181–2
mode of production, 106, 108, 111–13, 117–18, 123, 126–7, 134–6, 141
models of human nature, **11–12**, 20, 29, 64, 71, 82, 91, 97, 104, 107, 134, 139, 165, 166, 171
modernity, 31, 101, 150
moral culture, 15, 77
moral duties, 26–7, 34, 41
moral ends, 25, 26, 27, 37, 52–3, 54, 77
moral factor (the Webbs), 37
moral imperative of need (Heller), 132
moral neutrality of market (Hayek), 77–8
moral order, **13–15**, 17, 37, 54, 56, 65, 76–8, 88, 143
moral personality, 25, 167
moral purpose of welfare, 3, 26, 60–3, 65
moral qualities of human nature, 25–7, 36, **39–42** (Tawney), 61–3, 84, 86, 122, **152–4** (Gilligan), 179
morality, 37, 52–4, 56, 77, 78, 88, 89, 101, 122, 153
morbidity, 48, 52
mortality, 52
motivation, 3–4, 12, 13, 15, 31–3, 35, 55, 62, 64, 67, 75, 78, 80–3, 90–3, 96, 98, 102, 107–8, 163–5, 170, 174, 181
  see propositions, motivational
Mulhall, S. and Swift, A., 70

multi-national corporations, 6
Murray, C., 3, 81, 98, 102, 185
mutual exchange, 63, 174
mutual aid organizations, 20, 30, 42, 53, 64, 71, 82, 160–1, 166, 174, 182
  see friendly societies, self-help, co-operatives
mutual circles, 174
mutual insurance, 20, 48, 50, 53
mutual needs, 28, 46, 66, 67, 72, 73, 74, 107, 114, 115–17, 139, 166, 184
mutual recognition and understanding, 18, 53, 66, 67, 130, 155, 158–61
mutual welfare, 18, 28, 42, 46, 64, 160, 170, 174
mutualism, 5, 16–18, 20, 22, 23, 24–5, 28, 30, 39–40, 45, 48, 64, 69, 71–2, 77, 79, 91, 101, 104, 115, 116, 117, 134, 136, 139, 142, 148, 149, 154, 158, 161, 164–6, 170–1, 173–7, 180–1, 184
mutualism and exclusion, 160
mutualist model of human nature, 22–3, 48–9, 60, 62, 149

narratives, 12, 154, 157
National Audit Commission, 94
National Autistic Society, 128
National Health Service, 7, 33, 62, 63, 73, 94
  White Paper (1944), 35
national insurance, 7, 24, 28, 32–3, 38, 47, **50–4**, 90, 98, 145
  actuarial principles of, 51, 52
  compulsory insurance, 35, 51
  contributions, 7, 28, 34
national minimum, 20, 22, 24, 27–8, 29, 30, 31, 32–4, 35, 36, 38, 39, 42, 43, 46, 47–8, 50, 52, 54, 57, 64, 71, 87–8, 89–90, 96, 100, 102, 104, 114, 128, 146, 148, 161, 166–7, 169, 184
national minimum wage, 50
natural abilities, 40, 75
natural differences, 7, 143, 144
natural limits to human fulfilment, 121, 126, 155
naturalistic propositions, 31, 107, 108, 122, 133
naturalistic view of women, 8–9
naturalizing humanity (Marx), 119

nature, 105, **107–10**, 119, 121, 122–3, 129, 130, 133, 136, 137, 149
needs, 13, 44, 47, 48–9, 53, 60, 61, 63, 65, 67, 72, 95, 118, 123–9, 131–3, 135–8, 140–1, 145, 156, 160–1, 164–7, 169, 171, 175, 181 184
  thick and thin theories of needs, 68
  need as a category of value, 132
  needs assessments (local authority), 156, 158
  needs, aesthetic and cognitive, 123
  needs, higher, 18, 119, 121, 123–4, 126–9, 132–4, 138–9, 147–9, 157, 175, 181–3
  incommensurability of needs (Gray), 99
  limit concept of need, 126, 134
  need-satisfaction, 115, 116, 121, 123, 124, 125, 127–33, 135–8, 147
  need-satisfiers (Doyal and Gough), 70
negative income tax, 86
neo-liberalism, 1, 20, 66, 74, 78–9, 83–4, 98, 142, 166, 168, 176
neo-liberal economists, 60
New Deal, 9
New Labour, 1–2, 10, 23–4, 30, 41, 49, 56, 65, 71, 102, 167, 168, 173, 184, 186
New Liberals, 21–3, 25, 30, 35, 86, 89, 185
new political consensus, 9, 162, 179
new welfare state, 9
Noble, M. and Smith, G., 7
Nolan, P. and Walsh, J., 6
normative discourse in Marx (Soper), 120–1
normative propositions, 3, 13, 16, 17, 33, 37, 76, 80, 142, 163
normative standard of human nature, 119, 126, 129, 183
Novak, M., 77–9
Novak, M. and Preston, R., 79
Nozick, R., 185
nursery voucher scheme, 86

objectification (Marx), 109, 115, 121, 131
object-relations psychoanalysis, 149
O'Brien, M., 186
oedipus complex, resolution of, 150
one nation Toryism, 80

ontological individualism, 15;
  see epistemic individualism
ontology, 12, 14, 15, 41, 122, 129, 131, 140, 186
  anti-ontological reading, 119
Oppenheim, C., 186
Oppenheim, C. and Harker, L., 6
opted-out schools, 7
ordination of women to the Anglican priesthood, 144
organic, 17, 20, 21, 22, 24, 27, 28, 30, 39, 45, 62, 71, 82, 105, 107, 113, 136, 164, 165, 167, 168, 170, 173
  organic model of human nature, 17, 20, **21–2**, 24, 28, 30, 39, 62, 71, 144, 167, 173
  organic society, 27–8, 39, 45–6, 71, 82, 167–8, 170
original position (Rawls), 59, 66–8, 143
original sin, 37–8, 40, 77–8
otherness, 130, 150, 156, 159
out-of-wedlock births, 59
overlapping consensus (Rawls), 70
owners of the means of production, 27, 38, 106, 111, 114, 118

Page, R., 63, 164
paradox of equality, 58
parenting, 156
passive welfare state, 44
passive welfare subjects, 161
Pateman, C., 140, 146
paternalism, 36
patriarchy, 9, 139, 140–1, 143–4, 146, 150, 152, 176
pensioners, 7, 48
permeation (Fabian strategy), 145
perverse incentives, 81, 93
phenomenology, 180
philanthropy, 53, 83
philosophical anthropology in Marx, 120, 129
Plant, R., 2, 22, 25, 26, 27, 54, 65, 164, 171, 172, 185
plasticity in human nature, 166, 176–8, 181
politics of difference, 18, 119, 140–1, Ch. 7, **155–7**, 171
politics of recognition, 138, 159
politics of welfare, 164

pooling of risks, 51
poor, 7, 31, 32, 37–39, 44, 57, 59, 60, 73, 87, 89, 97, 98, 124, 169, 176, 184
  deserving and undeserving, 37–8
  corrigible and incorrigible poor, 38
Poor Law, 21, 38, 50, 87, 102, 114
  Commissioners (1834), 38, 50
  Commissioners (1909), 32, 36
  Royal Commission on the Poor Laws (1909), 32
population, 3, 4, 34, 41, 48, 52, 58, 59, 184
Portillo, M., 98
positive discrimination, 57–60, 65, 72
post-Enlightenment, 4, 98
postmodernism, 4, 11, 56, 176, 178, 179, 180, 186
postmodern critique of universal reason, 159
post-Thatcher era, 97
post-traditional society (Giddens), 10–11, 165, 176, 179
postwar consensus, 9, 24, 90
postwar Fabians, 31
postwar welfare state, 10, 60, 165
poverty, 4, 6–7, 11, 31, 39, 48, 54, 55, 56, 59, 64, 72, 90, 97, 114, 138, 157
Powell, M. and Hewitt, M., 186
Powell, M., 186
practical reasoning, 21, **85–6**, 91
  see pure reasoning
pragmatism, 4, 97, 98, 164, 165, 179
pragmatism in social policy, 5, 122
praxeology (Von Mises), 185
praxis, 5, 11, 16, 48, 90–2, 106–7, 108–9, 112, 113, 118, 121, 129, 130, 134, **136–8**, 142, 149, 160, 161, 165, 180, 181
pregnancy, 51
preschool provision, 152
prescription charges, 47
primary and secondary accounts, theories, propositions of human nature, 14, 16–17, 21, 29, 31, 75, 80, 82, 93, 102
Primary Care Groups, 170, 185
primary goods (Rawls), 30, 66, 67, 68, 69, 171
principles of justice, 29

principles to social policy, 65
private and occupational pension schemes, 48
private and state insurance provision, 50
Private Finance Initiatives, 170
private insurance, 50–2, 71
private property, 27, 113, 115
private provision, 32, 48, 55, 166, 170
 see mixed economy of welfare
privatization, 6, 74, 93, 98
production, 175, 176
professions in welfare, 45, 64, 145, 156–7, 158, 166
Prolegomena to Ethics (T.H. Green), 25, 26
proletariat as universal class (Marx), 150
propositions on human nature, 4, **11–7**, 14, 15, 29, 39, 108, 136
 factual, 75, 76, 107–8, 142
 motivational, 4, 75, 107–8, 142
 normative, 16, 17, 25, 35, 75, 76, 80, 107, 110, 120, 135, 142, 163
Pruger, R., 61
psychoanalytic feminism, 139
psychoanalytic theories of human nature, 18, 186
public and private spheres, 42, 139, 144, 145
 see mixed economy of welfare
public authorities, 32, 36, 37
public choice theory, 80, 95
public culture (Gray), 2, 77, 98, 100–2
public revenue, 43
public sector, 24, 30, 32, 34–5, 38, 42, 50, 52, 55, 90, 92–6, 102, 114, 128, 145, 158, 170–1, 172
public-choice theory, 80, 94, **95**
Pugh, M., 185
pure reasoning, 85–6
 see practical reasoning
purpose of social policy, 44, 47, 60–1, 63–4, 65
 see aims of social policy; social policy and human nature

quality assurance, 93
 see total quality management
quality of life, 124, 157
quasi-markets, 94, 102, 158, 168, 170
quid pro quo exchange, 60, 63

race, 18, 57, 58, 98, 119, 155, 156, 173
radical feminism, 139, 141
radical needs, 107, 131
 see truly human needs
rapprochement between basic and mutual needs, 64, 117, **159–62**
rational choice, 76, 81, 93
rational faculties, 142, 143
rationalism, 70, 80
 anti-rationalism, 78
Rawls, J., 18, 29, 49, 59, **65–71**, 72, 140, 156, 163, 167, 171–2, 186
Rawls' theory of justice, 65–71
Rawls' approach to human nature, 65–71
Raz, J., 99
reading human nature, 11–17
Reagan, R. 23
reciprocity, 5, 22, 25, 26, 30, 44, 45, 51, 62–5, 71, 92, 116, 139, 149, 158, 171, 174–5, 184
recognition, 11,18, 25, 26, 48, 53, 104, 116–7, 130, 140, 149, 150, 152, 154, **155–8, 159–62**, 165, 184
reconstructed welfare state, 9
rediscovery of poverty, 56
redistribution, policies for, 140
reflexive modernization (Giddens), 176
reflexivity, 11, 16, 161, 177–80, 186
regulative ideals (Benhabib), 154, 158
relations of production, 106, 108, 111, 112, 113, 125, 127
relativism, 70, 98, 102
reproduction of labour power, 118
reproduction of mothering (Chodorow), 151
Republican approach to citizenship, 185
residual welfare minimum, 80, 88, 89, 100, 161, 169
residual needs, 9, 73, 89, 169
residual view of human need, 21, 22, 47, 59
respite care, 145
retirement, 9, 51, 52
reversibility of perspectives and roles, 154, 155, 186
the Right (New Right, Radical Right), 1–2, 3, 5, 9, 10, 12, 13, 20–1, 24, 44, 56, 59, 72, **Ch. 4**, 104, 105, 142, 163, 164, 165, 169, 176, 184, 185

Index 207

the Right's account of human nature, 12–13, 14–17, 20–1, Ch. 4, **75–79**,
right relationships (Tawney), 40
rights, 7, 9, 10, 25, 26, 27, 29, 30, 34, 35, 45, 49, 62, 63, 64, 70, 71, 86, 96, 99, 139, 140, 143, 145, 150, 153, 161, 167, 172, 173, 182, 184
rights of women, 143, 145
risk, 11, 14, 51–2, 60, 61, 78, 177, 179, 180
Robson, W.A., 65
robust approach to human motivation (Le Grand), 163–4
rogue propositions, 16, 80
role reversibility, 152, 153
Rose, N., 40
Rousseau, J.J., 37, 59
Rowntree, S., 31, 114, 185
rule of law, 13, 14, 15, 17, 76–7, 78, 84, 88, 89, 96, 143, 153, 172
Runciman, W.G., 65

sacredness, 25, 79
Sandel, M., 68
satiable needs (Gray), 98, 99–100, 101, 102
schooling, 52, 57, 86, 152
science, 83, 85, 91, 99, 106, 110, 130, 133, 144, 179
scientific administration, 38
scientific Marxism, 119
scientific method, 85
scientific rationality, 159
Scott, J. *et al.*, 9
secondary account of human nature *see* primary accounts
selective welfare, 22, 47, 57, 59, 65, 100, 158
see universal welfare
self and other, 62
self-help, 30, 33, 45, 48, 71
self-interest, 2, 10, 12–16, 21, 23, 52, 55, 56, 75, 76, 79–83, 87, 91, 92, 93, 95–8, 101, 102, 115, 142, 163, 165, 168, 169, 174
self-reflexivity (Giddens), 11, 179
sexuality, 119
sickness, 47, 51, 52
Smith, Adam, 12, 91, 114
Smith, (Hon.) C., 41

social administration, 31–2
social capital, 43
social class, 16, 45, 106, 114
social conscience, 53
social construction (Butler), 178
Social Democracy, 1, 5, 6, 8, 9–10, 13, 18, 20, 21–22, 23–4, 25, 27–8, **Ch. 2** (pre-war Social Democracy), **Ch. 3** (postwar Social Democracy), 86–9, 90, 96, 102, 104, 105, 107, 112, 113–16, 126–7, 128, 134, 135, 136, 138, 139, 142–9, 158, 163–8, 169–71, 172–3, 176–77, 182, 184,
Social Democratic account of human nature, 23, 25, **31–40**, 49, 51, 72
Social Democratic compact, 74
social democratic feminism, 141, **142–9**
Social Democratic social policy, 56, 141, 148
Social Democratic thinkers, 8, Ch. 2, **Ch. 3**, 185
social difference, 18, 28, 40, 49, 155, 161
social diversity, 41, 54, 183
social engineering, 55
social exclusion, 11, 35, 39, 139, 143, 160, 182
social inclusion, 33, 63, 140
social insurance, 7, 49, 51–3, 90
Social Insurance and Allied Services (Beveridge), 49
social justice, 86, 99, 140, 171–3, 183, 184
social market, 97
social movements, 16, 104, 119, 140
social organizations, 61
social partners of social insurance, 53
social policy
feminist, 8, 9, **Ch. 7**, 139, 141, 142, 144, 149, 150, 152, 155–6, 158, 160
human nature and, 2–5, 11, 17–18, 20–1, 24, 48–9, 62–3, 72, 87, 93, 104, 135, 136, 138, 139, 163–4, 165–6, 170–1, 183, 192
Marx and Marxist, 104, 105, 107, 113, 116, 118, 119, 121, 122, 124, 127, 128–9, 133, 136–8
New Labour, 10, 23, 24, 30, 41, 49, 65, 168, 170, 173, 186

social policy – *continued*
  new thinking on, 170, 171, 183
  purpose of, 44, 47, 60–1, 64, 65
  the Right and, 74, 81, 90, 97, 98
  Social Democratic, 17, 28–9, 30, 32, 35, 44, 45, 56–7, 63, 70, 114, 128, 141, 148, 161, 175
social policy ideologies, 1, 2, 8, 29, 47, 163–4
social provision, 5, 32, 45, 50, 102, 124, 146, 150, 170, 156
Social Reconstruction (the Webbs), 37
social security, 1, 3, 7, 27, 43, 47, 48, 54, 67
social services, 40, 41, 42, 43, 45, 54, 55, 57, 94
social structure, 4, 39, 152
social theory, 16, 105
social wage, 43
social workers, 24, 67, 93, 96, 156
socialism, 2, 23–4, 54–5, 57, 78, 84, 106, 129, 168
  critique of, 78
  ethical (Christian), 23, 30, 39, 41, 45, 60, 167
  Fabian, 23, 30
  feminist, 139, 141–2
solidarity, 11, 22, 42, 53, 61, 62, 63, 80, 95, 171, 184
Soper, K., 119, 120–2, 125, 126, 129, 134–5, 183
special needs provision, 128
species, 123, 124, 141
species character (Honneth and Joas), 129
spiritual needs, 15, 25, 113, 131, 132
spoiled identities (Titmuss), 61
spontaneous order (Hayek), 85, 86
Springborg, P., 126, 134
standards of human fulfilment (of living, need-satisfaction, welfare), 29, 33, 34, 51, 55, 67, 94, 99, 106–7, 111–12, 116, 118, 119, 120, 121–2, 124, 125–7, 129, 132, 134–5, 138, 158, 162, 183
state, 4, 6, 8, 10, 23, 26–7, 29, 31, 33–6, 38–40, 44–6, 48–54, 61, 63–4, 73–5, 80, 83, 87, 98, 90, 94, 100–1, 128, 142, 145, 148, 159, 161, 167–8, 170–2, 174, 176, 179, 181, 183, 185
  and private and voluntary sectors, *see* mixed economy of welfare; hegemony, 73, 186
state of nature, 75
Stewart, J. *et al.*, 138
stigma, 14, 59, 61, 63, 81, 158
stranger and stranger relations (Titmuss), 175, 158
strategy of equality (Tawney), 40, 43
structures, economic and social, 145
struggle, 104, 106, 111, 115, 118, 127, 129, 131, 136, 141, 149, 154
struggle for recognition, 18, 65, 104, 115, 136, 149, 161, 162
submission to nature, 11
subsistence, 22, 31, 34, 50, 89, 90, 99, 169
supported living, 128, 133, 182
Supporting People (DSS), 182
surplus value, 114, 116, 131
suture (Laclau and Mouffe), 166, 169, 186
sweated workshops, 38
Swedish Social Democracy, 167
Swedish social policy, 148
symbolic forms of value, 63
symmetrical reciprocity (Young), 186
synoptic delusion, 85, 89, 92

tacit knowledge (Hayek), 17, 85–6, 91–2
Tawney, 17, 21, 22, 30, 33–4, 39, 40–6, 48, 54, 55, 57, 58, 60, 101, 146, 166, 172, 173
taxation, 28, 34, 42, 43, 64, 69, 86
Taylor, C., 160
Taylor-Gooby, P. and Lawson, R., 10
teachers, 43, 145
technology, 10, 17, 48, 54–5, 60, 84, 100, 106, 110, 121, 124, 130, 133, 148, 156, 179
teleology, 111, 120, 135
Terrill, R., 40, 41, 44, 173
Thair, T. and Risdon, A., 8
Thatcher, M., 23
Thatcherism, 2, 82, 97
The German Ideology (Marx and Engels), 105, 108, 126
The Gift Relationship (Titmuss), 62, 64
The Phenomenology of Spirit (Hegel), 115
The Road to Serfdom (Hayek), 75

theology, 25, 37, 77–8, 84
theoretical reconstruction, 16
Theory of Communicative Action (Habermas), 91
A Theory of Justice (Rawls), 65, 156
Third Way, 27, 53, 168, 184
Thorne, M.J., 75
Timmins, N., 47, 98
Titmuss, R.M., 8, 18, 21, 22, 34, 39, 41, 45, 48–9, 55, **60–5**, 70, 88, 114, 115–16, 149, 158, 175
Tories, 1, 80, 82, 93, 98, 167, 170
Tory governments, 43, 86, 94, 184
Tory social policy, 3, 97
total quality management, 93
Touraine, A., 179, 180
Townsend, P., 31, 48, 59, 124, 167
trade unions, 6, 20
training, 3, 38, 128, 168, 174
transcendent beliefs, 79, 179
transcendent notions of universalism, 107, 149–50, 153–4, 158, 159, 160
  see immanent notions
transhistorical accounts of human nature, 111, 118, 119, 121, 129
trickle down thesis, 44
truly human needs (Marx), 107, 115, 118–19, 120, 128, 131, 135, 161, 165, 175

underclass, 3, 81
unemployment, 32, 38, 47, 48, 51, 57, 59, 98, 168
universal human nature and needs, 9–10, 11, 22, 25–6, 29, 32, 34, 39, 47, 49, 52, 56, 60, 63, 65, 68, 70, 72, 80, 87, 89, 93, 104, 107, 108, 114, 121, 123–4, 125–6, 129–31, 139–41, 142–5, 148–55, 166, 178, 180, 182–3
universal welfare, 1, 4, 5, 7, 9–10, 20, 22, 24, 26, 29–30, 32–6, 41–2, 47, 49, 55–6, 57, 61, 63–4, 92, 96, 100, 101, 128, 141–2, 146, 148, 154, 166, 169, 171, 182, 184, 185
universal *versus* uniform welfare (the Webbs and Tawney), 32–5
universal stranger (Titmuss), 63, 116
urbanization, 22
USA social policy, 57, 59, 98

use- and exchange-values, 60, 65, 132, 174, 157, 175
utilitarianism, 35, 95, 96
utility-maximization, 35

value forms of capitalist production, 131
value neutrality, 140
value-neutrality of the market, 81
veil of ignorance (Rawls), 66, 140
Veit-Wilson, J.H., 185
Vincent, A. and Plant, R., 2, 22, 26–7, 35, 54, 185
voluntary action, 15, 36, 47–9, 51, 53, 62–3, 71, 74, 79, 80, 92, 97, 166
  organizations, 12, 21, 22, 30, 32, 36, 45, 46, 50, 52, 54, 71, 128, 169, 171, 182
  sector, 8, 9, 20, 34, 51, 62, 64, 90, 148, 166
Von Mises, L., 185
vouchers, 24, 86, 99

wage-labour, 118
wages, 7, 8, 50, 67, 69, 170
wages for housework, 156
Wainwright, H., 2, 17, 92
Wallerstein, I., 6, 24
Waters, M., 6
Weale, A., 65
wealth, 39, 43, 44
Webb, S., 7, 17, 32, 33, 34, 36
the Webbs, 8, 21, 22, 27, 28, 29, 30–8, 40, 41, 44–6, 53–5, 57, 61, 71, 88, 96, 114, 146, 166, 168, 172, 182
Weiss, L., 185
welfare capitalism, 116
welfare feminism, 145
welfare reform, 1, 98, 166
welfare society, 65
welfare state, 1, 4, 5, 6, 7, 9–10, 13, 24–5, 28–9, 34, 44–5, 47–8, 54–6, 60, 62, 64–5, 71, 73–4, 80, 87–8, 92, 98–100, 137, 139–40, 145, 160–1, 164–6, 169, 172, 176, 184
welfare to work, 50, 88, 168
well-women programmes, 141
widows, 47, 51, 52
Wilding, P., 10
Willetts, D., 77, 91, 97

Williams, F., 7, 8, 139, 176
Wilson, W.J., 59
women, demands of, 140, 143–6, 148, 152, 156
   and gender differences, 7, 8, 9, 140, 143, 146, 148, 151–3, 155, 176
   and inequalities, 8, 47, 58, 104, 139, 141, 143, 146, 151
   in labour force, 8–9, 147
   returners, 9

work, 3, 8, 9, 50, 52, 58, 78, 81, 89, 90, 96, 105, 122, 124, 128, 130, 136–7, 144, 145, 147, 148, 152, 156, 176
workers, 30, 53, 106, 108, 114, 118, 120, 121, 168
work and welfare, 3, 50, 83, 87, 88, 169, 174
world system (Wallerstein), 6, 176

Young, I.M., 144, 152, 186